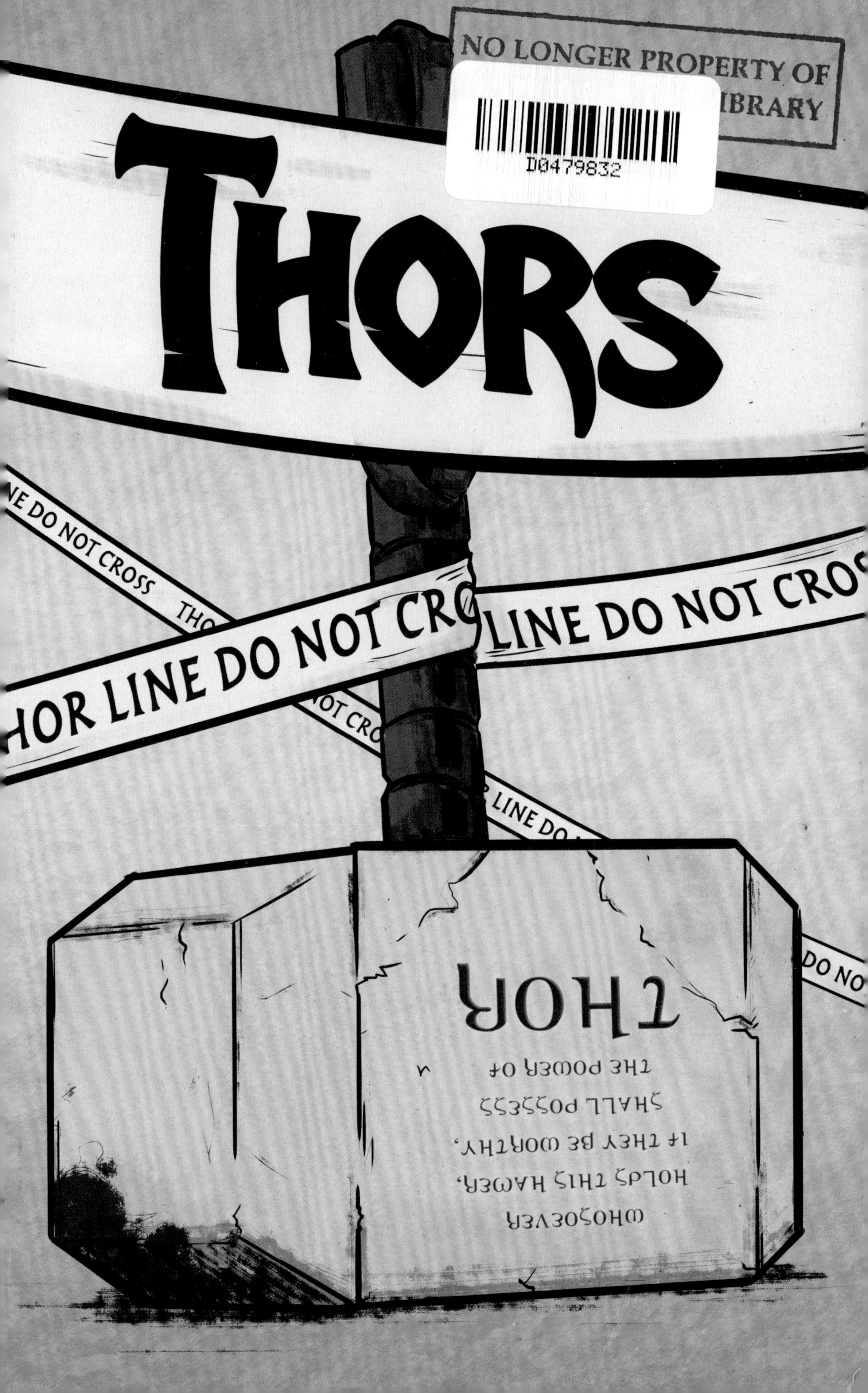

THORS

LINE DO NOT CROSS • THOR LINE DO NOT CROSS • LINE DO NOT CROSS • NOT CRO • LINE DO • DO NO

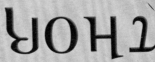

THOR

WHOSOEVER
HOLDS THIS HAMMER,
IF THEY BE WORTHY,
SHALL POSSESS
THE POWER OF

IN DOOM WE TRUST

OFFICER IN CHARGE: ULTIMATE THOR
CASE NO.: 7851-9889-5

WRITER: **JASON AARON**

PENCILERS: **CHRIS SPROUSE** (#1-4) &
GORAN SUDŽUKA (#2-3)

INKERS: **KARL STORY** (#1-4) & **DEXTER VINES** (#2-3)

COLOR ARTISTS: **MARTE GRACIA** (#1-3) & **ISRAEL SILVA** (#3-4)

LETTERER: **JOE SABINO**

COVER ART: **CHRIS SPROUSE, KARL STORY & DAVE MCCAIG**

ASSISTANT EDITORS: **JON MOISAN & CHRIS ROBINSON**

EDITOR: **WIL MOSS**

THOR CREATED BY **STAN LEE, LARRY LIEBER & JACK KIRBY**

COLLECTION EDITOR: JENNIFER GRÜNWALD
ASSOCIATE EDITOR: SARAH BRUNSTAD
ASSOCIATE MANAGING EDITOR: ALEX STARBUCK
EDITOR, SPECIAL PROJECTS: MARK D. BEAZLEY
VP, PRODUCTION AND SPECIAL PROJECTS: JEFF YOUNGQUIST
SVP PRINT, SALES & MARKETING: DAVID GABRIEL
BOOK DESIGNER: ADAM DEL RE

EDITOR IN CHIEF: AXEL ALONSO
CHIEF CREATIVE OFFICER: JOE QUESADA
PUBLISHER: DAN BUCKLEY
EXECUTIVE PRODUCER: ALAN FINE

THORS. Contains material originally published in magazine form as THORS #1-4 and THOR #364-365. First printing 2016. ISBN# 978-0-7851-9889-5. Published by MARVEL WORLDWIDE, INC., a subsidiary of MARVEL ENTERTAINMENT, LLC. OFFICE OF PUBLICATION: 135 West 50th Street, New York, NY 10020. Copyright © 2016 MARVEL No similarity between any of the names, characters, persons, and/or institutions in this magazine with those of any living or dead person or institution is intended, and any such similarity which may exist is purely coincidental. **Printed in Canada.** ALAN FINE, President, Marvel Entertainment; DAN BUCKLEY, President, TV, Publishing and Brand Management; JOE QUESADA, Chief Creative Officer; TOM BREVOORT, SVP of Publishing; DAVID BOGART, SVP of Operations & Procurement, Publishing; C.B. CEBULSKI, VP of International Development & Brand Management; DAVID GABRIEL, SVP Print, Sales & Marketing; JIM O'KEEFE, VP of Operations & Logistics; DAN CARR, Executive Director of Publishing Technology; SUSAN CRESPI, Editorial Operations Manager; ALEX MORALES, Publishing Operations Manager; STAN LEE, Chairman Emeritus. For information regarding advertising in Marvel Comics or on Marvel.com, please contact Jonathan Rheingold, VP of Custom Solutions & Ad Sales, at jrheingold@marvel.com. For Marvel subscription inquiries, please call 800-217-9158. **Manufactured between 1/15/2016 and 2/22/2016 by SOLISCO PRINTERS, SCOTT, QC, CANADA.**

10 9 8 7 6 5 4 3 2 1

SECRET WARS

THE MULTIVERSE WAS DESTROYED!

·

THE HEROES OF EARTH-616 AND EARTH-1610
WERE POWERLESS TO SAVE IT!

·

NOW, ALL THAT REMAINS...IS BATTLEWORLD

·

A MASSIVE, PATCHWORK PLANET COMPOSED OF
THE FRAGMENTS OF WORLDS THAT NO LONGER
EXIST, MAINTAINED BY THE IRON WILL OF ITS
GOD AND MASTER, VICTOR VON DOOM!

·

EACH REGION IS A DOMAIN UNTO ITSELF!

THORS

WATCHING OVER THE DOMAINS
OF BATTLEWORLD ARE THE STEADFAST
MEN AND WOMEN OF THE THORS!

·

THESE EXTRAORDINARY CITIZENS OF BATTLEWORLD
HAVE BEEN DEEMED WORTHY OF THEIR OWN HAMMERS
AND KEEP THE PEACE IN THE NAME OF DOOM,
THE ALL-FATHER!

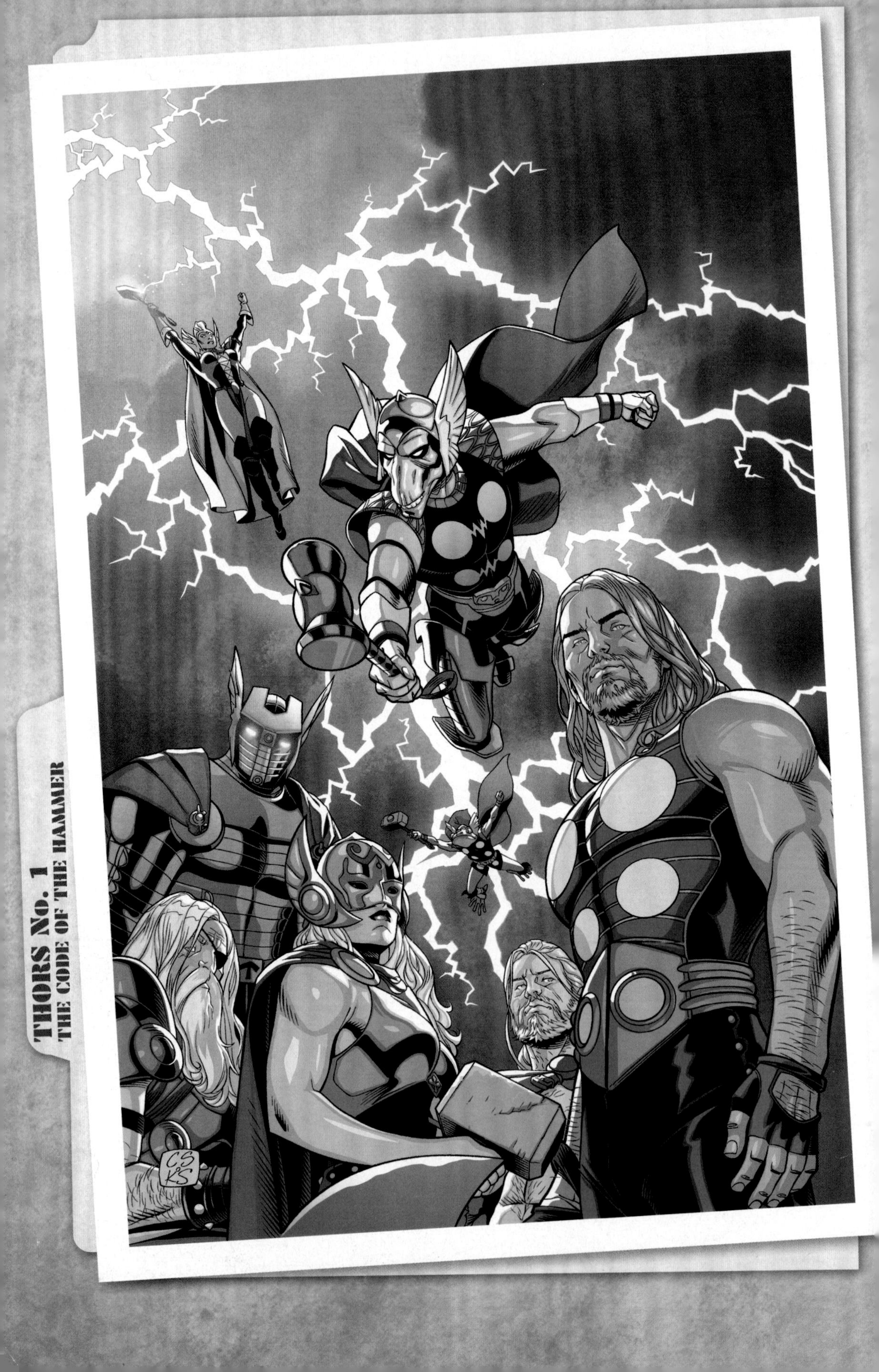
THORS No. 1
THE CODE OF THE HAMMER

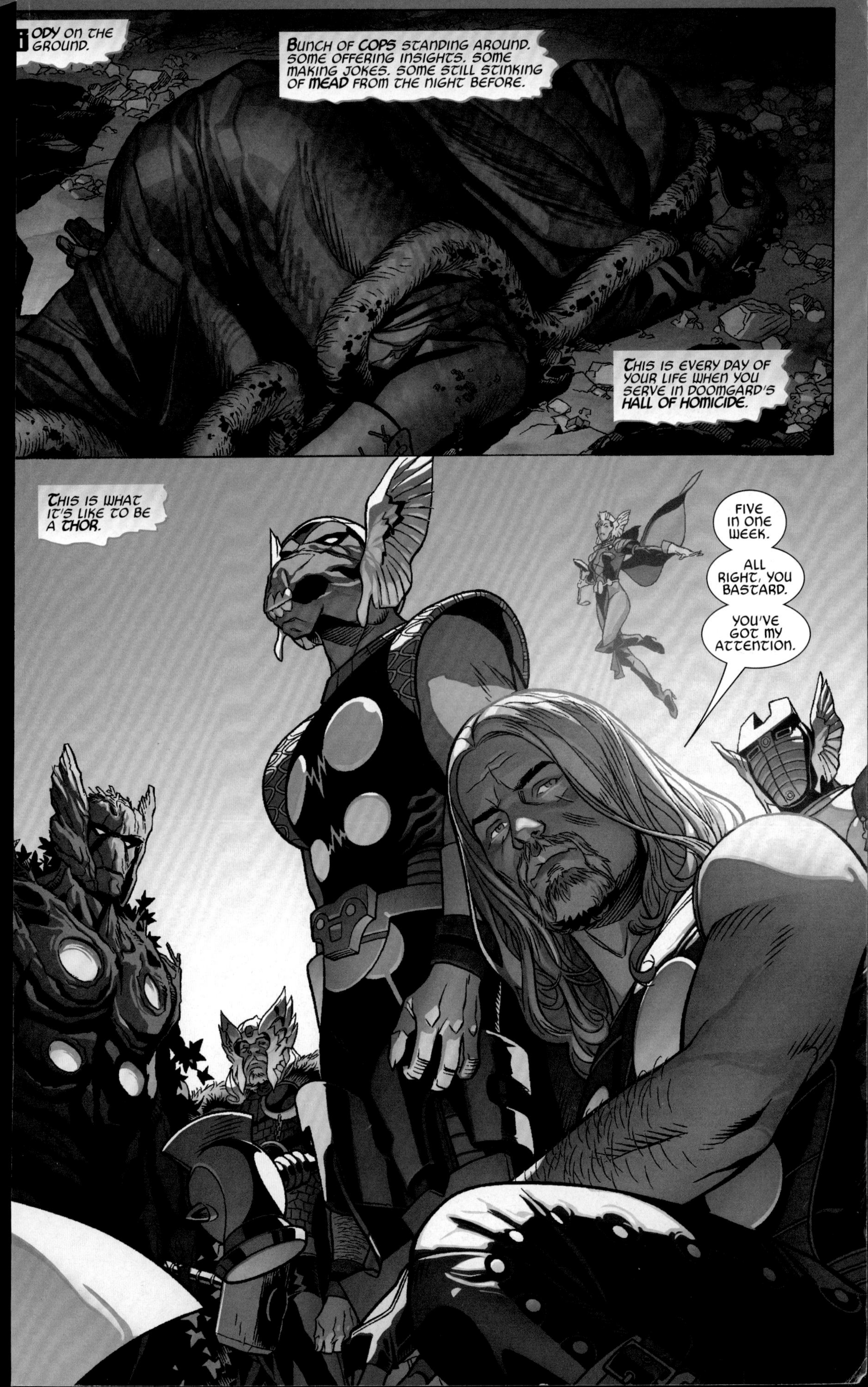

BODY ON THE GROUND.
BUNCH OF COPS STANDING AROUND. SOME OFFERING INSIGHTS. SOME MAKING JOKES. SOME STILL STINKING OF MEAD FROM THE NIGHT BEFORE.
THIS IS EVERY DAY OF YOUR LIFE WHEN YOU SERVE IN DOOMGARD'S HALL OF HOMICIDE.
THIS IS WHAT IT'S LIKE TO BE A THOR.
FIVE IN ONE WEEK.
ALL RIGHT, YOU BASTARD.
YOU'VE GOT MY ATTENTION.

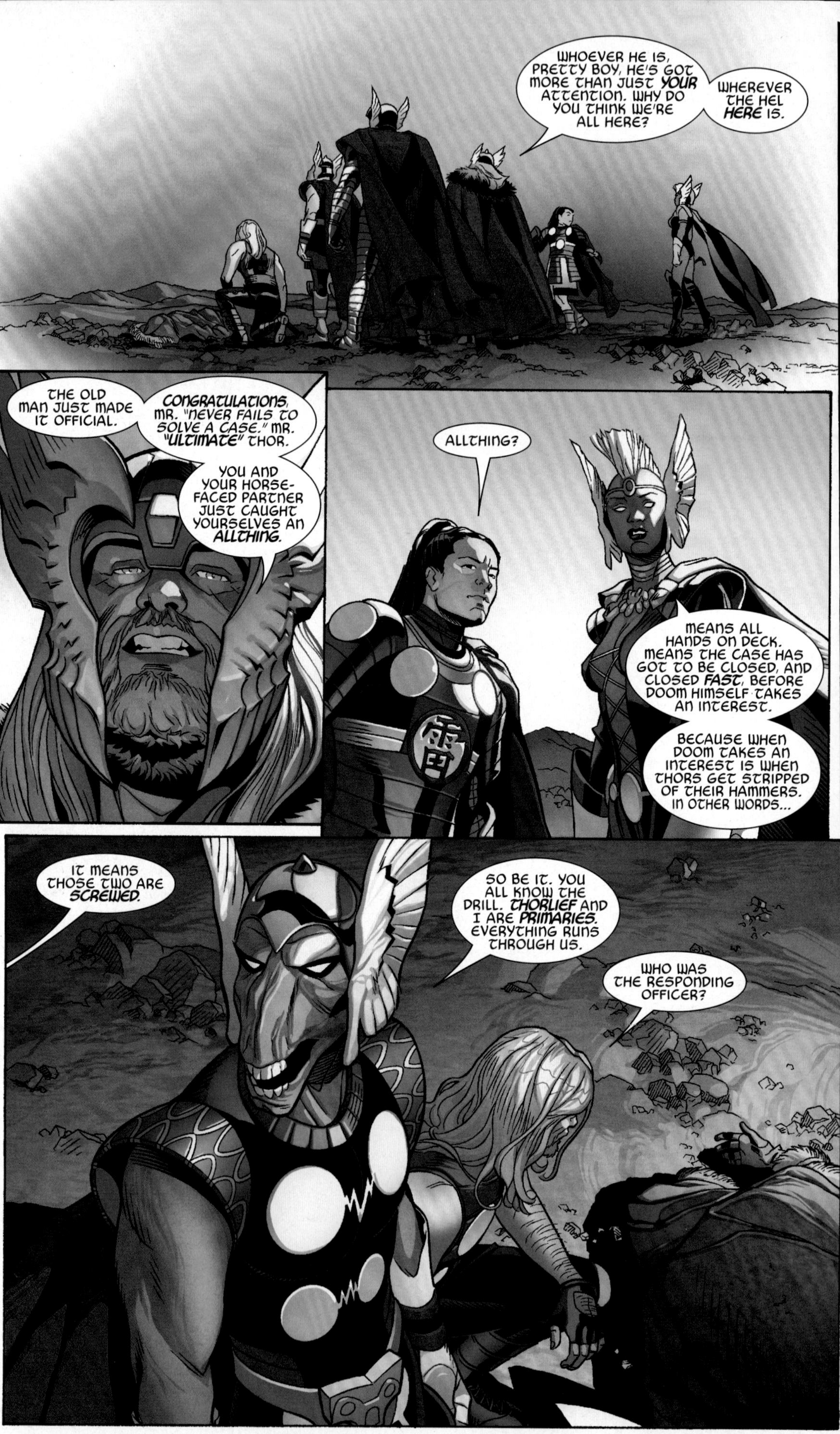
WHOEVER HE IS, PRETTY BOY, HE'S GOT MORE THAN JUST YOUR ATTENTION. WHY DO YOU THINK WE'RE ALL HERE?
WHEREVER THE HEL HERE IS.
THE OLD MAN JUST MADE IT OFFICIAL.
CONGRATULATIONS, MR. "NEVER FAILS TO SOLVE A CASE." MR. "ULTIMATE" THOR.
YOU AND YOUR HORSE-FACED PARTNER JUST CAUGHT YOURSELVES AN ALLTHING.
ALLTHING?
MEANS ALL HANDS ON DECK. MEANS THE CASE HAS GOT TO BE CLOSED, AND CLOSED FAST, BEFORE DOOM HIMSELF TAKES AN INTEREST.
BECAUSE WHEN DOOM TAKES AN INTEREST IS WHEN THORS GET STRIPPED OF THEIR HAMMERS. IN OTHER WORDS...
IT MEANS THOSE TWO ARE SCREWED.
SO BE IT. YOU ALL KNOW THE DRILL. THORLIEF AND I ARE PRIMARIES. EVERYTHING RUNS THROUGH US.
WHO WAS THE RESPONDING OFFICER?

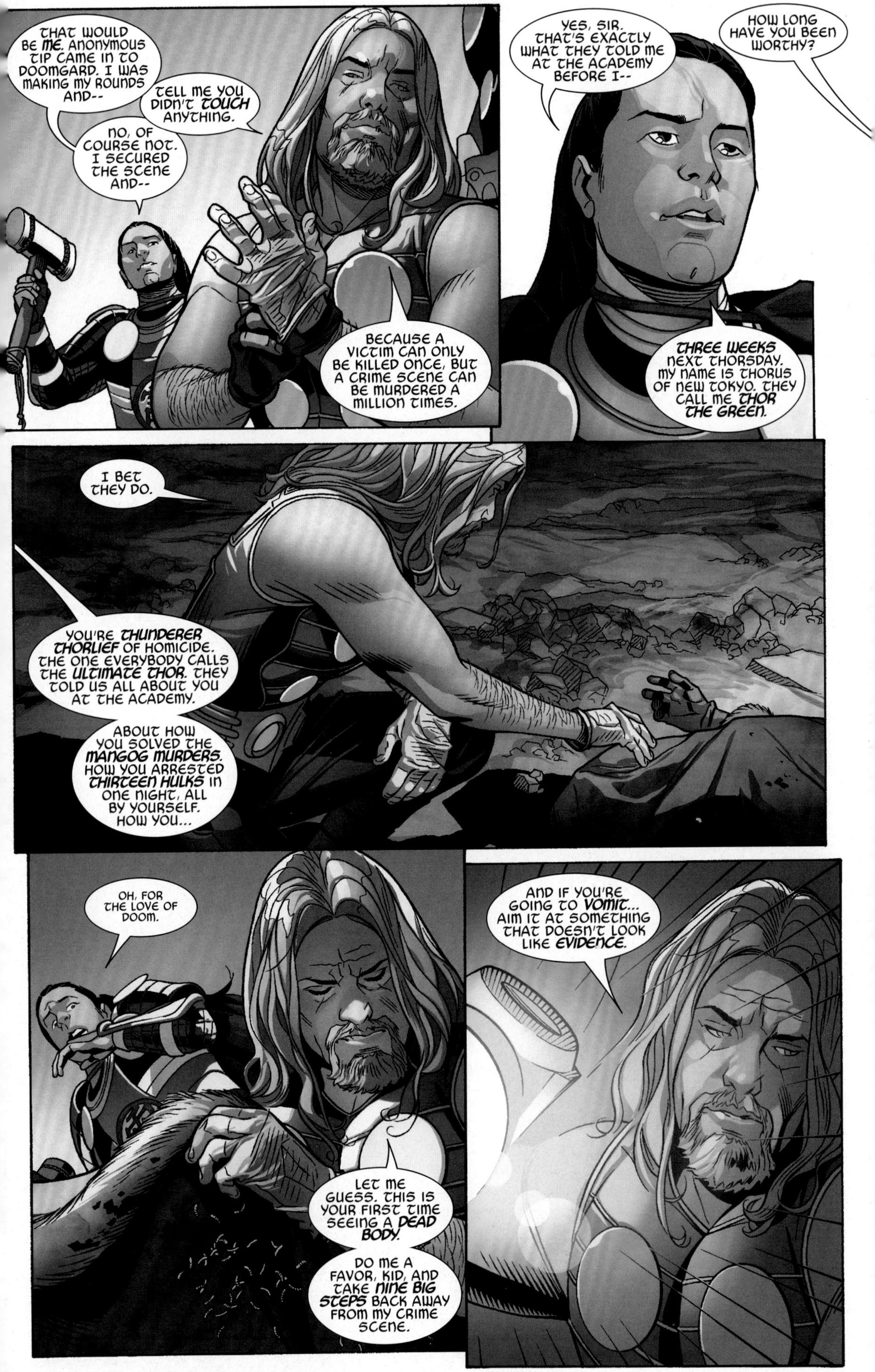
THAT WOULD BE ME. ANONYMOUS TIP CAME IN TO DOOMGARD. I WAS MAKING MY ROUNDS AND--
TELL ME YOU DIDN'T TOUCH ANYTHING.
NO, OF COURSE NOT. I SECURED THE SCENE AND--
BECAUSE A VICTIM CAN ONLY BE KILLED ONCE, BUT A CRIME SCENE CAN BE MURDERED A MILLION TIMES.
YES, SIR. THAT'S EXACTLY WHAT THEY TOLD ME AT THE ACADEMY BEFORE I--
HOW LONG HAVE YOU BEEN WORTHY?
THREE WEEKS NEXT THORSDAY. MY NAME IS THORUS OF NEW TOKYO. THEY CALL ME THOR THE GREEN.
I BET THEY DO.
YOU'RE THUNDERER THORLIEF OF HOMICIDE. THE ONE EVERYBODY CALLS THE ULTIMATE THOR. THEY TOLD US ALL ABOUT YOU AT THE ACADEMY.
ABOUT HOW YOU SOLVED THE MANGOG MURDERS. HOW YOU ARRESTED THIRTEEN HULKS IN ONE NIGHT, ALL BY YOURSELF. HOW YOU...
OH, FOR THE LOVE OF DOOM.
LET ME GUESS. THIS IS YOUR FIRST TIME SEEING A DEAD BODY.
DO ME A FAVOR, KID, AND TAKE NINE BIG STEPS BACK AWAY FROM MY CRIME SCENE.
AND IF YOU'RE GOING TO VOMIT... AIM IT AT SOMETHING THAT DOESN'T LOOK LIKE EVIDENCE.

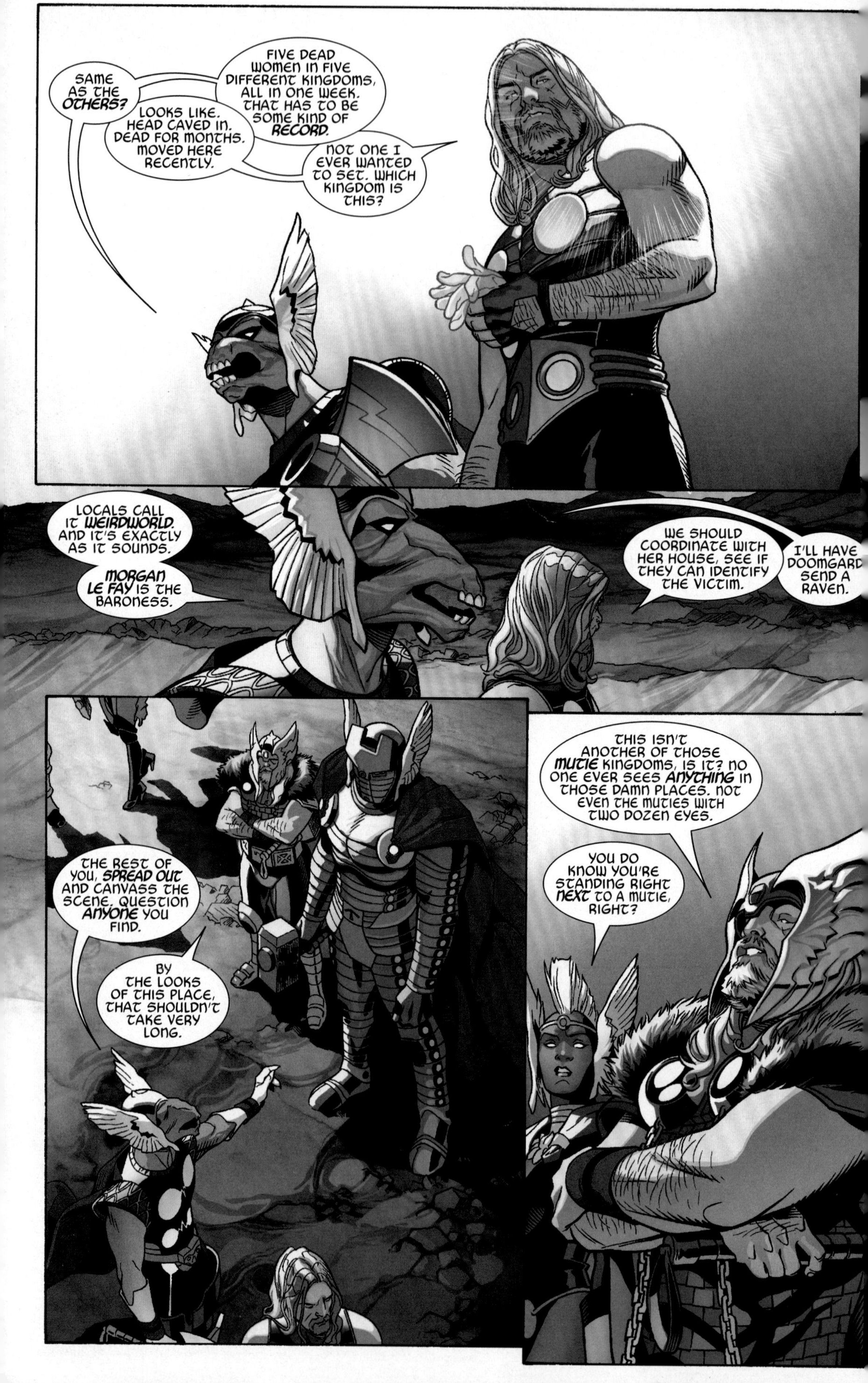
SAME AS THE OTHERS?
FIVE DEAD WOMEN IN FIVE DIFFERENT KINGDOMS, ALL IN ONE WEEK. THAT HAS TO BE SOME KIND OF RECORD.
LOOKS LIKE. HEAD CAVED IN. DEAD FOR MONTHS. MOVED HERE RECENTLY.
NOT ONE I EVER WANTED TO SET. WHICH KINGDOM IS THIS?
LOCALS CALL IT WEIRDWORLD. AND IT'S EXACTLY AS IT SOUNDS.
MORGAN LE FAY IS THE BARONESS.
WE SHOULD COORDINATE WITH HER HOUSE, SEE IF THEY CAN IDENTIFY THE VICTIM.
I'LL HAVE DOOMGARD SEND A RAVEN.
THE REST OF YOU, SPREAD OUT AND CANVASS THE SCENE. QUESTION ANYONE YOU FIND.
BY THE LOOKS OF THIS PLACE, THAT SHOULDN'T TAKE VERY LONG.
THIS ISN'T ANOTHER OF THOSE MUTIE KINGDOMS, IS IT? NO ONE EVER SEES ANYTHING IN THOSE DAMN PLACES. NOT EVEN THE MUTIES WITH TWO DOZEN EYES.
YOU DO KNOW YOU'RE STANDING RIGHT NEXT TO A MUTIE, RIGHT?

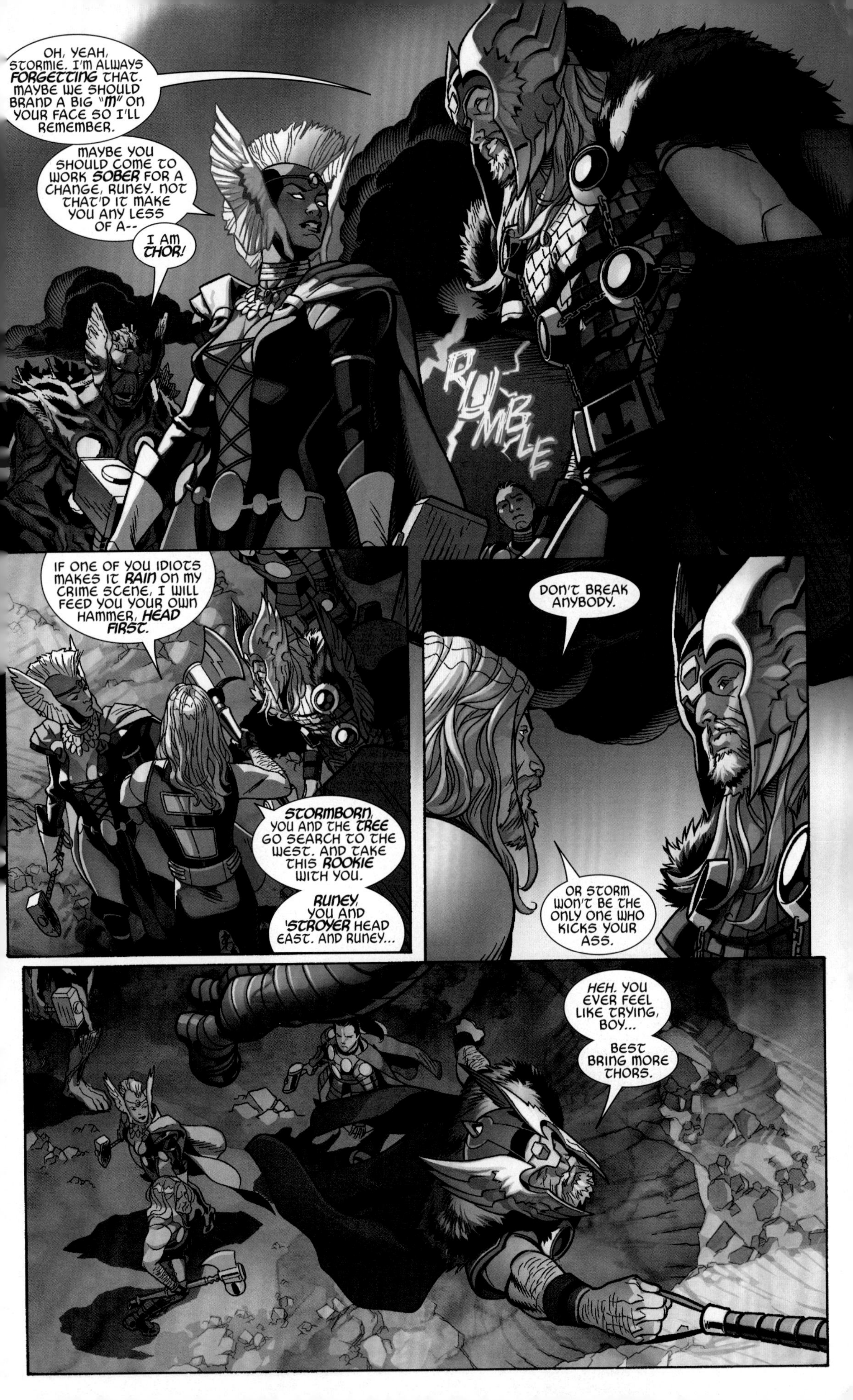

OH, YEAH, STORMIE. I'M ALWAYS FORGETTING THAT. MAYBE WE SHOULD BRAND A BIG "M" ON YOUR FACE SO I'LL REMEMBER.
MAYBE YOU SHOULD COME TO WORK SOBER FOR A CHANGE, RUNEY. NOT THAT'D IT MAKE YOU ANY LESS OF A--
I AM THOR!
RUMBLE
IF ONE OF YOU IDIOTS MAKES IT RAIN ON MY CRIME SCENE, I WILL FEED YOU YOUR OWN HAMMER, HEAD FIRST.
STORMBORN, YOU AND THE TREE GO SEARCH TO THE WEST. AND TAKE THIS ROOKIE WITH YOU.
RUNEY, YOU AND 'STROYER HEAD EAST. AND RUNEY...
DON'T BREAK ANYBODY.
OR STORM WON'T BE THE ONLY ONE WHO KICKS YOUR ASS.
HEH. YOU EVER FEEL LIKE TRYING, BOY...
BEST BRING MORE THORS.

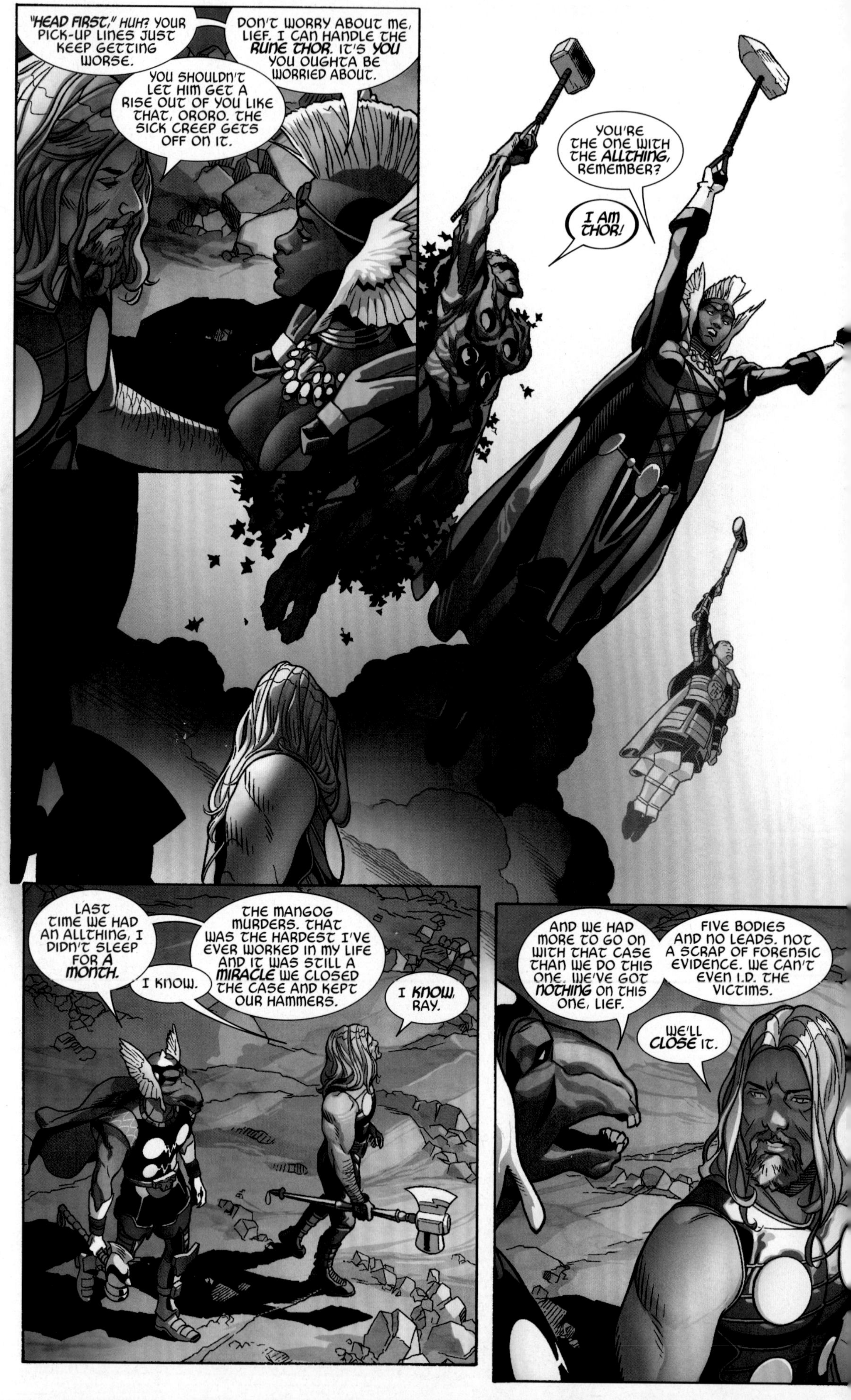
"HEAD FIRST," HUH? YOUR PICK-UP LINES JUST KEEP GETTING WORSE.
DON'T WORRY ABOUT ME, LIEF. I CAN HANDLE THE RUNE THOR. IT'S YOU YOU OUGHTA BE WORRIED ABOUT.
YOU SHOULDN'T LET HIM GET A RISE OUT OF YOU LIKE THAT, ORORO. THE SICK CREEP GETS OFF ON IT.
YOU'RE THE ONE WITH THE ALLTHING, REMEMBER?
I AM THOR!
LAST TIME WE HAD AN ALLTHING, I DIDN'T SLEEP FOR A MONTH.
THE MANGOG MURDERS. THAT WAS THE HARDEST I'VE EVER WORKED IN MY LIFE AND IT WAS STILL A MIRACLE WE CLOSED THE CASE AND KEPT OUR HAMMERS.
I KNOW.
I KNOW, RAY.
AND WE HAD MORE TO GO ON WITH THAT CASE THAN WE DO THIS ONE. WE'VE GOT NOTHING ON THIS ONE, LIEF.
FIVE BODIES AND NO LEADS. NOT A SCRAP OF FORENSIC EVIDENCE. WE CAN'T EVEN I.D. THE VICTIMS.
WE'LL CLOSE IT.

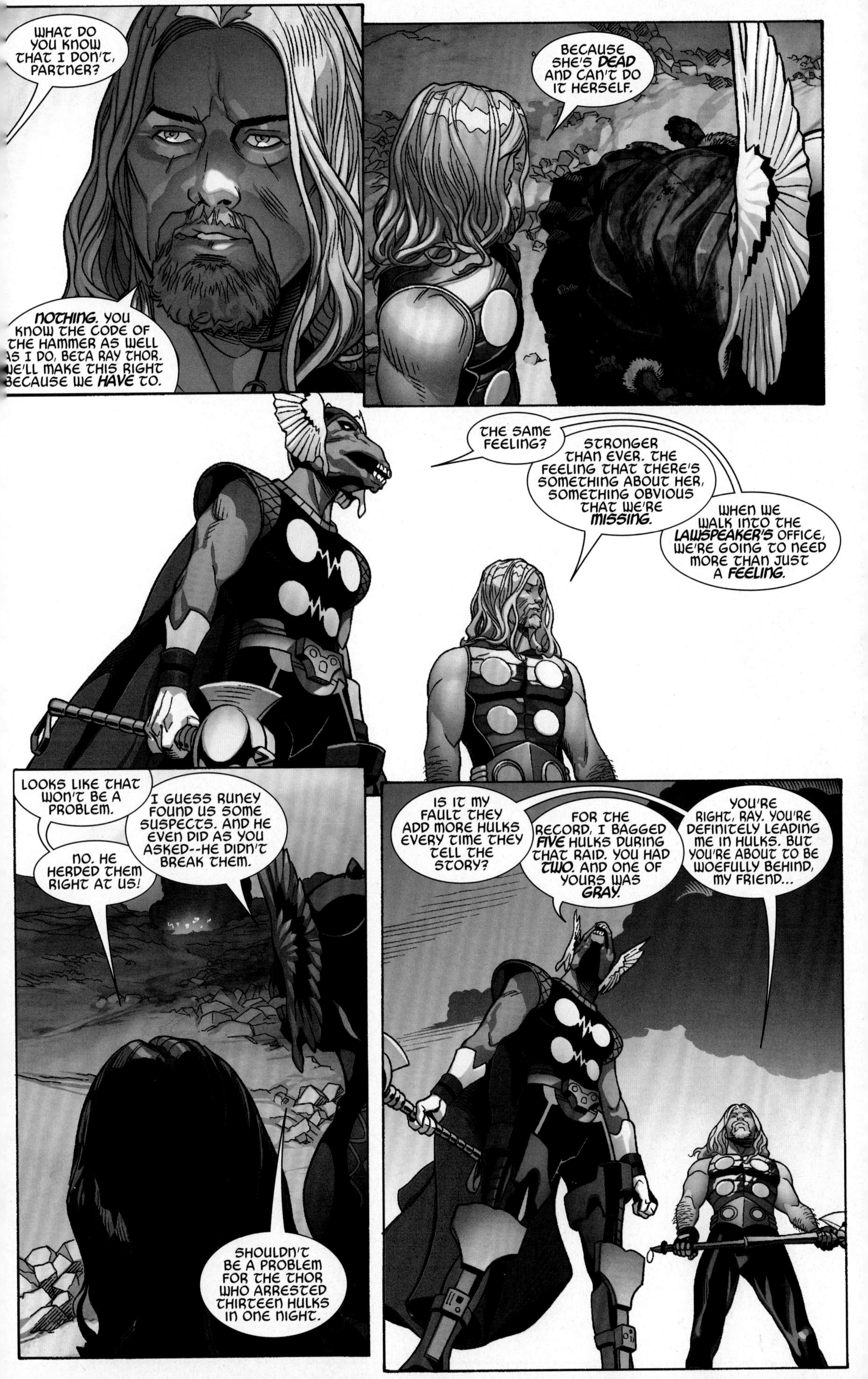
WHAT DO YOU KNOW THAT I DON'T, PARTNER?
NOTHING. YOU KNOW THE CODE OF THE HAMMER AS WELL AS I DO, BETA RAY THOR. WE'LL MAKE THIS RIGHT BECAUSE WE HAVE TO.
BECAUSE SHE'S DEAD AND CAN'T DO IT HERSELF.
THE SAME FEELING?
STRONGER THAN EVER. THE FEELING THAT THERE'S SOMETHING ABOUT HER, SOMETHING OBVIOUS THAT WE'RE MISSING.
WHEN WE WALK INTO THE LAWSPEAKER'S OFFICE, WE'RE GOING TO NEED MORE THAN JUST A FEELING.
LOOKS LIKE THAT WON'T BE A PROBLEM.
NO. HE HERDED THEM RIGHT AT US!
I GUESS RUNEY FOUND US SOME SUSPECTS. AND HE EVEN DID AS YOU ASKED--HE DIDN'T BREAK THEM.
SHOULDN'T BE A PROBLEM FOR THE THOR WHO ARRESTED THIRTEEN HULKS IN ONE NIGHT.
IS IT MY FAULT THEY ADD MORE HULKS EVERY TIME THEY TELL THE STORY?
FOR THE RECORD, I BAGGED FIVE HULKS DURING THAT RAID. YOU HAD TWO. AND ONE OF YOURS WAS GRAY.
YOU'RE RIGHT, RAY. YOU'RE DEFINITELY LEADING ME IN HULKS. BUT YOU'RE ABOUT TO BE WOEFULLY BEHIND, MY FRIEND...

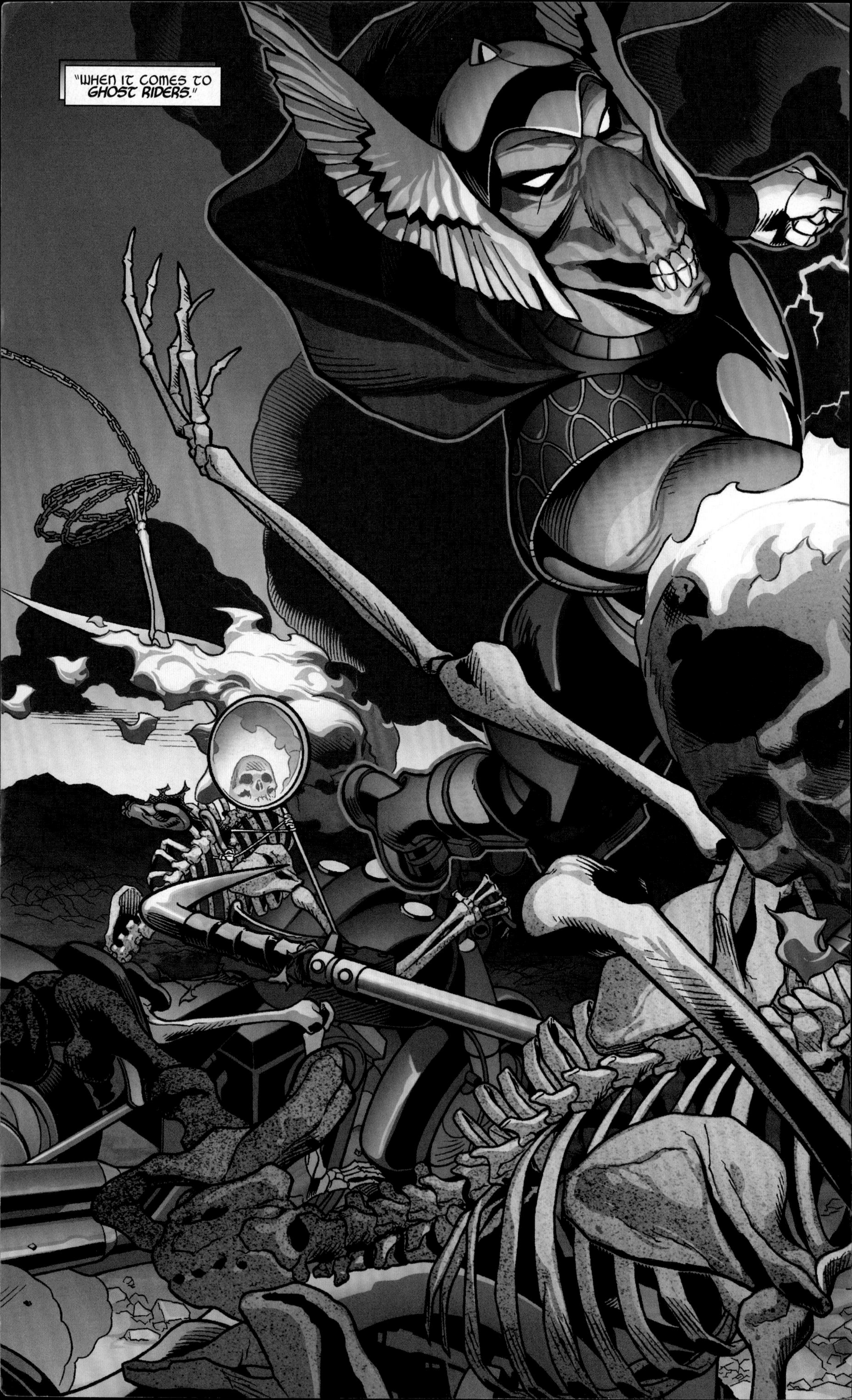
"WHEN IT COMES TO GHOST RIDERS."

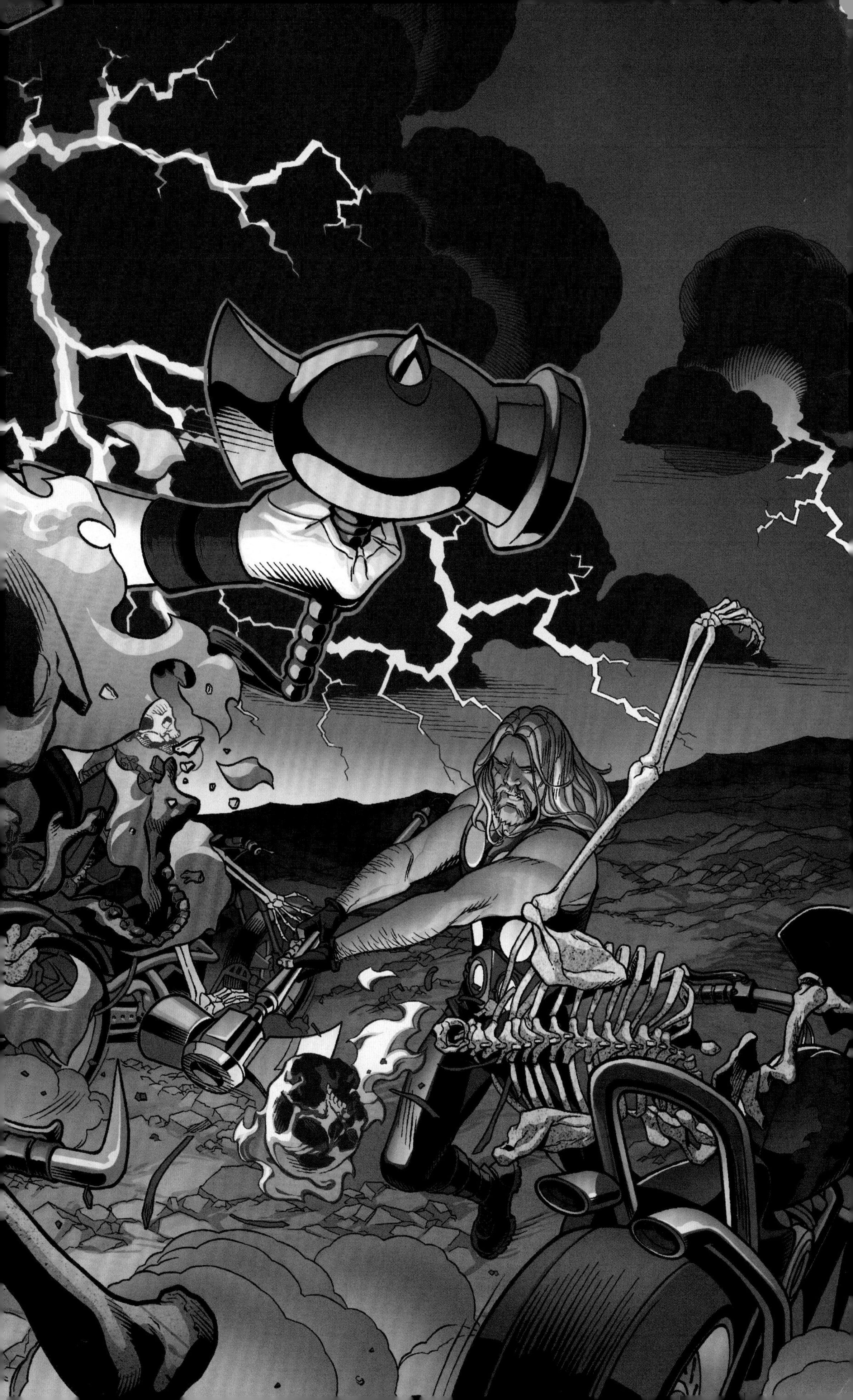

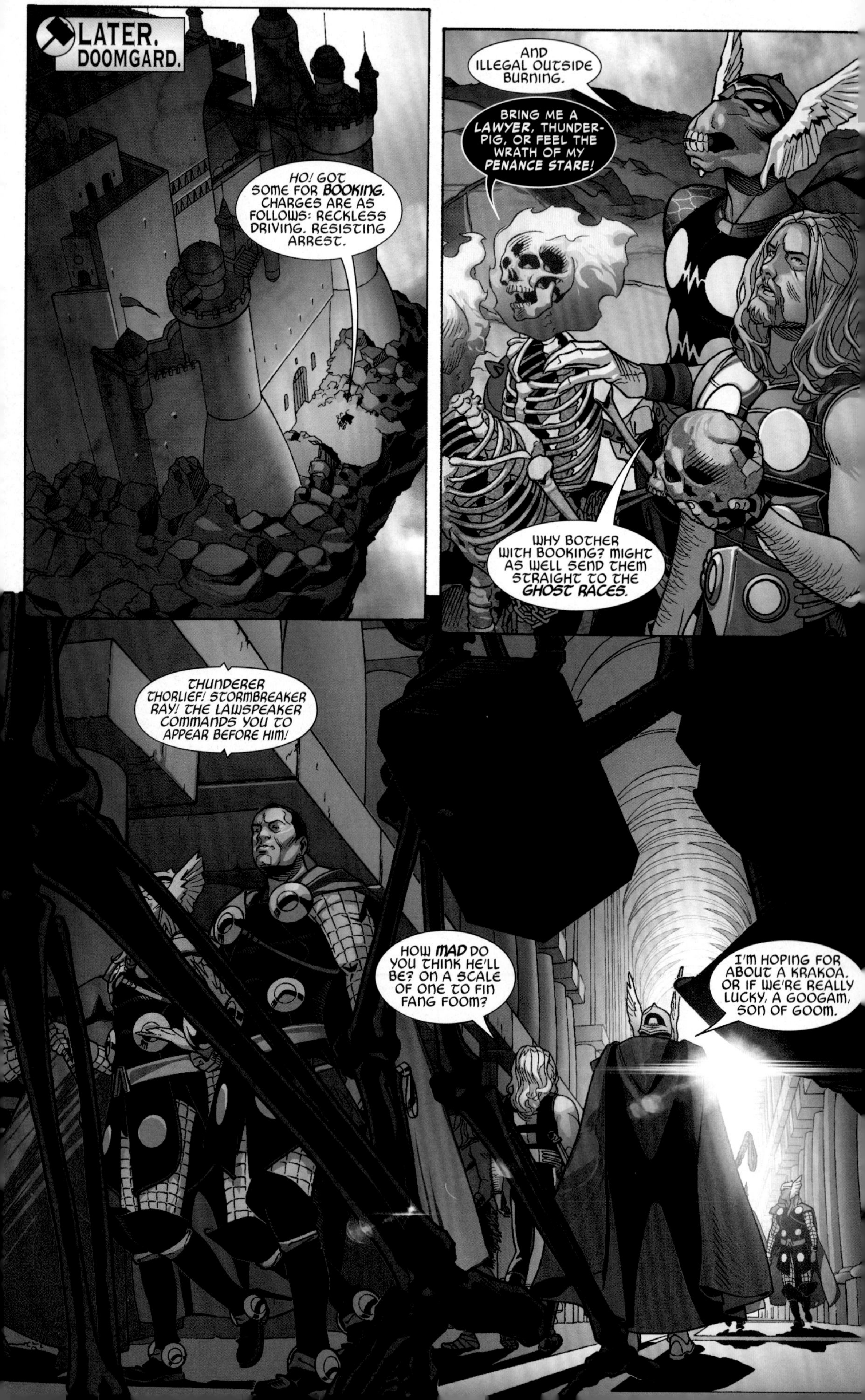
LATER. DOOMGARD.
HO! GOT SOME FOR BOOKING. CHARGES ARE AS FOLLOWS: RECKLESS DRIVING. RESISTING ARREST.
AND ILLEGAL OUTSIDE BURNING.
BRING ME A LAWYER, THUNDER-PIG, OR FEEL THE WRATH OF MY PENANCE STARE!
WHY BOTHER WITH BOOKING? MIGHT AS WELL SEND THEM STRAIGHT TO THE GHOST RACES.
THUNDERER THORLIEF! STORMBREAKER RAY! THE LAWSPEAKER COMMANDS YOU TO APPEAR BEFORE HIM!
HOW MAD DO YOU THINK HE'LL BE? ON A SCALE OF ONE TO FIN FANG FOOM?
I'M HOPING FOR ABOUT A KRAKOA. OR IF WE'RE REALLY LUCKY, A GOOGAM, SON OF GOOM.

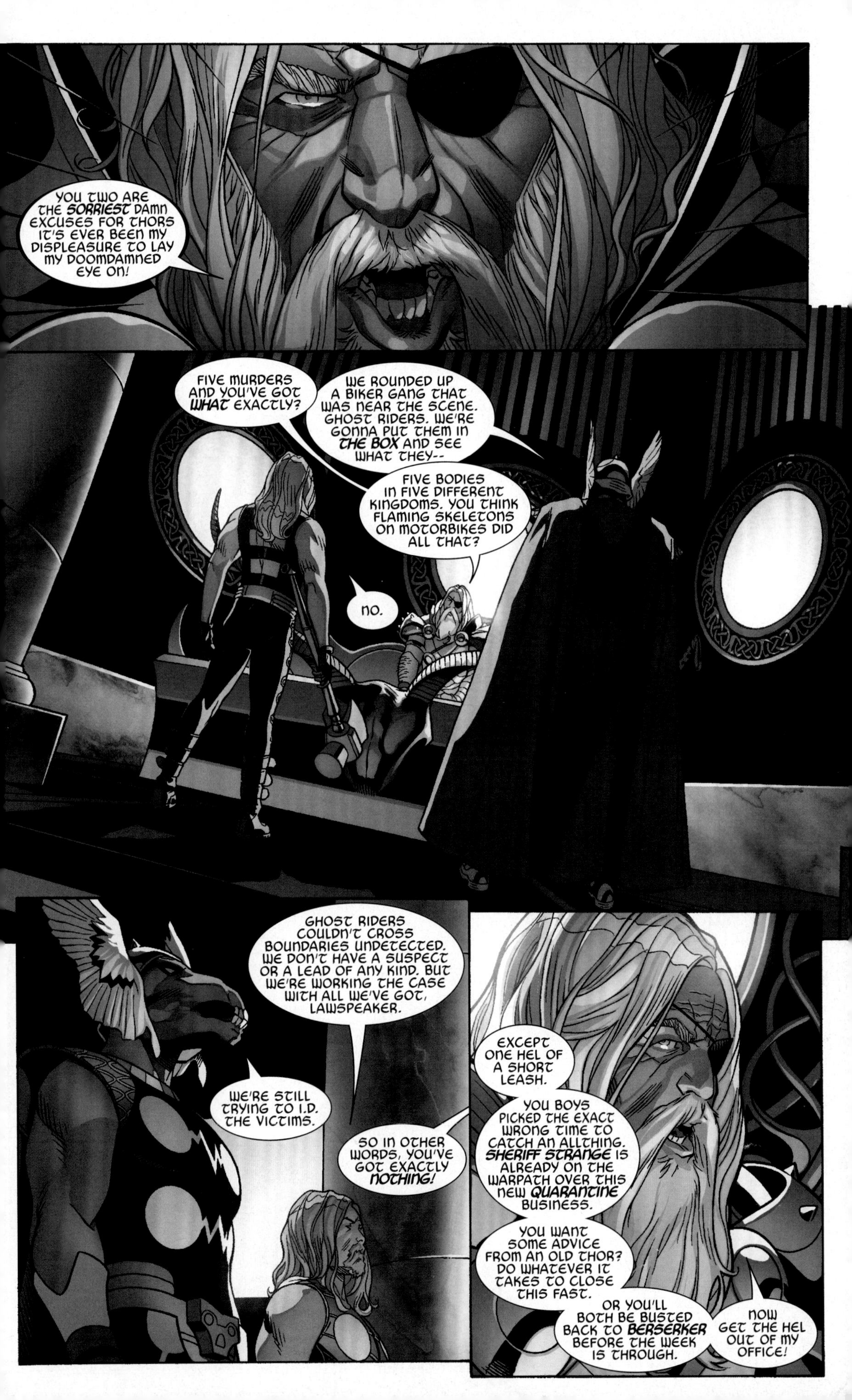
YOU TWO ARE THE SORRIEST DAMN EXCUSES FOR THORS IT'S EVER BEEN MY DISPLEASURE TO LAY MY DOOMDAMNED EYE ON!
FIVE MURDERS AND YOU'VE GOT WHAT EXACTLY?
WE ROUNDED UP A BIKER GANG THAT WAS NEAR THE SCENE. GHOST RIDERS. WE'RE GONNA PUT THEM IN THE BOX AND SEE WHAT THEY--
FIVE BODIES IN FIVE DIFFERENT KINGDOMS. YOU THINK FLAMING SKELETONS ON MOTORBIKES DID ALL THAT?
NO.
GHOST RIDERS COULDN'T CROSS BOUNDARIES UNDETECTED. WE DON'T HAVE A SUSPECT OR A LEAD OF ANY KIND. BUT WE'RE WORKING THE CASE WITH ALL WE'VE GOT, LAWSPEAKER.
WE'RE STILL TRYING TO I.D. THE VICTIMS.
SO IN OTHER WORDS, YOU'VE GOT EXACTLY NOTHING!
EXCEPT ONE HEL OF A SHORT LEASH.
YOU BOYS PICKED THE EXACT WRONG TIME TO CATCH AN ALLTHING. SHERIFF STRANGE IS ALREADY ON THE WARPATH OVER THIS NEW QUARANTINE BUSINESS.
YOU WANT SOME ADVICE FROM AN OLD THOR? DO WHATEVER IT TAKES TO CLOSE THIS FAST.
OR YOU'LL BOTH BE BUSTED BACK TO BERSERKER BEFORE THE WEEK IS THROUGH.
NOW GET THE HEL OUT OF MY OFFICE!

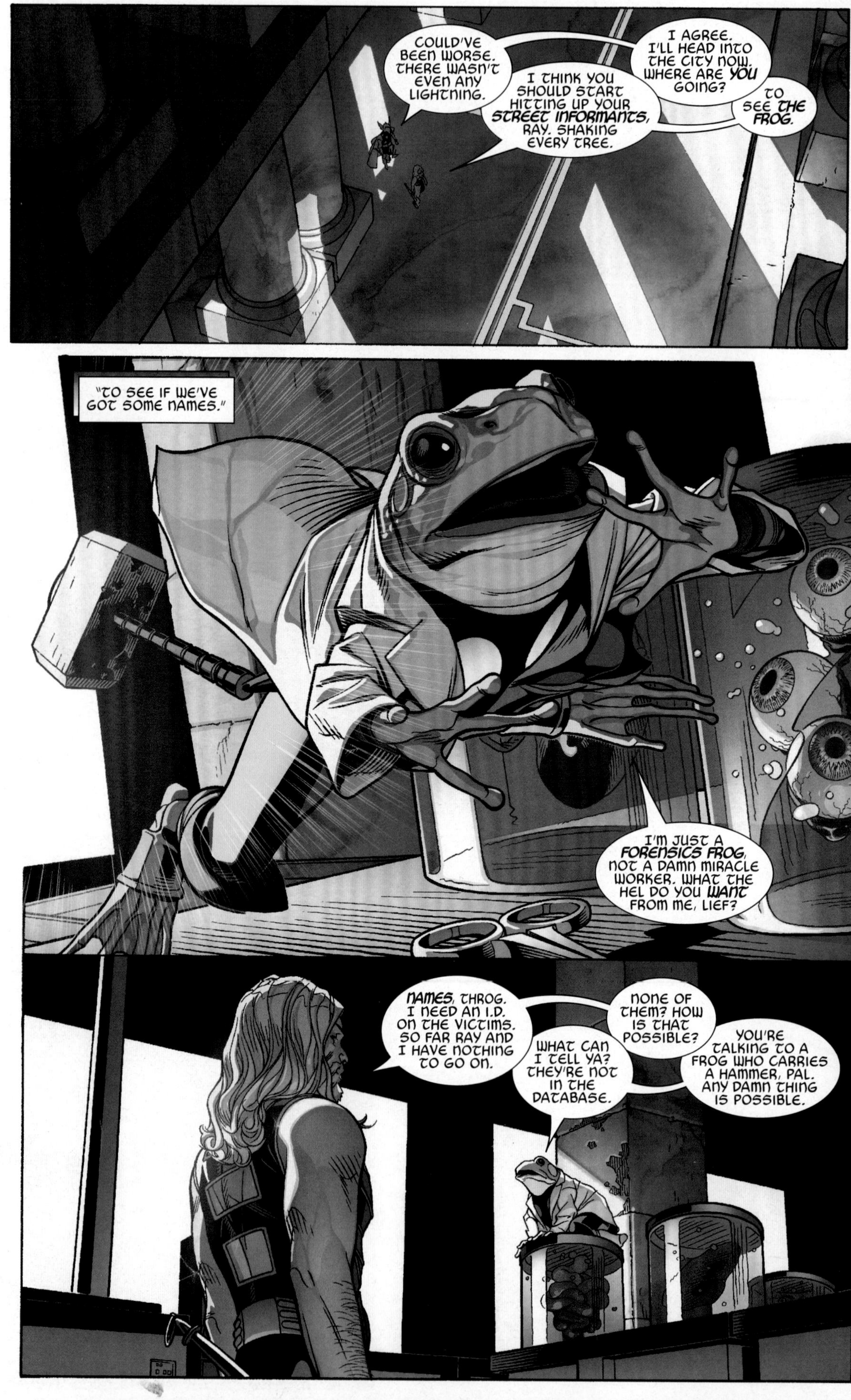
COULD'VE BEEN WORSE. THERE WASN'T EVEN ANY LIGHTNING.
I THINK YOU SHOULD START HITTING UP YOUR STREET INFORMANTS, RAY. SHAKING EVERY TREE.
I AGREE. I'LL HEAD INTO THE CITY NOW. WHERE ARE YOU GOING?
TO SEE THE FROG.
"TO SEE IF WE'VE GOT SOME NAMES."
I'M JUST A FORENSICS FROG, NOT A DAMN MIRACLE WORKER. WHAT THE HEL DO YOU WANT FROM ME, LIEF?
NAMES, THROG. I NEED AN I.D. ON THE VICTIMS. SO FAR RAY AND I HAVE NOTHING TO GO ON.
WHAT CAN I TELL YA? THEY'RE NOT IN THE DATABASE.
NONE OF THEM? HOW IS THAT POSSIBLE?
YOU'RE TALKING TO A FROG WHO CARRIES A HAMMER, PAL. ANY DAMN THING IS POSSIBLE.

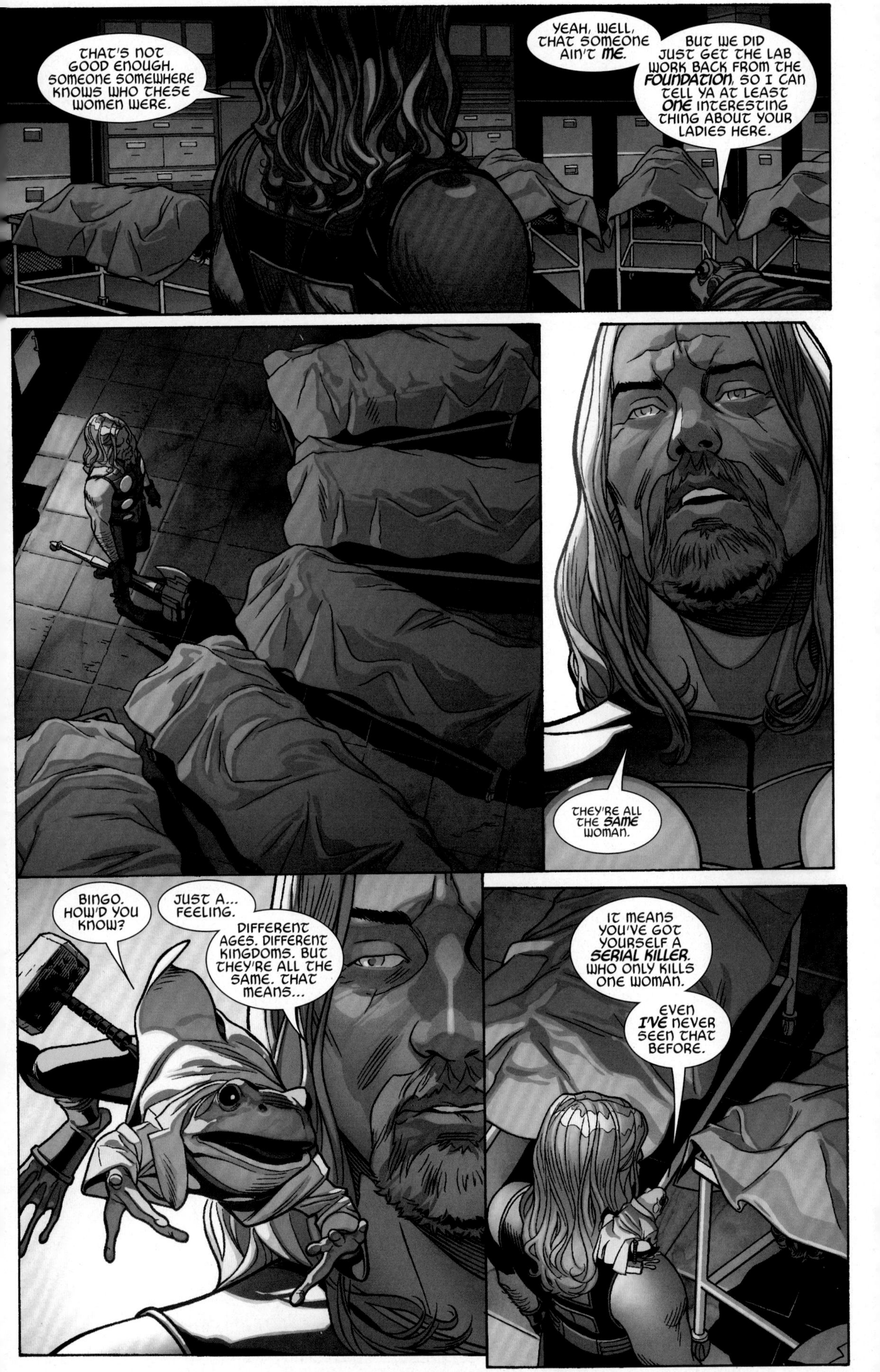
THAT'S NOT GOOD ENOUGH. SOMEONE SOMEWHERE KNOWS WHO THESE WOMEN WERE.
YEAH, WELL, THAT SOMEONE AIN'T ME.
BUT WE DID JUST GET THE LAB WORK BACK FROM THE FOUNDATION, SO I CAN TELL YA AT LEAST ONE INTERESTING THING ABOUT YOUR LADIES HERE.
THEY'RE ALL THE SAME WOMAN.
BINGO. HOW'D YOU KNOW?
JUST A... FEELING.
DIFFERENT AGES. DIFFERENT KINGDOMS. BUT THEY'RE ALL THE SAME. THAT MEANS...
IT MEANS YOU'VE GOT YOURSELF A SERIAL KILLER. WHO ONLY KILLS ONE WOMAN.
EVEN I'VE NEVER SEEN THAT BEFORE.

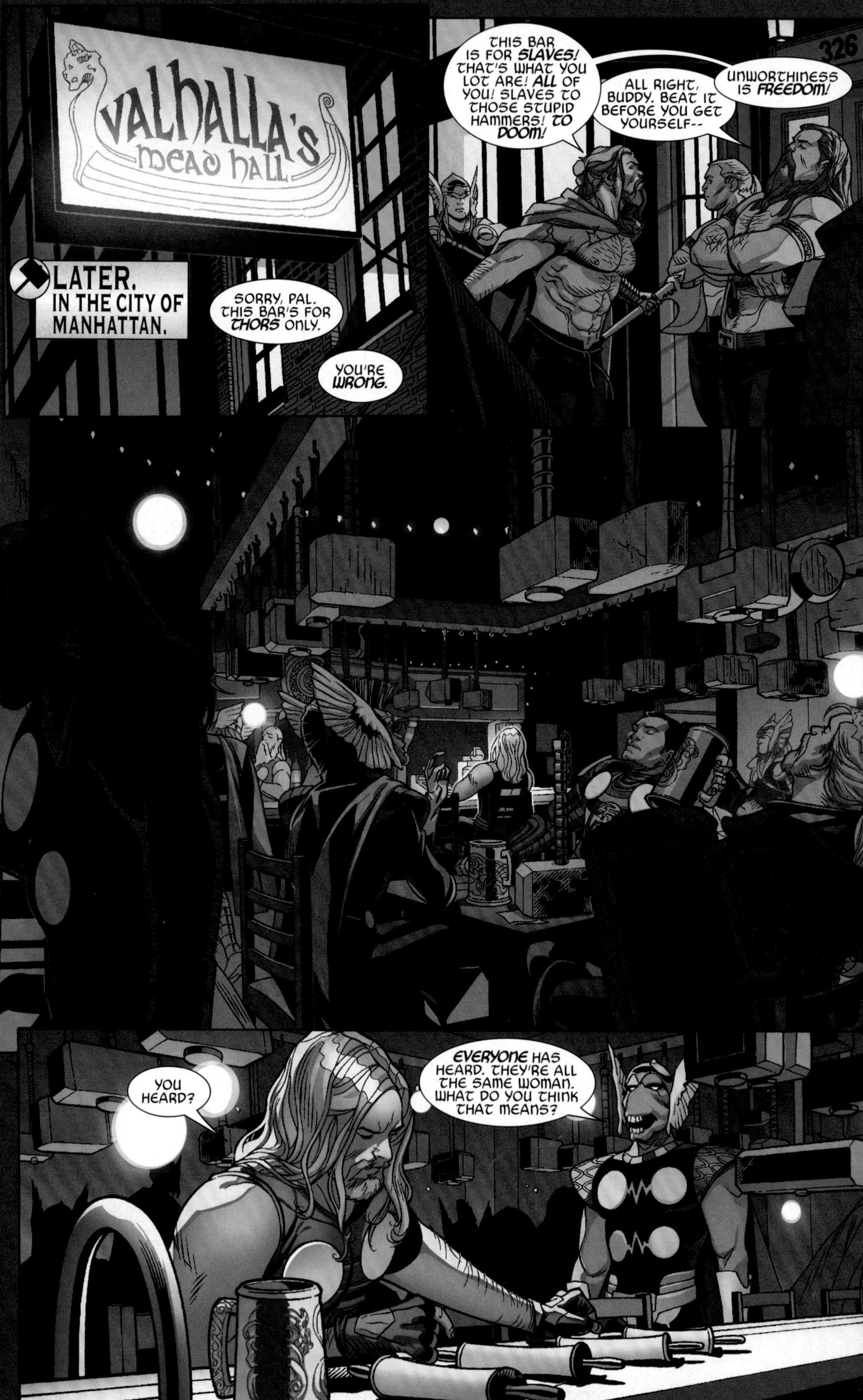
VALHALLA'S MEAD HALL
LATER. IN THE CITY OF MANHATTAN.
SORRY, PAL. THIS BAR'S FOR THORS ONLY.
YOU'RE WRONG.
THIS BAR IS FOR SLAVES! THAT'S WHAT YOU LOT ARE! ALL OF YOU! SLAVES TO THOSE STUPID HAMMERS! TO DOOM!
ALL RIGHT, BUDDY. BEAT IT BEFORE YOU GET YOURSELF--
UNWORTHINESS IS FREEDOM!
326
YOU HEARD?
EVERYONE HAS HEARD. THEY'RE ALL THE SAME WOMAN. WHAT DO YOU THINK THAT MEANS?

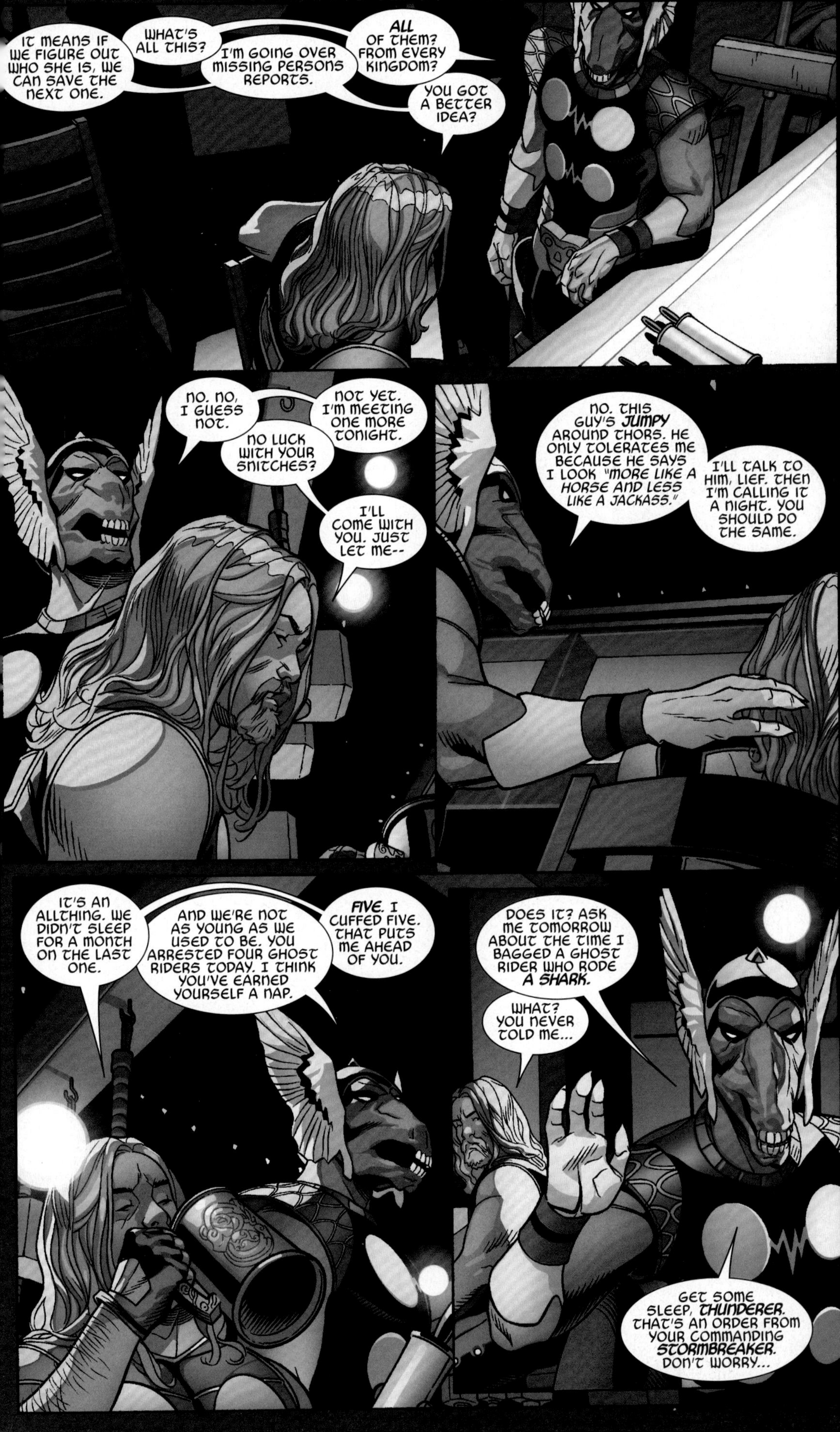

IT MEANS IF WE FIGURE OUT WHO SHE IS, WE CAN SAVE THE NEXT ONE.
WHAT'S ALL THIS?
I'M GOING OVER MISSING PERSONS REPORTS.
ALL OF THEM? FROM EVERY KINGDOM?
YOU GOT A BETTER IDEA?
NO. NO, I GUESS NOT.
NO LUCK WITH YOUR SNITCHES?
NOT YET. I'M MEETING ONE MORE TONIGHT.
I'LL COME WITH YOU. JUST LET ME--
NO. THIS GUY'S JUMPY AROUND THORS. HE ONLY TOLERATES ME BECAUSE HE SAYS I LOOK "MORE LIKE A HORSE AND LESS LIKE A JACKASS."
I'LL TALK TO HIM, LIEF. THEN I'M CALLING IT A NIGHT. YOU SHOULD DO THE SAME.
IT'S AN ALLTHING. WE DIDN'T SLEEP FOR A MONTH ON THE LAST ONE.
AND WE'RE NOT AS YOUNG AS WE USED TO BE. YOU ARRESTED FOUR GHOST RIDERS TODAY. I THINK YOU'VE EARNED YOURSELF A NAP.
FIVE. I CUFFED FIVE. THAT PUTS ME AHEAD OF YOU.
DOES IT? ASK ME TOMORROW ABOUT THE TIME I BAGGED A GHOST RIDER WHO RODE A SHARK.
WHAT? YOU NEVER TOLD ME...
GET SOME SLEEP, THUNDERER. THAT'S AN ORDER FROM YOUR COMMANDING STORMBREAKER. DON'T WORRY...

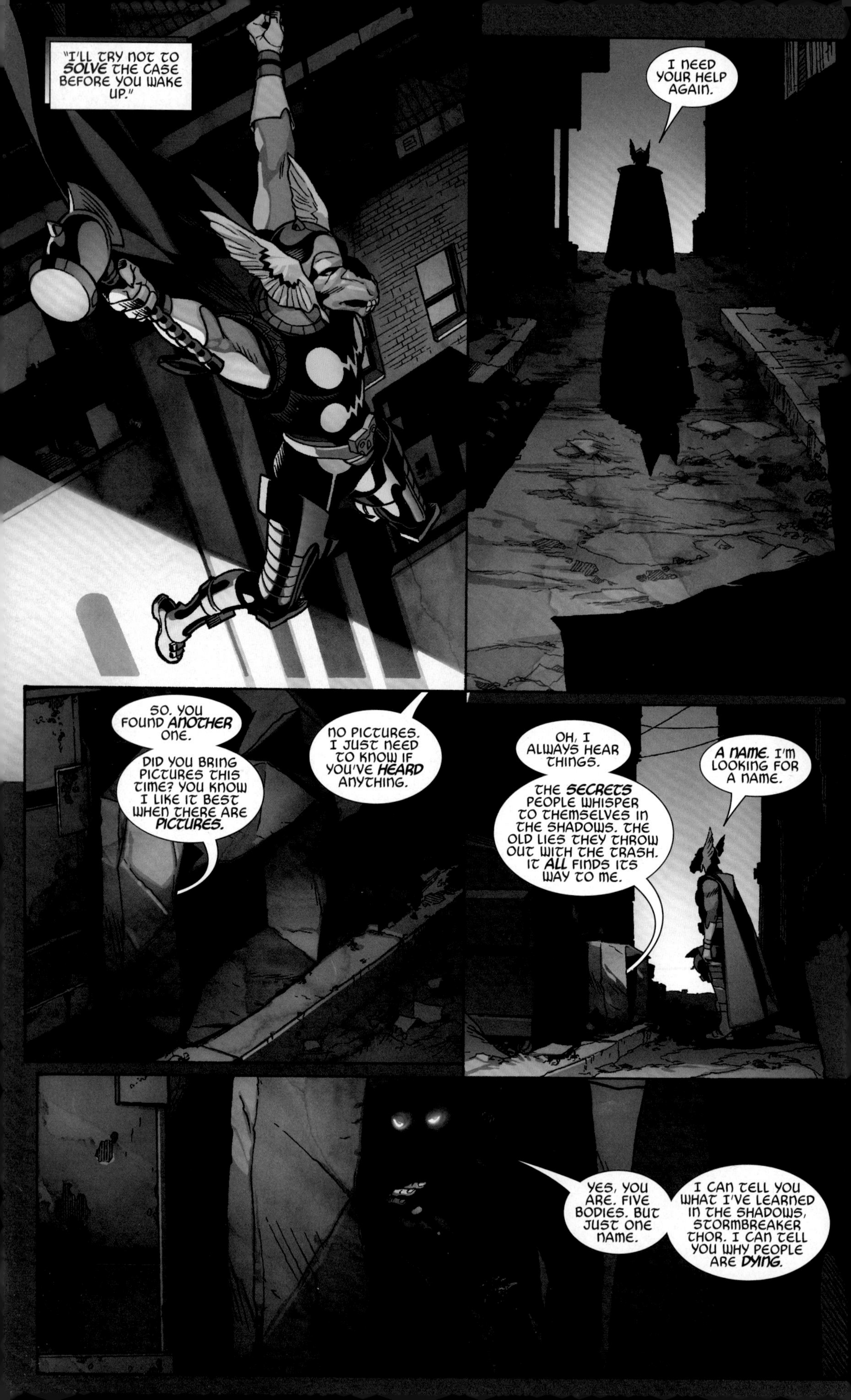
"I'LL TRY NOT TO SOLVE THE CASE BEFORE YOU WAKE UP."
I NEED YOUR HELP AGAIN.
SO. YOU FOUND ANOTHER ONE.
DID YOU BRING PICTURES THIS TIME? YOU KNOW I LIKE IT BEST WHEN THERE ARE PICTURES.
NO PICTURES. I JUST NEED TO KNOW IF YOU'VE HEARD ANYTHING.
OH, I ALWAYS HEAR THINGS.
THE SECRETS PEOPLE WHISPER TO THEMSELVES IN THE SHADOWS. THE OLD LIES THEY THROW OUT WITH THE TRASH. IT ALL FINDS ITS WAY TO ME.
A NAME. I'M LOOKING FOR A NAME.
YES, YOU ARE. FIVE BODIES. BUT JUST ONE NAME.
I CAN TELL YOU WHAT I'VE LEARNED IN THE SHADOWS, STORMBREAKER THOR. I CAN TELL YOU WHY PEOPLE ARE DYING.

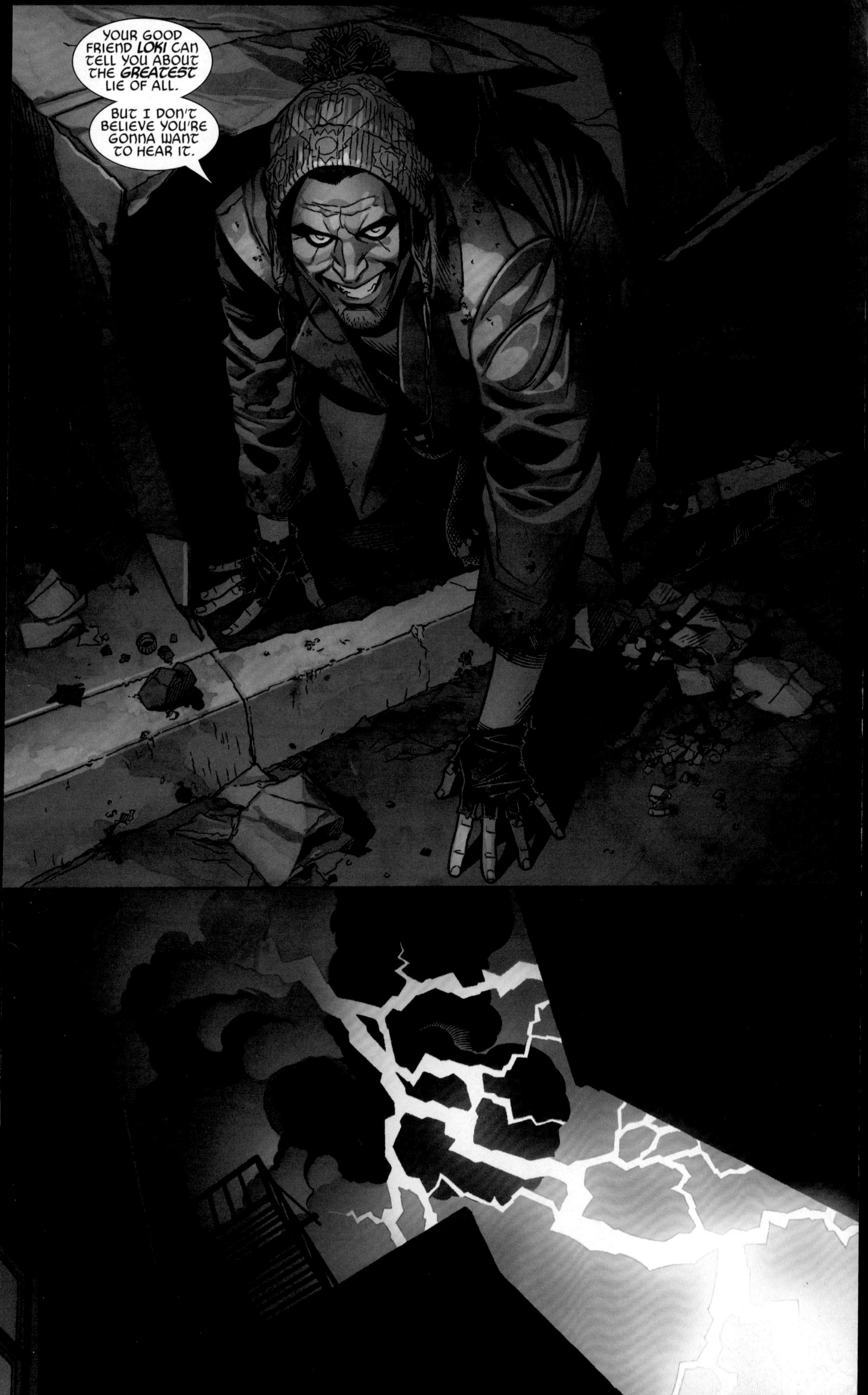
YOUR GOOD FRIEND LOKI CAN TELL YOU ABOUT THE GREATEST LIE OF ALL.
BUT I DON'T BELIEVE YOU'RE GONNA WANT TO HEAR IT.

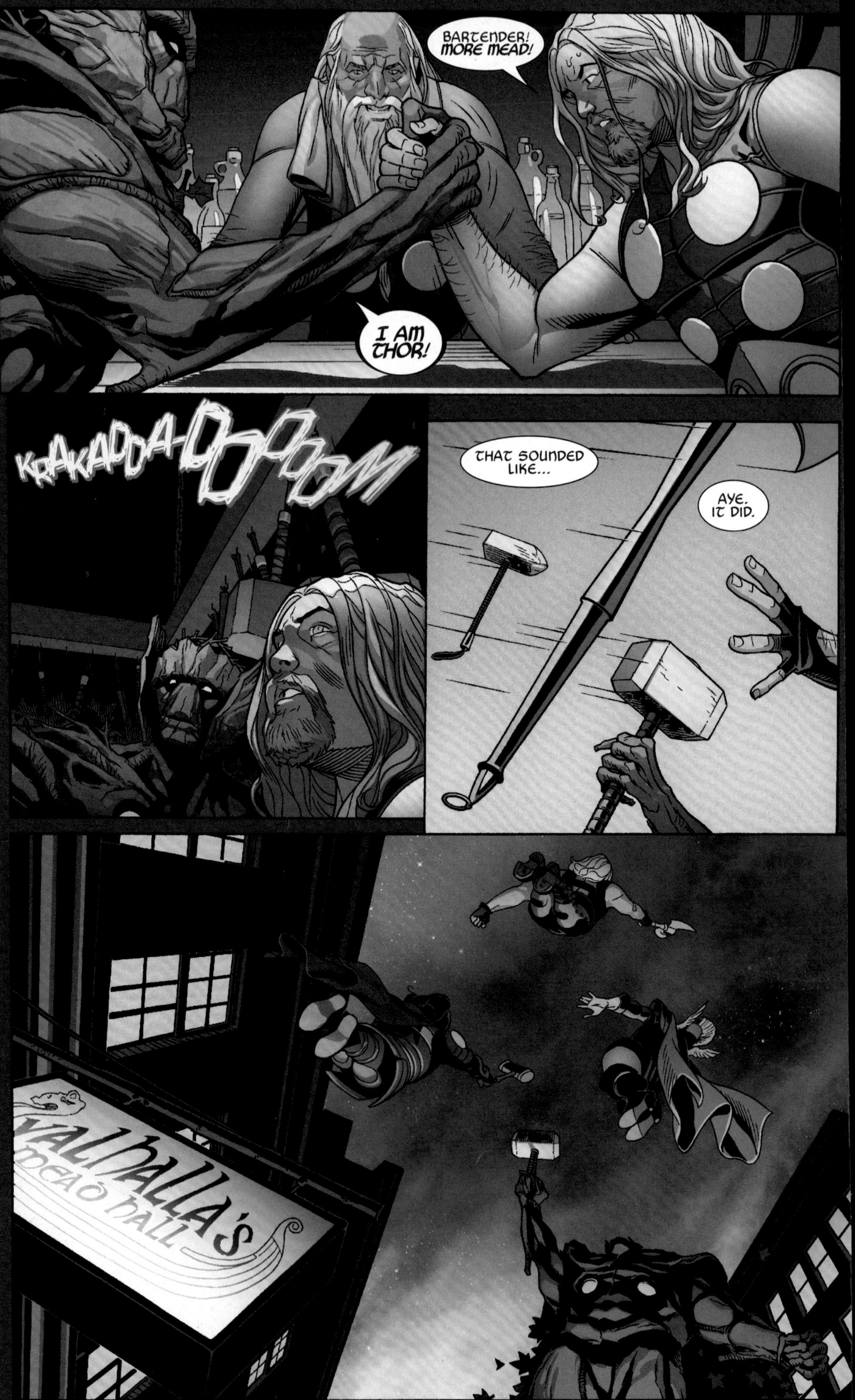
BARTENDER! MORE MEAD!
I AM THOR!
KRAKADDA-DOOOOOM
THAT SOUNDED LIKE...
AYE. IT DID.
VALHALLA'S MEAD HALL

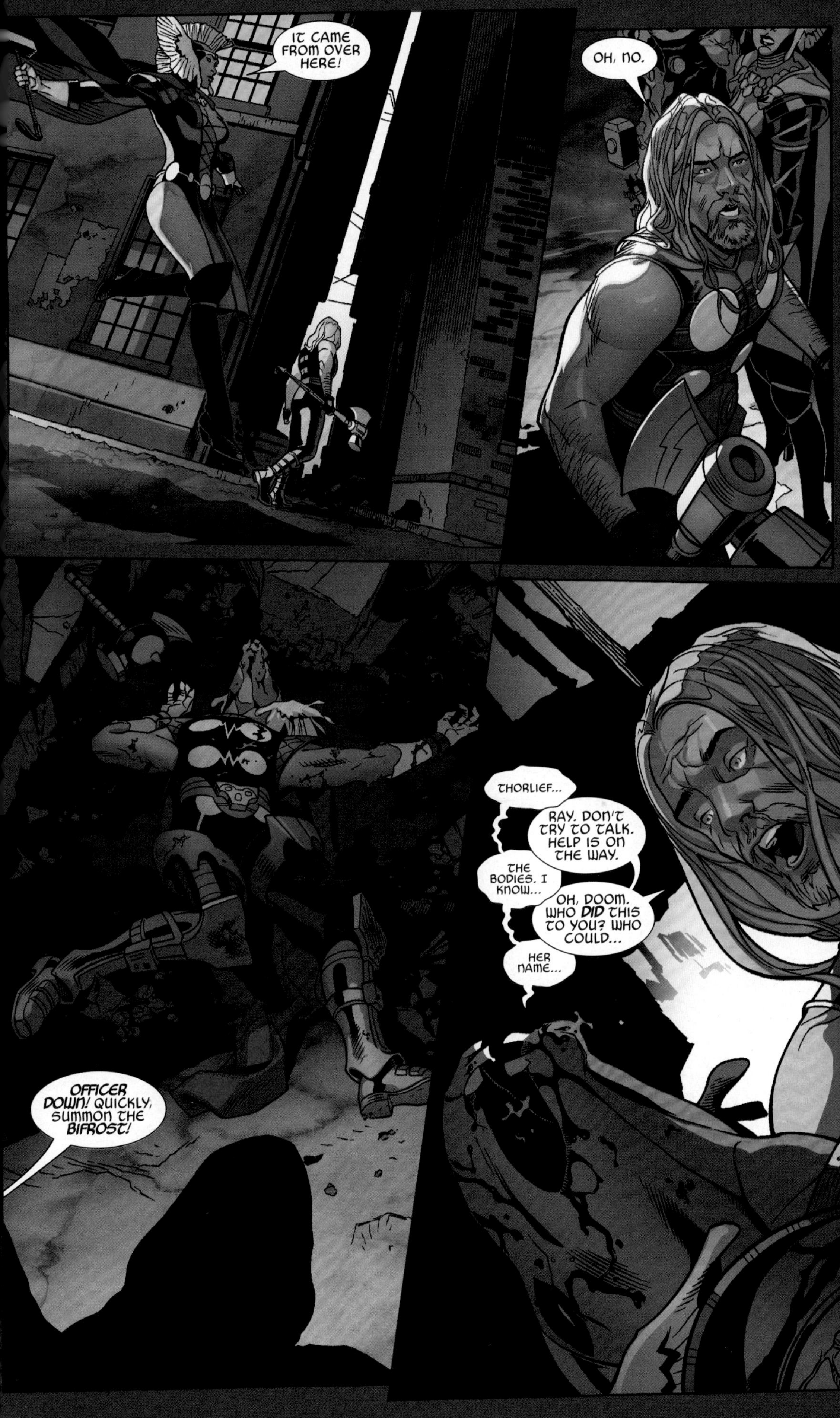
IT CAME FROM OVER HERE!
OH, NO.
THORLIEF...
RAY. DON'T TRY TO TALK. HELP IS ON THE WAY.
THE BODIES. I KNOW...
OH, DOOM. WHO **DID** THIS TO YOU? WHO COULD...
HER NAME...
OFFICER DOWN! QUICKLY, SUMMON THE **BIFROST!**

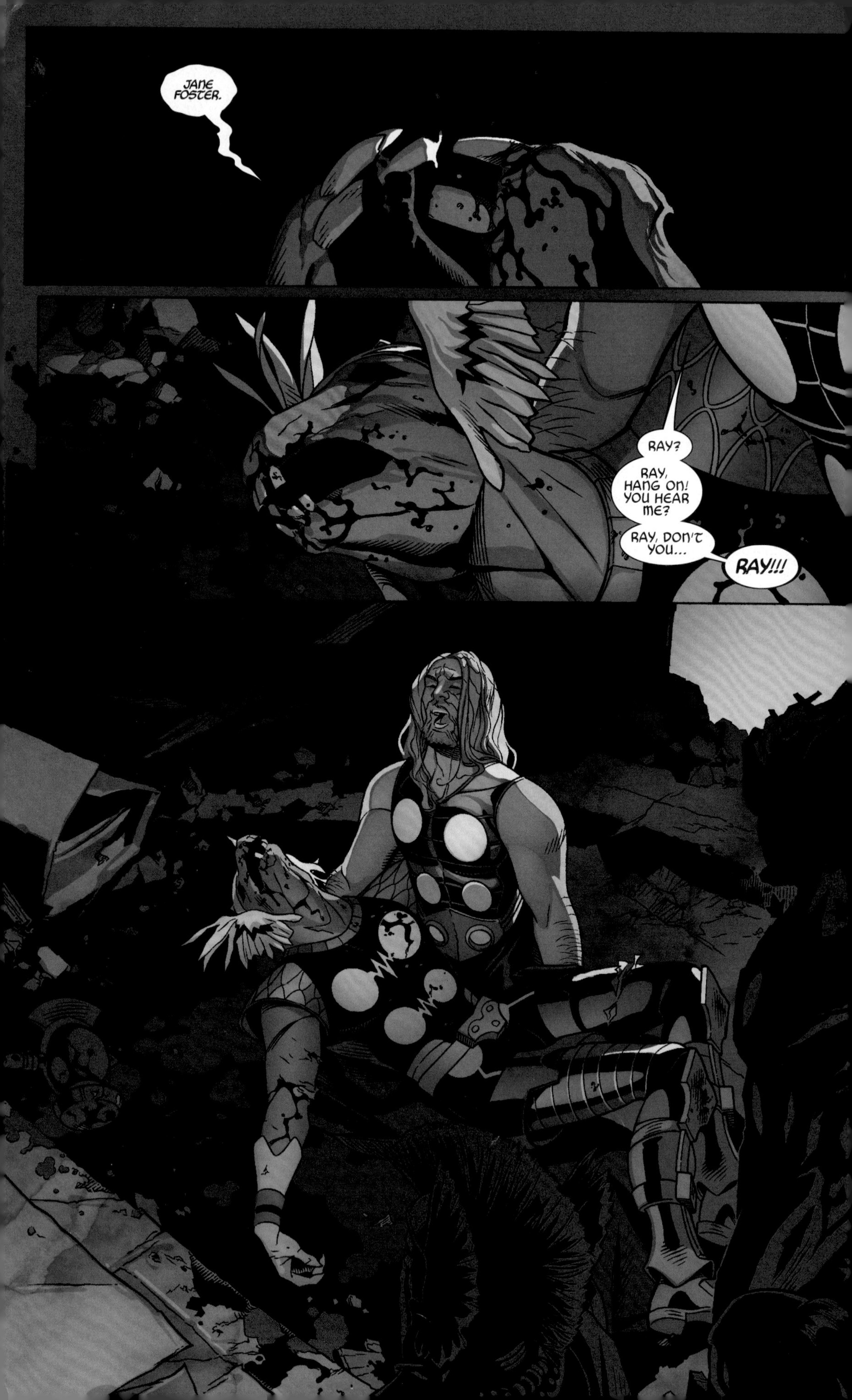
JANE FOSTER.
RAY?
RAY, HANG ON! YOU HEAR ME?
RAY, DON'T YOU...
RAY!!!

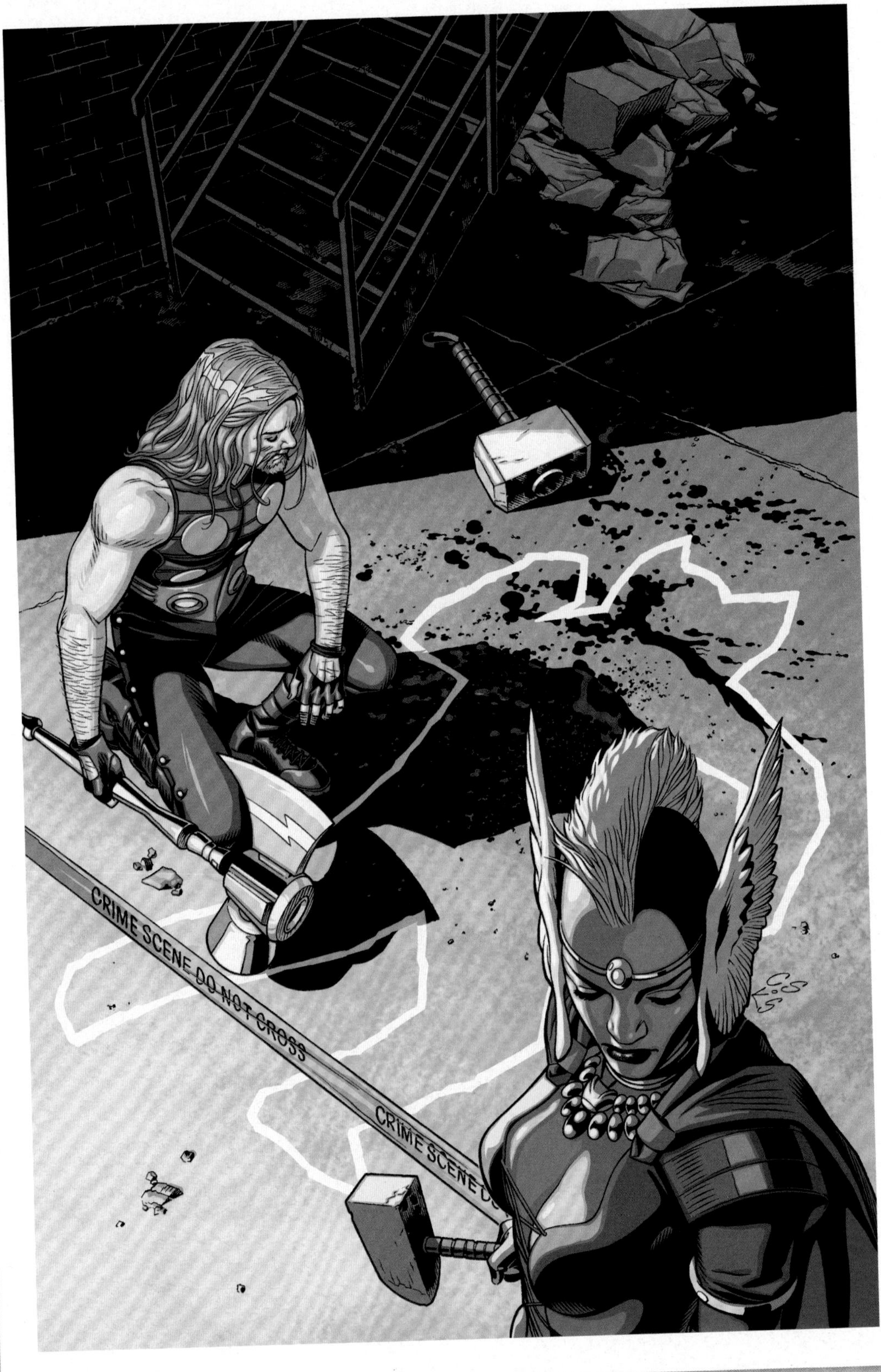
CRIME SCENE DO NOT CROSS
CRIME SCENE DO

THORS No. 2
THE JANE FOSTER MURDERS

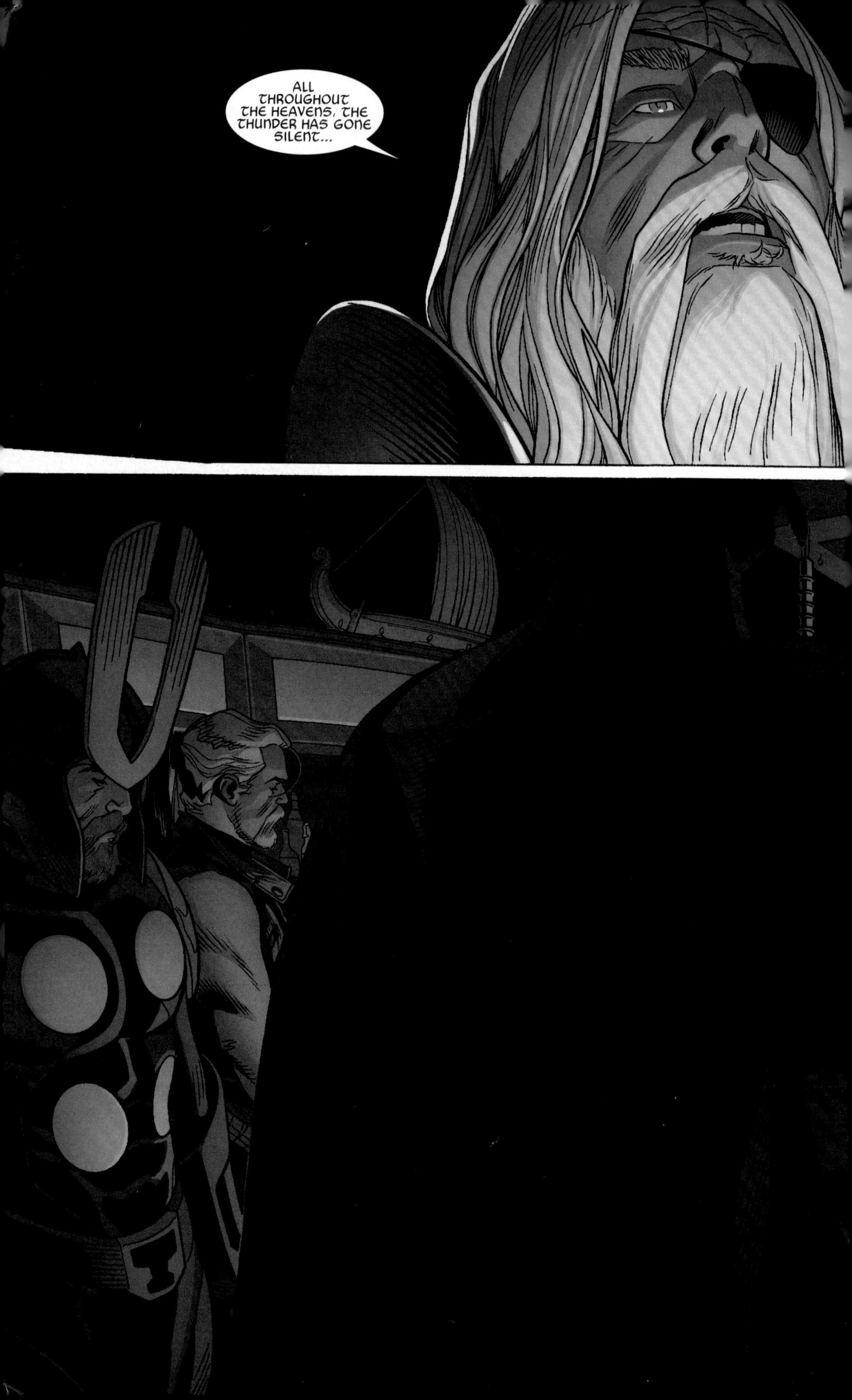
ALL THROUGHOUT THE HEAVENS, THE THUNDER HAS GONE SILENT...

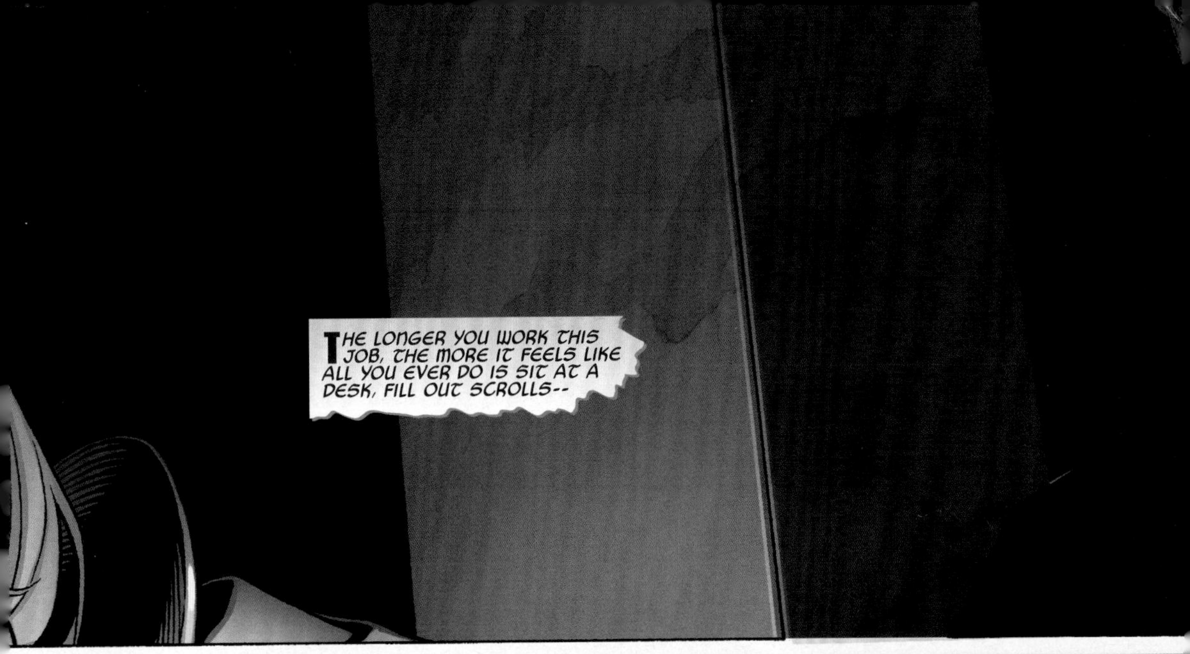
THE LONGER YOU WORK THIS JOB, THE MORE IT FEELS LIKE ALL YOU EVER DO IS SIT AT A DESK, FILL OUT SCROLLS--

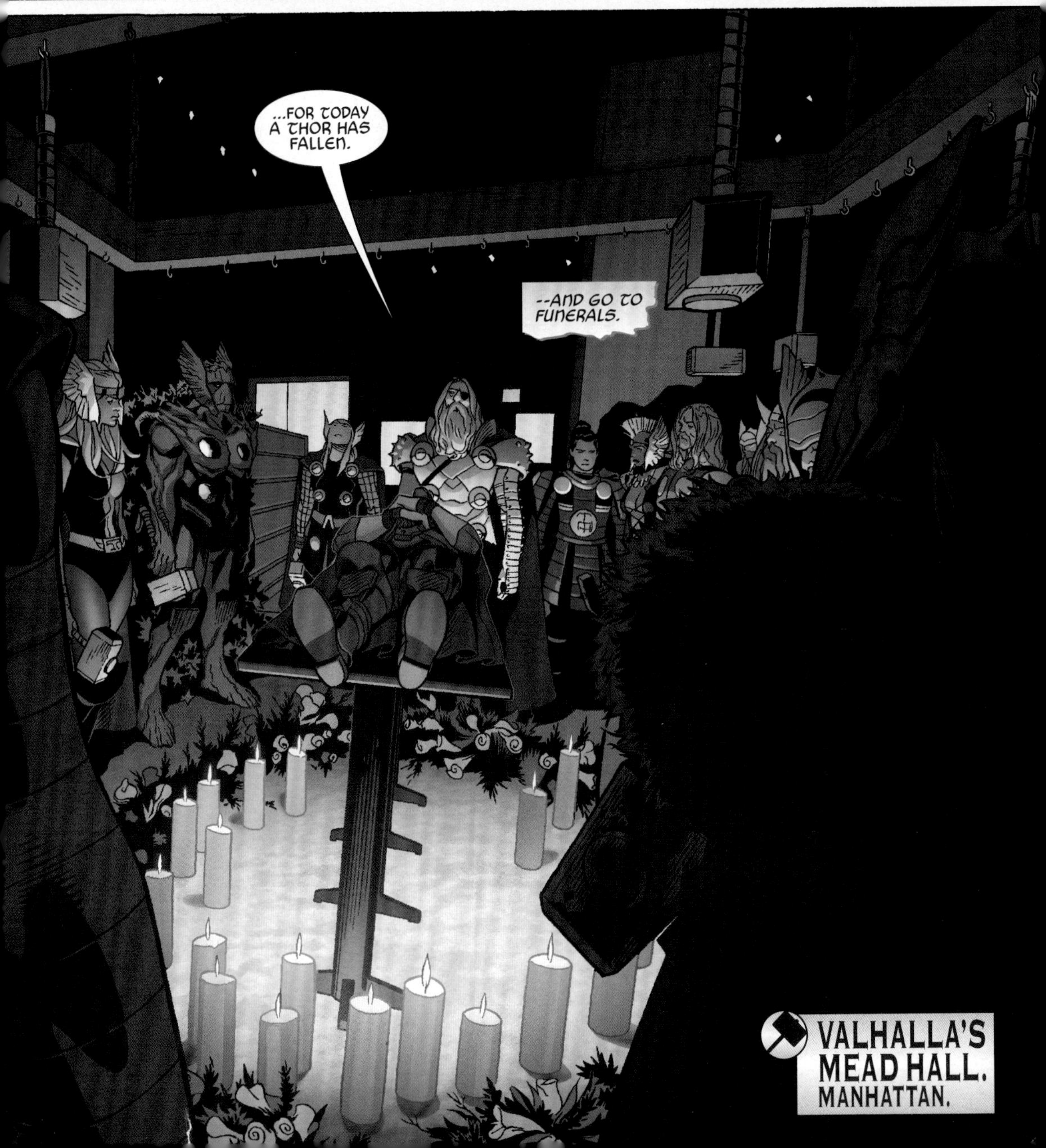
...FOR TODAY A THOR HAS FALLEN.
--AND GO TO FUNERALS.
VALHALLA'S MEAD HALL.
MANHATTAN.

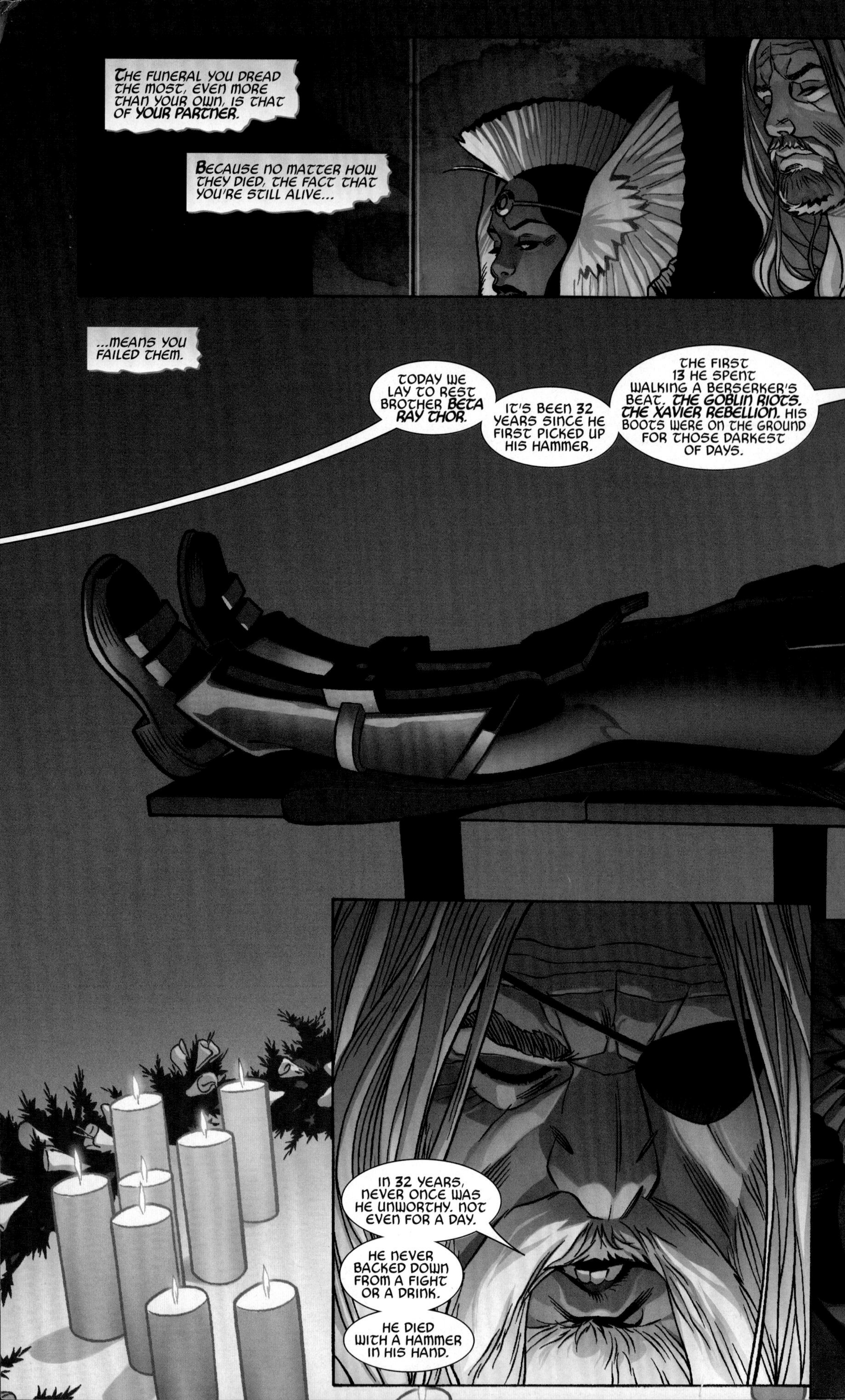
THE FUNERAL YOU DREAD THE MOST, EVEN MORE THAN YOUR OWN, IS THAT OF YOUR PARTNER.
BECAUSE NO MATTER HOW THEY DIED, THE FACT THAT YOU'RE STILL ALIVE...
...MEANS YOU FAILED THEM.
TODAY WE LAY TO REST BROTHER BETA RAY THOR.
IT'S BEEN 32 YEARS SINCE HE FIRST PICKED UP HIS HAMMER.
THE FIRST 13 HE SPENT WALKING A BERSERKER'S BEAT. THE GOBLIN RIOTS. THE XAVIER REBELLION. HIS BOOTS WERE ON THE GROUND FOR THOSE DARKEST OF DAYS.
IN 32 YEARS, NEVER ONCE WAS HE UNWORTHY. NOT EVEN FOR A DAY.
HE NEVER BACKED DOWN FROM A FIGHT OR A DRINK.
HE DIED WITH A HAMMER IN HIS HAND.

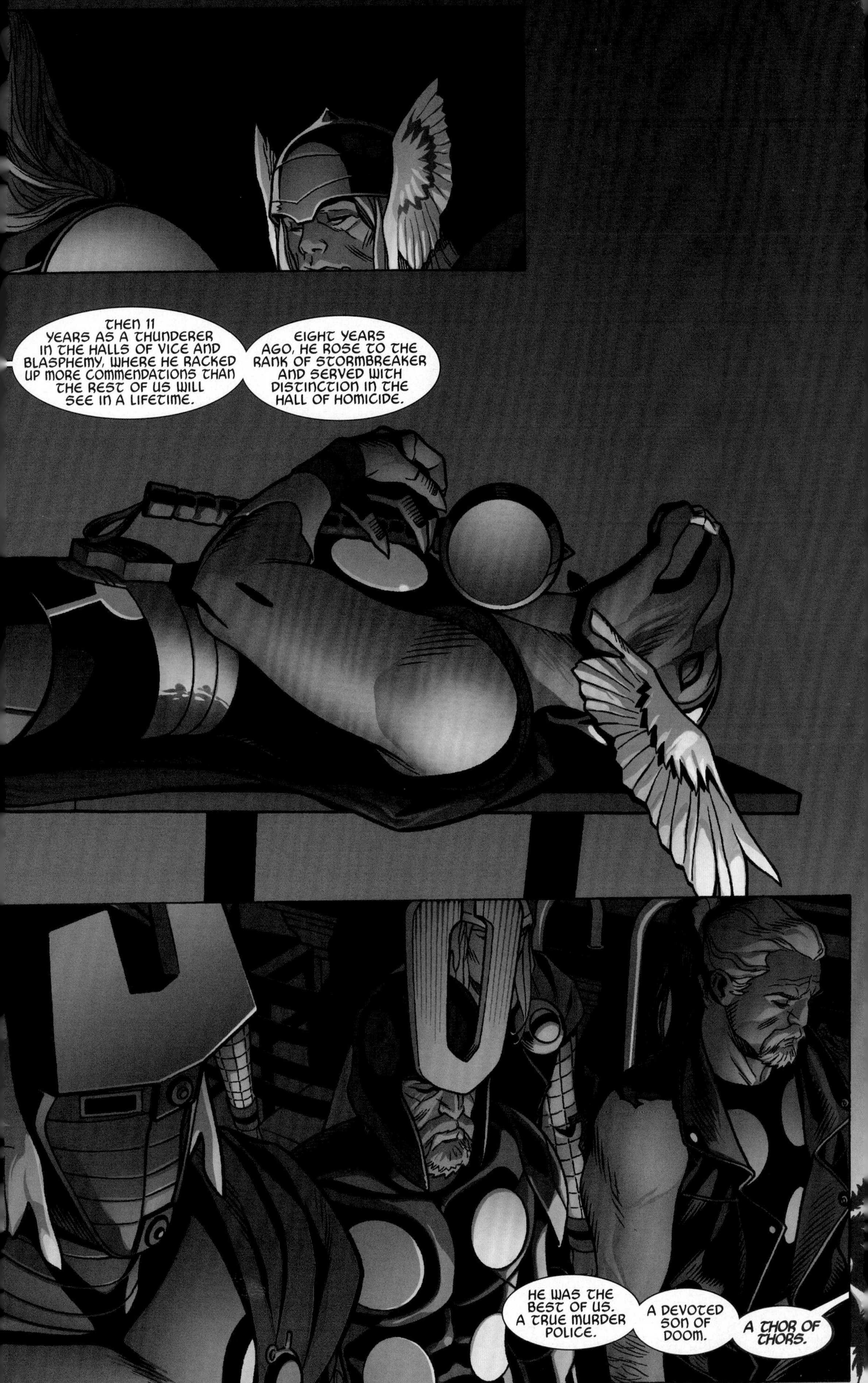
THEN 11 YEARS AS A THUNDERER IN THE HALLS OF VICE AND BLASPHEMY, WHERE HE RACKED UP MORE COMMENDATIONS THAN THE REST OF US WILL SEE IN A LIFETIME.
EIGHT YEARS AGO, HE ROSE TO THE RANK OF STORMBREAKER AND SERVED WITH DISTINCTION IN THE HALL OF HOMICIDE.
HE WAS THE BEST OF US. A TRUE MURDER POLICE.
A DEVOTED SON OF DOOM.
A THOR OF THORS.

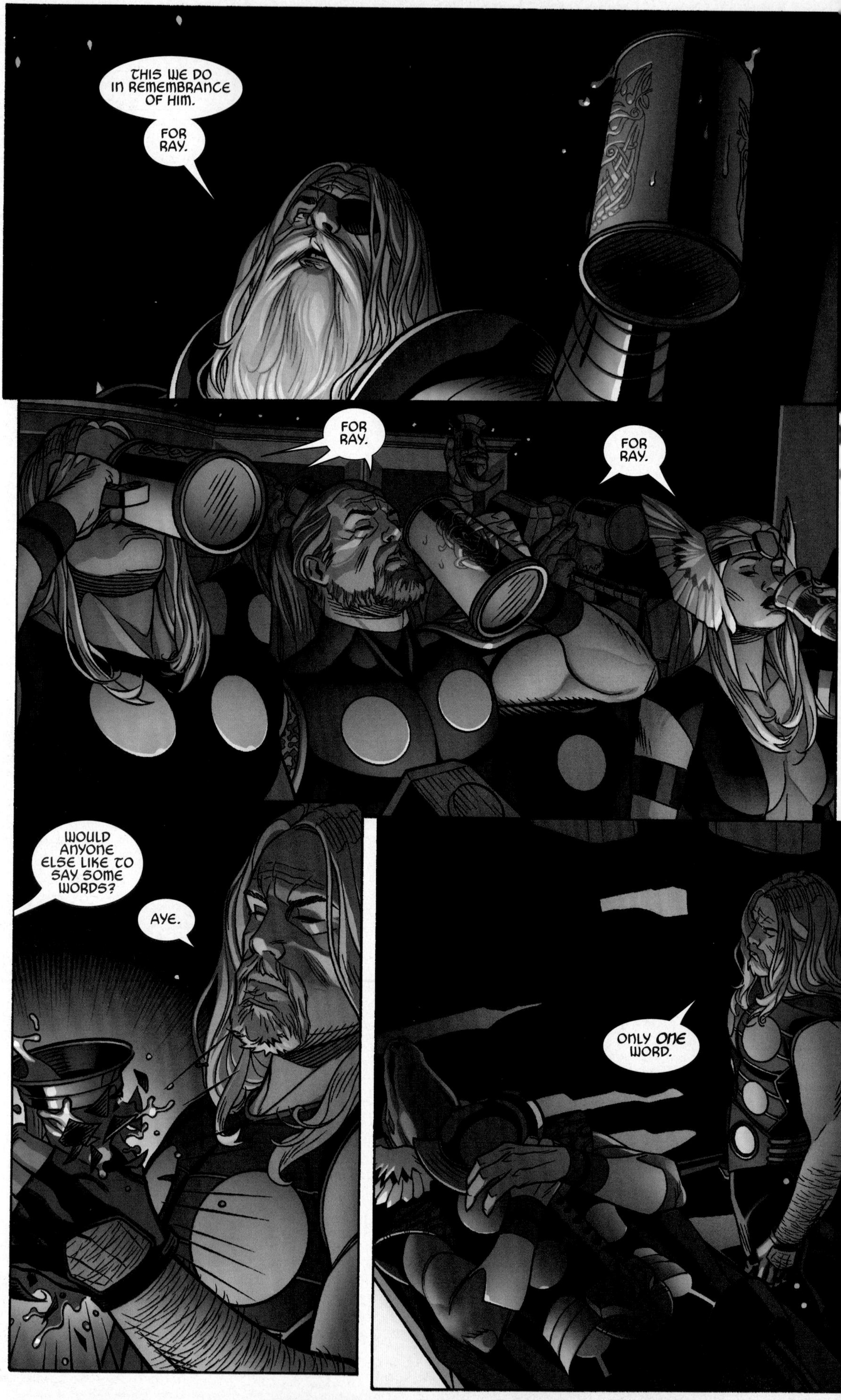
THIS WE DO IN REMEMBRANCE OF HIM.
FOR RAY.
FOR RAY.
FOR RAY.
WOULD ANYONE ELSE LIKE TO SAY SOME WORDS?
AYE.
ONLY ONE WORD.

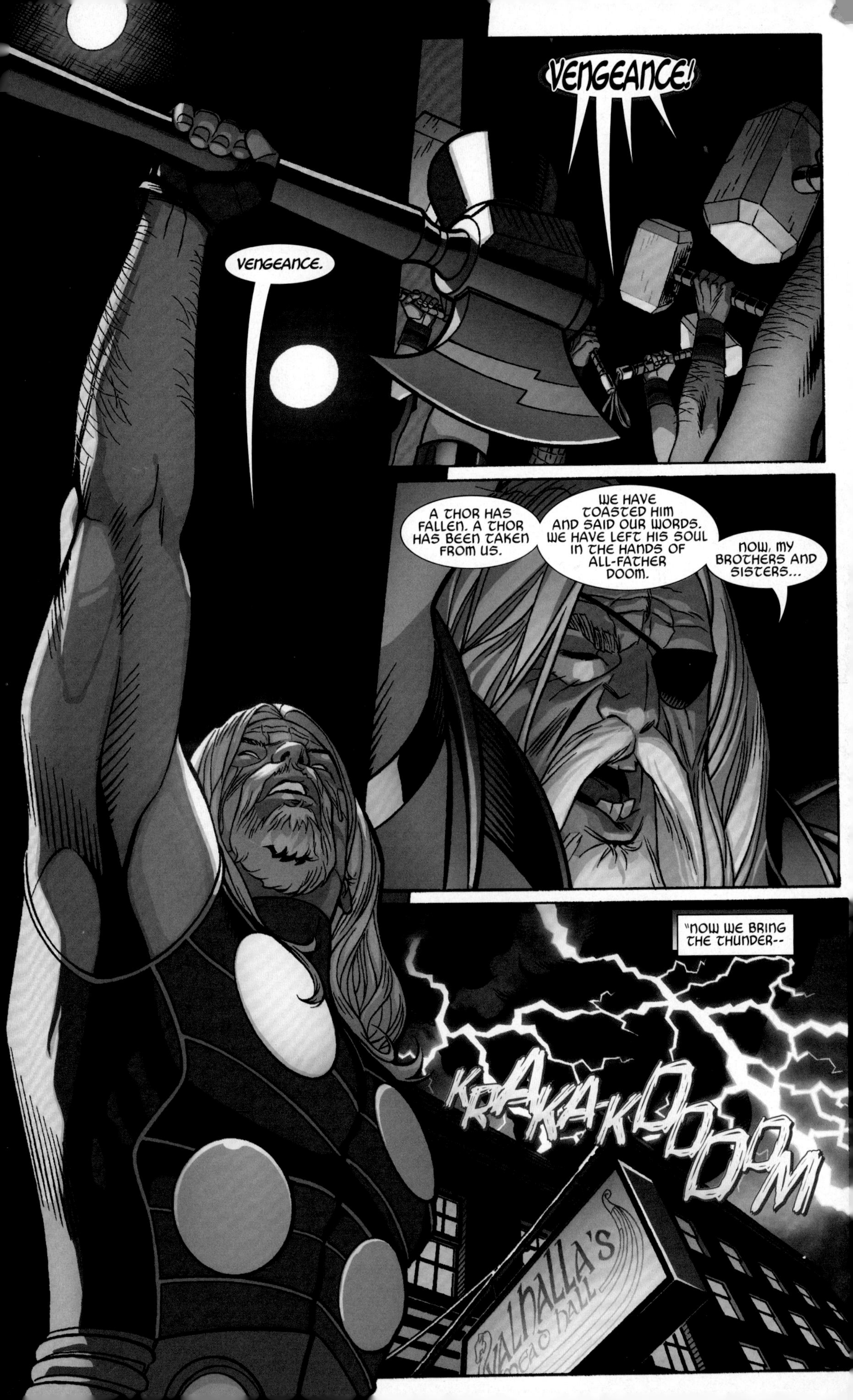
VENGEANCE!
VENGEANCE.
A THOR HAS FALLEN. A THOR HAS BEEN TAKEN FROM US.
WE HAVE TOASTED HIM AND SAID OUR WORDS. WE HAVE LEFT HIS SOUL IN THE HANDS OF ALL-FATHER DOOM.
NOW, MY BROTHERS AND SISTERS...
"NOW WE BRING THE THUNDER--
KRAKAKOOOOM
VALHALLA'S MEAD HALL

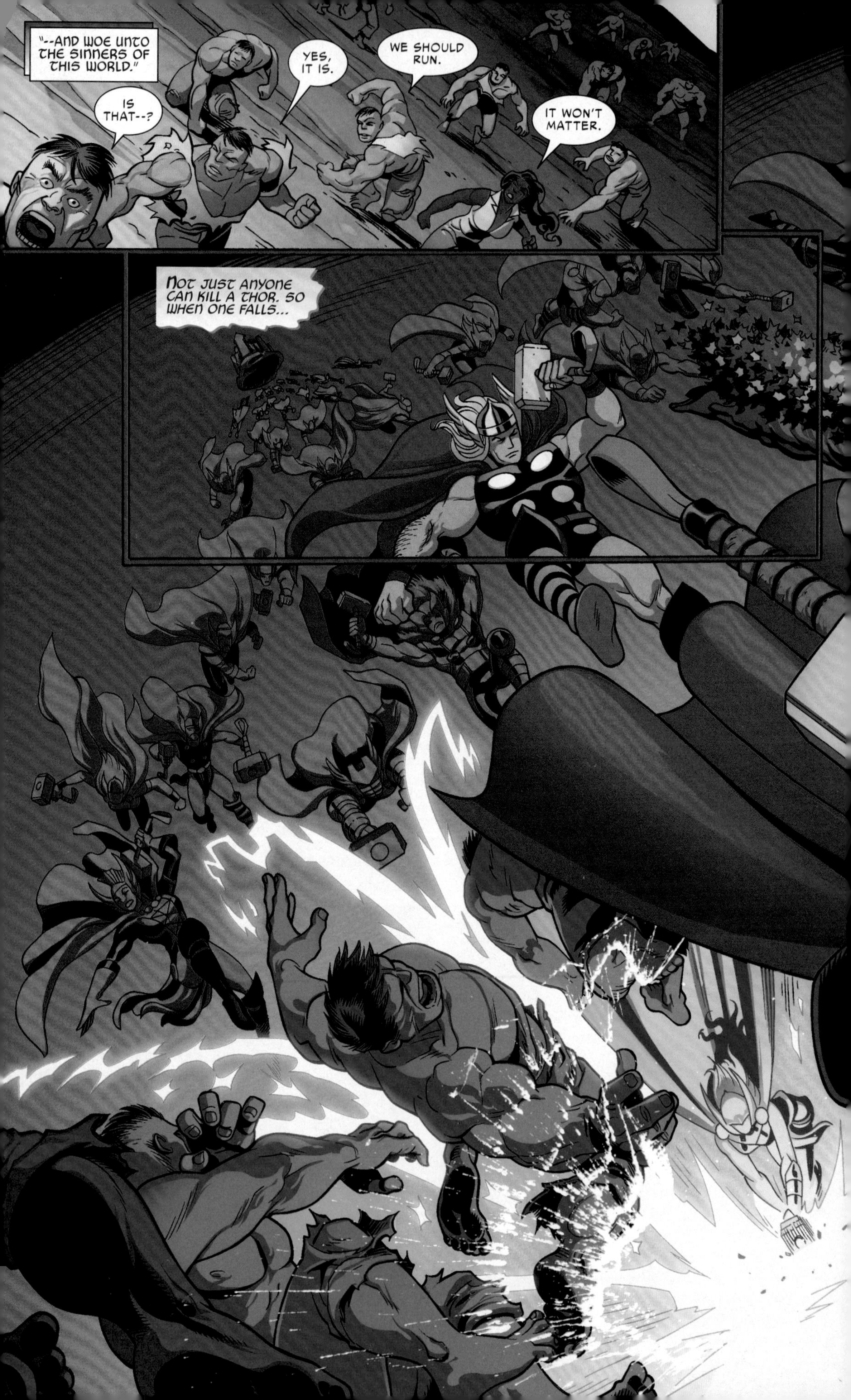

"--AND WOE UNTO THE SINNERS OF THIS WORLD."
IS THAT--?
YES, IT IS.
WE SHOULD RUN.
IT WON'T MATTER.
NOT JUST ANYONE CAN KILL A THOR. SO WHEN ONE FALLS...

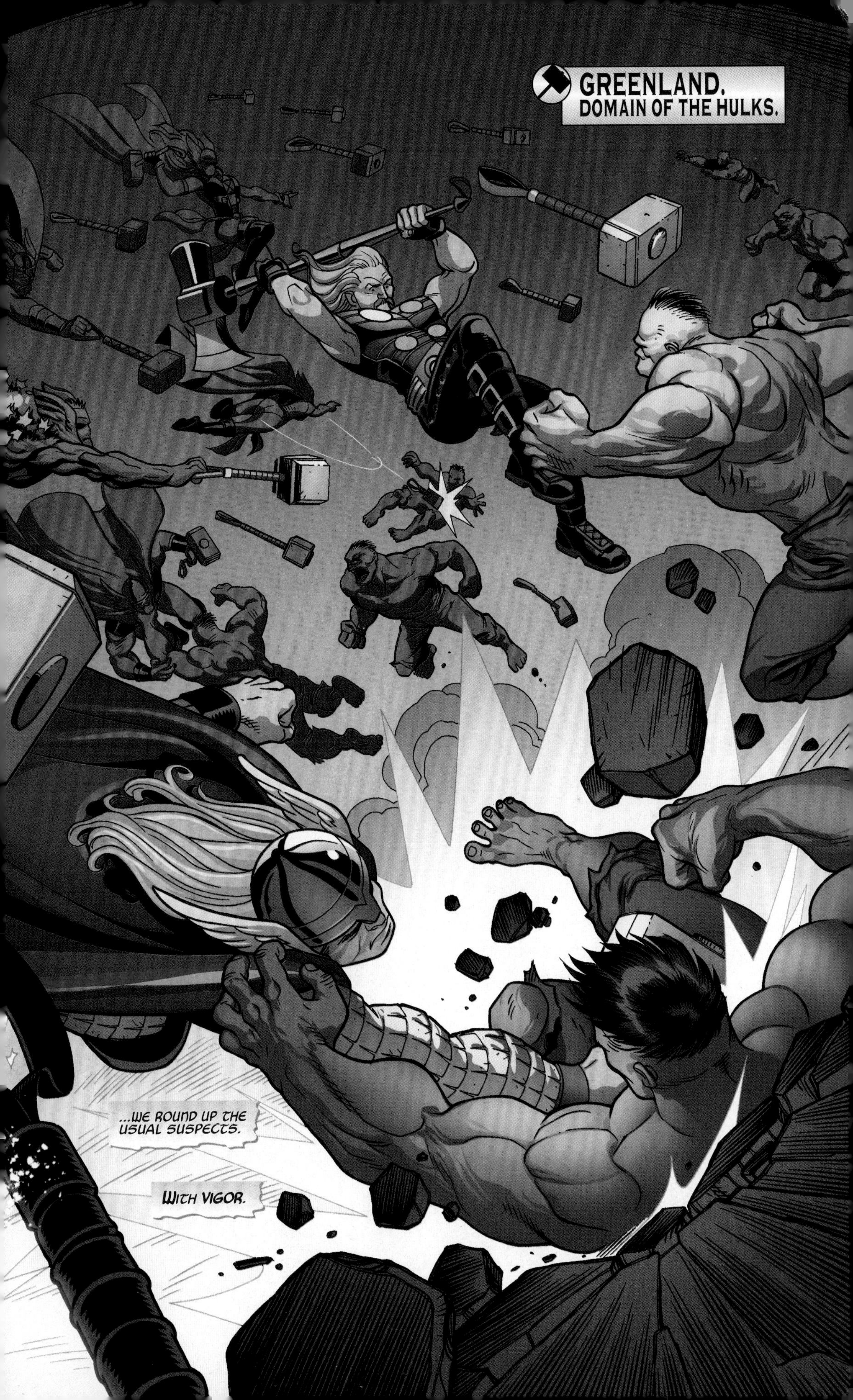
GREENLAND.
DOMAIN OF THE HULKS.
...WE ROUND UP THE USUAL SUSPECTS.
WITH VIGOR.

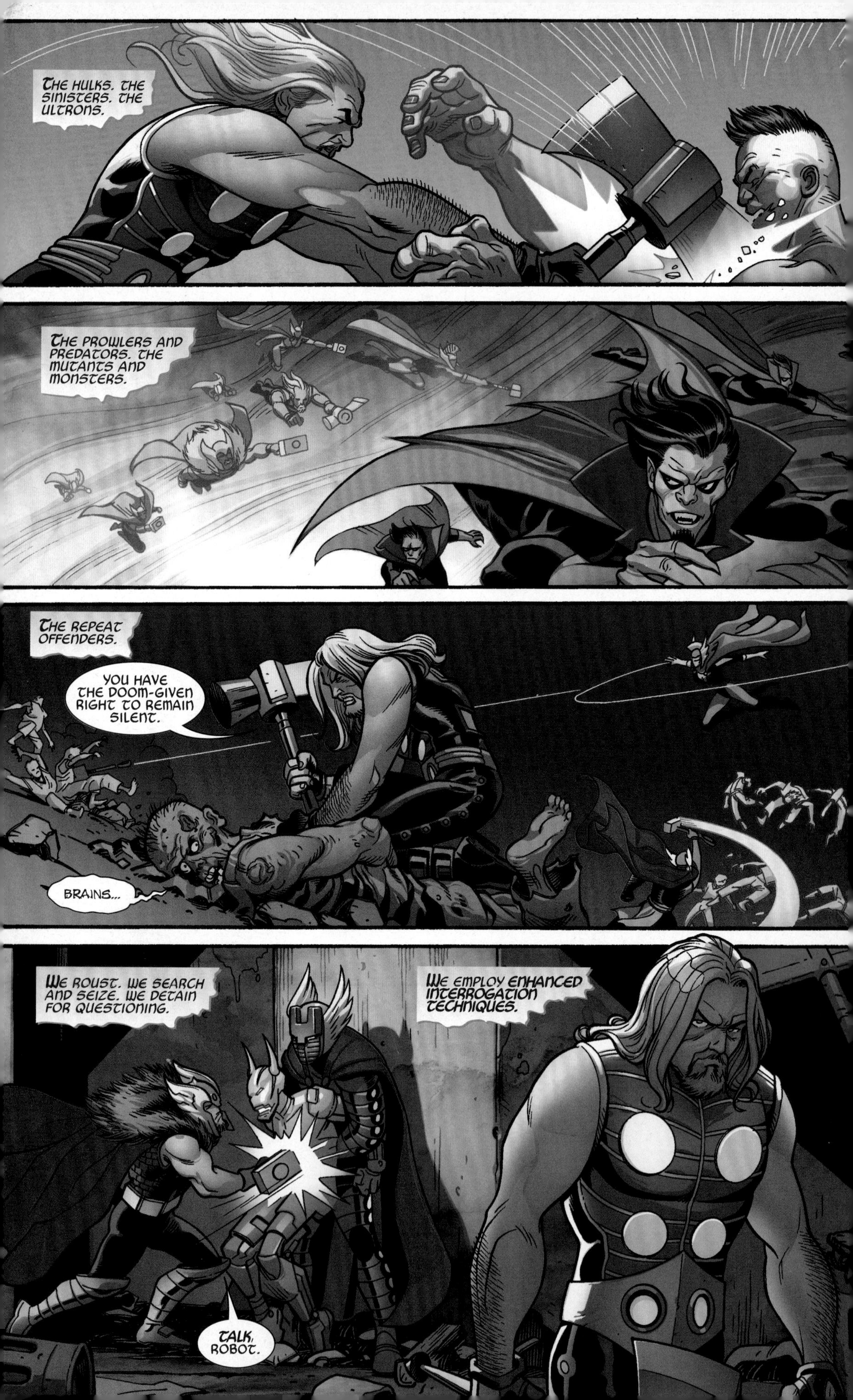
THE HULKS. THE SINISTERS. THE ULTRONS.
THE PROWLERS AND PREDATORS. THE MUTANTS AND MONSTERS.
THE REPEAT OFFENDERS.
YOU HAVE THE DOOM-GIVEN RIGHT TO REMAIN SILENT.
BRAINS...
WE ROUST. WE SEARCH AND SEIZE. WE DETAIN FOR QUESTIONING.
WE EMPLOY ENHANCED INTERROGATION TECHNIQUES.
TALK, ROBOT.

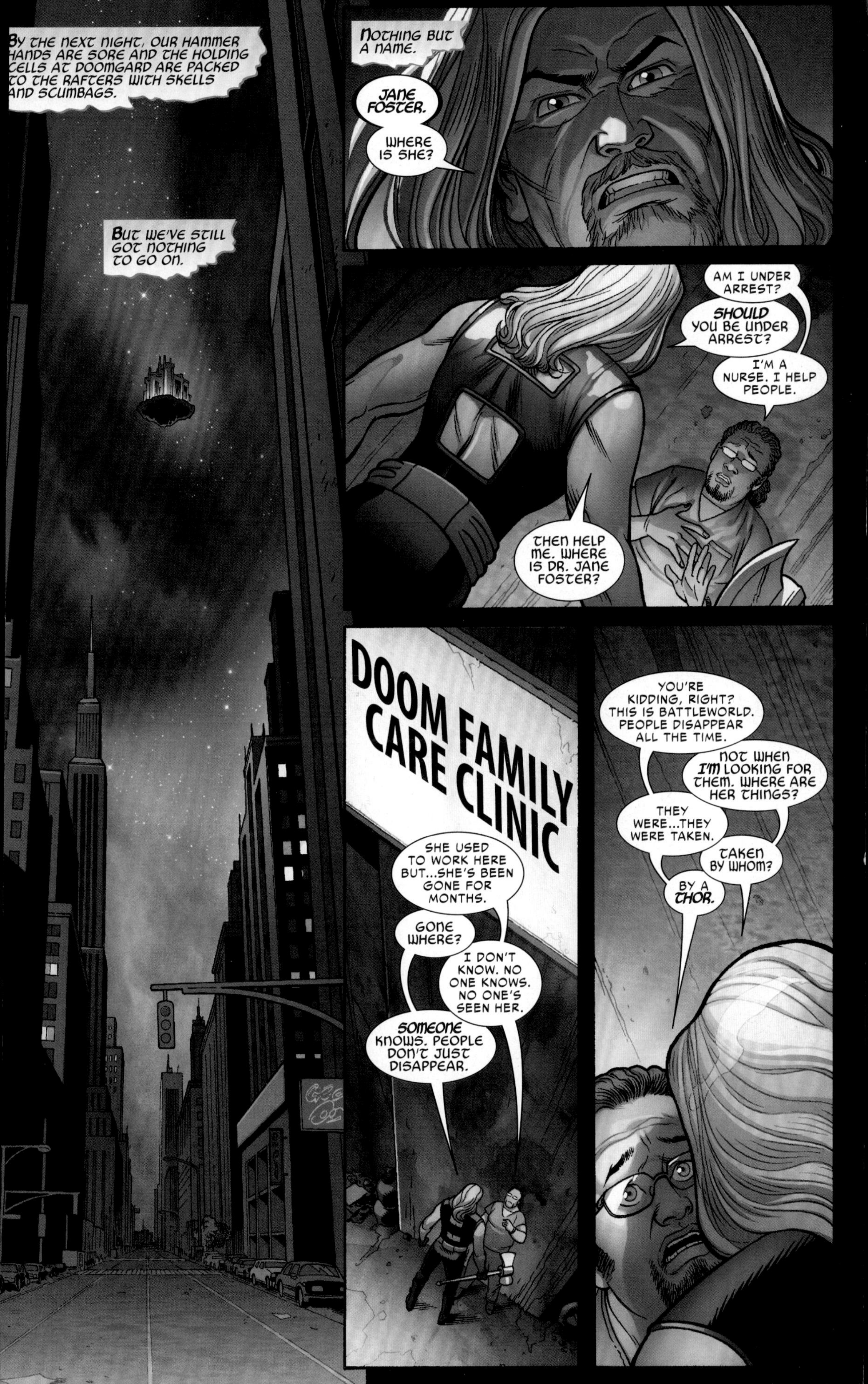
BY THE NEXT NIGHT, OUR HAMMER HANDS ARE SORE AND THE HOLDING CELLS AT DOOMGARD ARE PACKED TO THE RAFTERS WITH SKELLS AND SCUMBAGS.
BUT WE'VE STILL GOT NOTHING TO GO ON.
NOTHING BUT A NAME.
JANE FOSTER.
WHERE IS SHE?
AM I UNDER ARREST?
SHOULD YOU BE UNDER ARREST?
I'M A NURSE. I HELP PEOPLE.
THEN HELP ME. WHERE IS DR. JANE FOSTER?
DOOM FAMILY CARE CLINIC
SHE USED TO WORK HERE BUT...SHE'S BEEN GONE FOR MONTHS.
GONE WHERE?
I DON'T KNOW. NO ONE KNOWS. NO ONE'S SEEN HER.
SOMEONE KNOWS. PEOPLE DON'T JUST DISAPPEAR.
YOU'RE KIDDING, RIGHT? THIS IS BATTLEWORLD. PEOPLE DISAPPEAR ALL THE TIME.
NOT WHEN I'M LOOKING FOR THEM. WHERE ARE HER THINGS?
THEY WERE...THEY WERE TAKEN.
TAKEN BY WHOM?
BY A THOR.

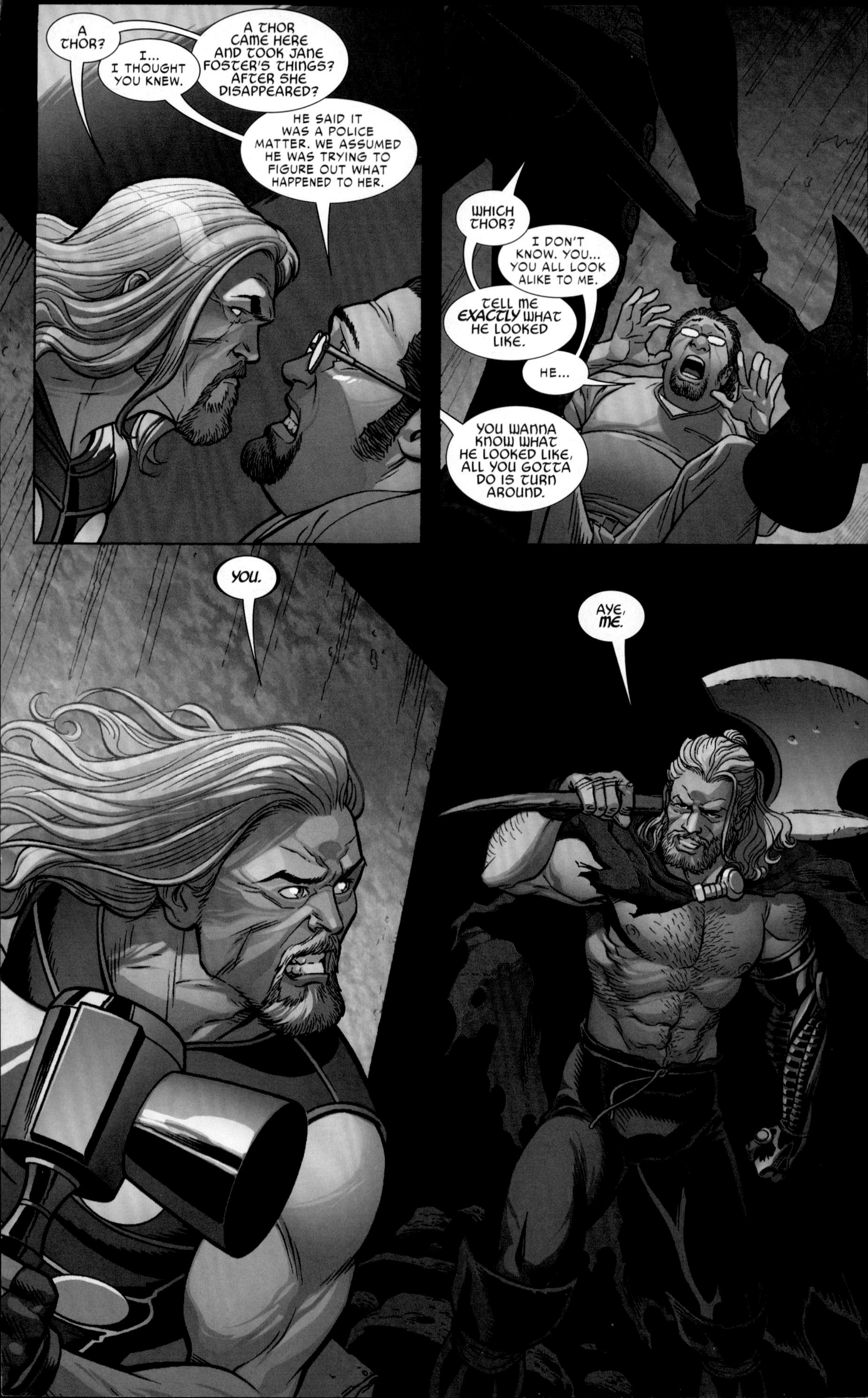
A THOR?
I... I THOUGHT YOU KNEW.
A THOR CAME HERE AND TOOK JANE FOSTER'S THINGS? AFTER SHE DISAPPEARED?
HE SAID IT WAS A POLICE MATTER. WE ASSUMED HE WAS TRYING TO FIGURE OUT WHAT HAPPENED TO HER.
WHICH THOR?
I DON'T KNOW. YOU... YOU ALL LOOK ALIKE TO ME.
TELL ME EXACTLY WHAT HE LOOKED LIKE.
HE...
YOU WANNA KNOW WHAT HE LOOKED LIKE, ALL YOU GOTTA DO IS TURN AROUND.
YOU.
AYE, ME.

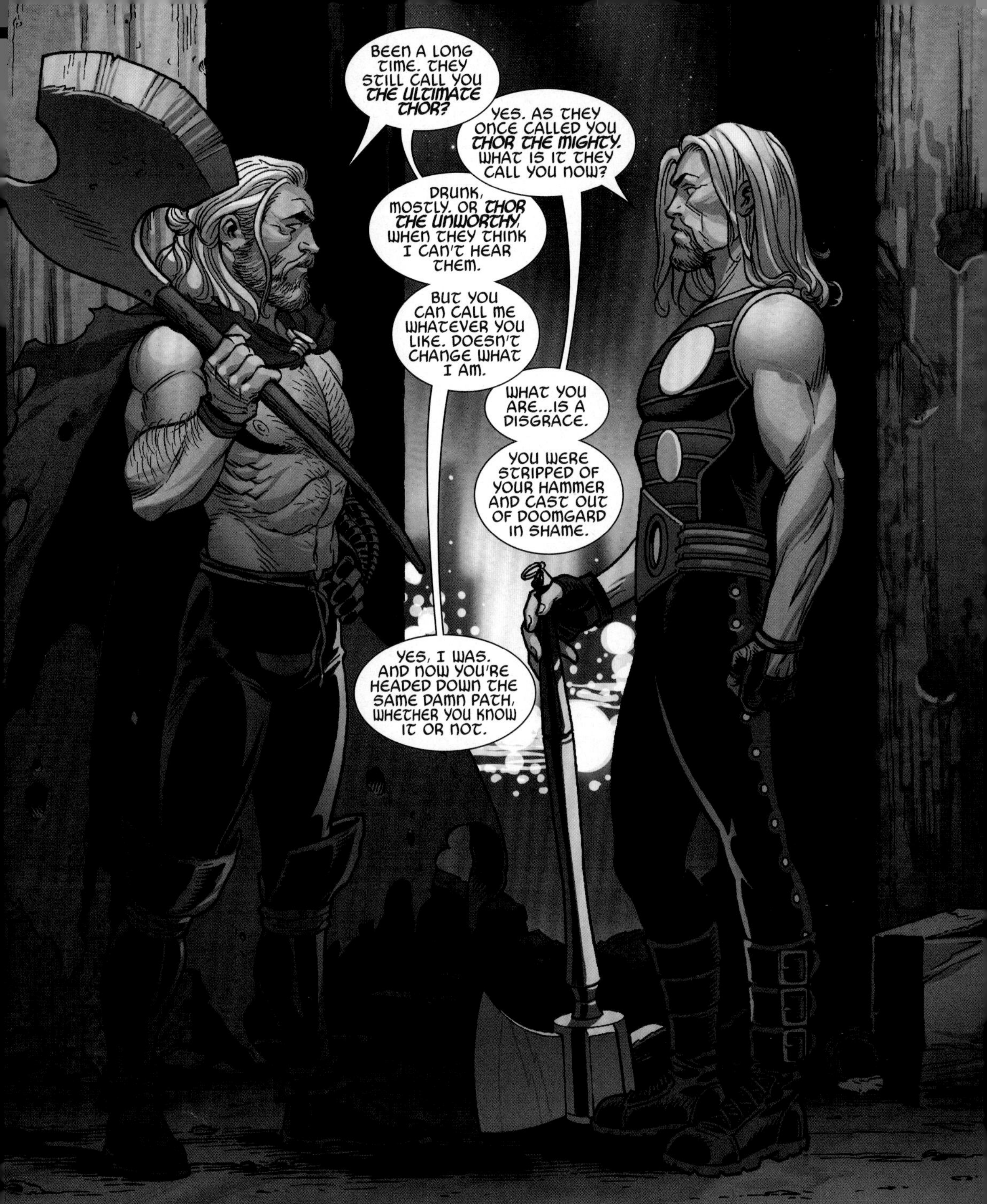
BEEN A LONG TIME. THEY STILL CALL YOU THE ULTIMATE THOR?
YES. AS THEY ONCE CALLED YOU THOR THE MIGHTY. WHAT IS IT THEY CALL YOU NOW?
DRUNK, MOSTLY. OR THOR THE UNWORTHY, WHEN THEY THINK I CAN'T HEAR THEM.
BUT YOU CAN CALL ME WHATEVER YOU LIKE. DOESN'T CHANGE WHAT I AM.
WHAT YOU ARE...IS A DISGRACE.
YOU WERE STRIPPED OF YOUR HAMMER AND CAST OUT OF DOOMGARD IN SHAME.
YES, I WAS. AND NOW YOU'RE HEADED DOWN THE SAME DAMN PATH, WHETHER YOU KNOW IT OR NOT.
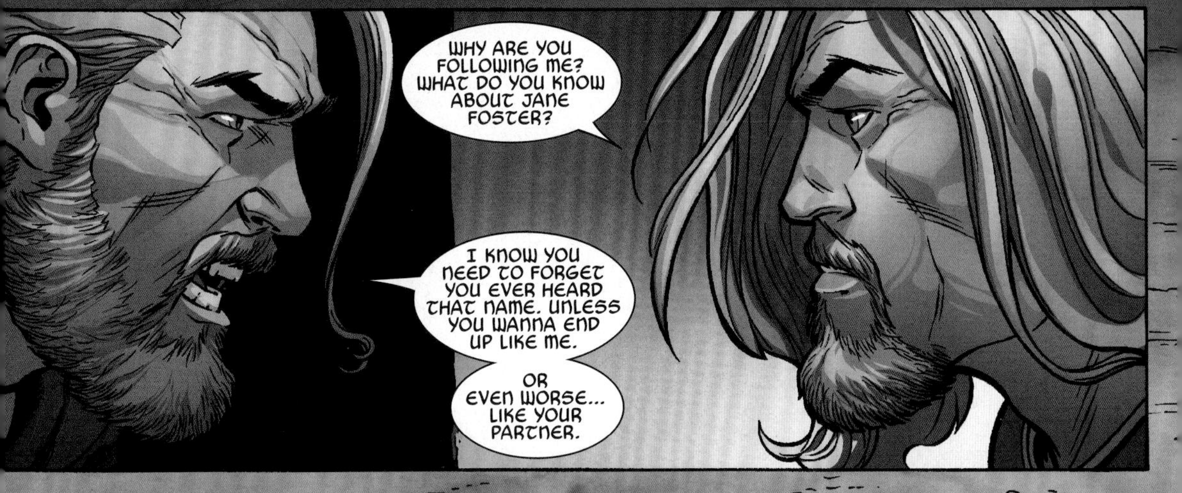
WHY ARE YOU FOLLOWING ME? WHAT DO YOU KNOW ABOUT JANE FOSTER?
I KNOW YOU NEED TO FORGET YOU EVER HEARD THAT NAME. UNLESS YOU WANNA END UP LIKE ME.
OR EVEN WORSE... LIKE YOUR PARTNER.

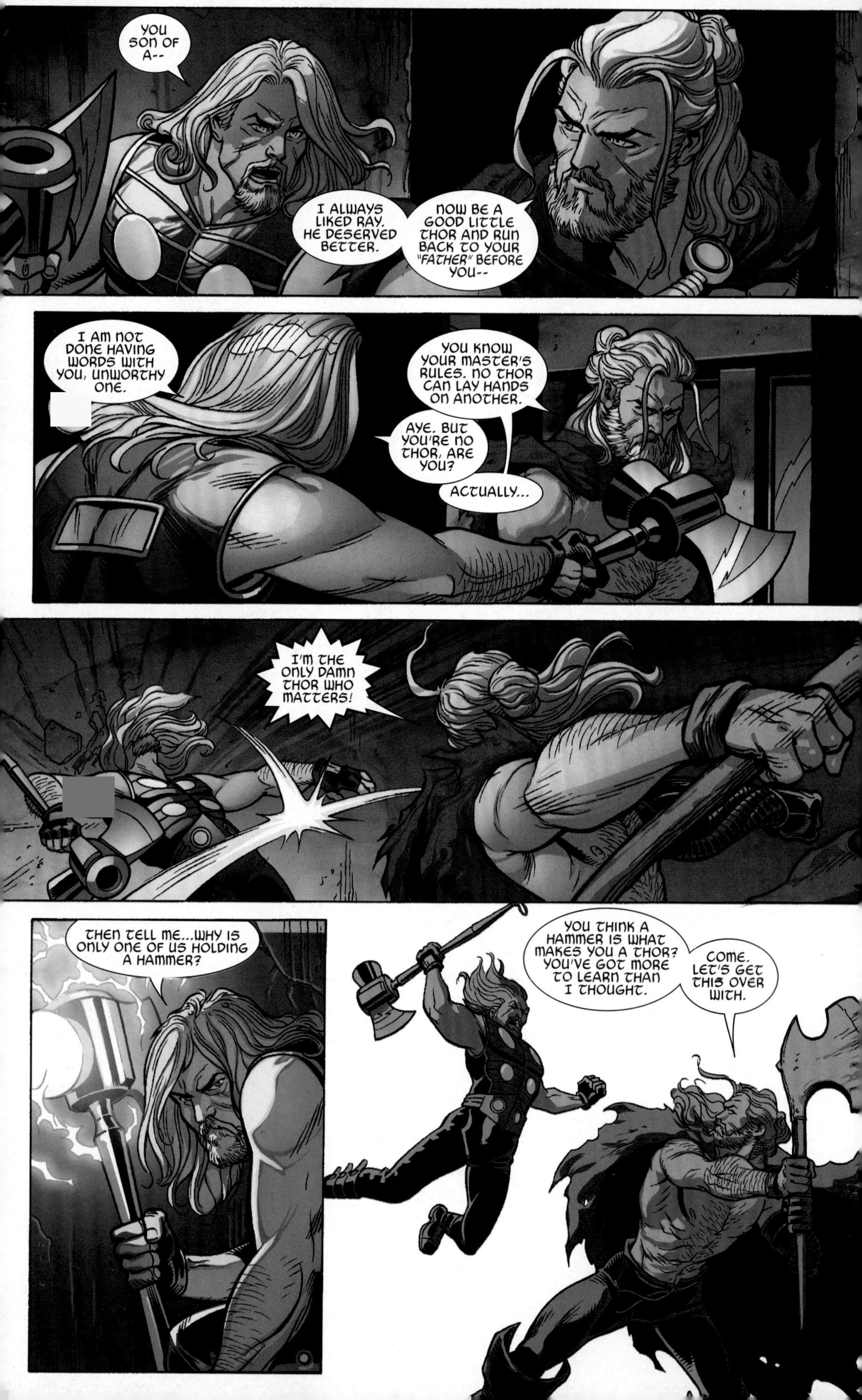
YOU SON OF A--
I ALWAYS LIKED RAY. HE DESERVED BETTER.
NOW BE A GOOD LITTLE THOR AND RUN BACK TO YOUR "FATHER" BEFORE YOU--
I AM NOT DONE HAVING WORDS WITH YOU, UNWORTHY ONE.
YOU KNOW YOUR MASTER'S RULES. NO THOR CAN LAY HANDS ON ANOTHER.
AYE. BUT YOU'RE NO THOR, ARE YOU?
ACTUALLY...
I'M THE ONLY DAMN THOR WHO MATTERS!
THEN TELL ME...WHY IS ONLY ONE OF US HOLDING A HAMMER?
YOU THINK A HAMMER IS WHAT MAKES YOU A THOR? YOU'VE GOT MORE TO LEARN THAN I THOUGHT.
COME. LET'S GET THIS OVER WITH.

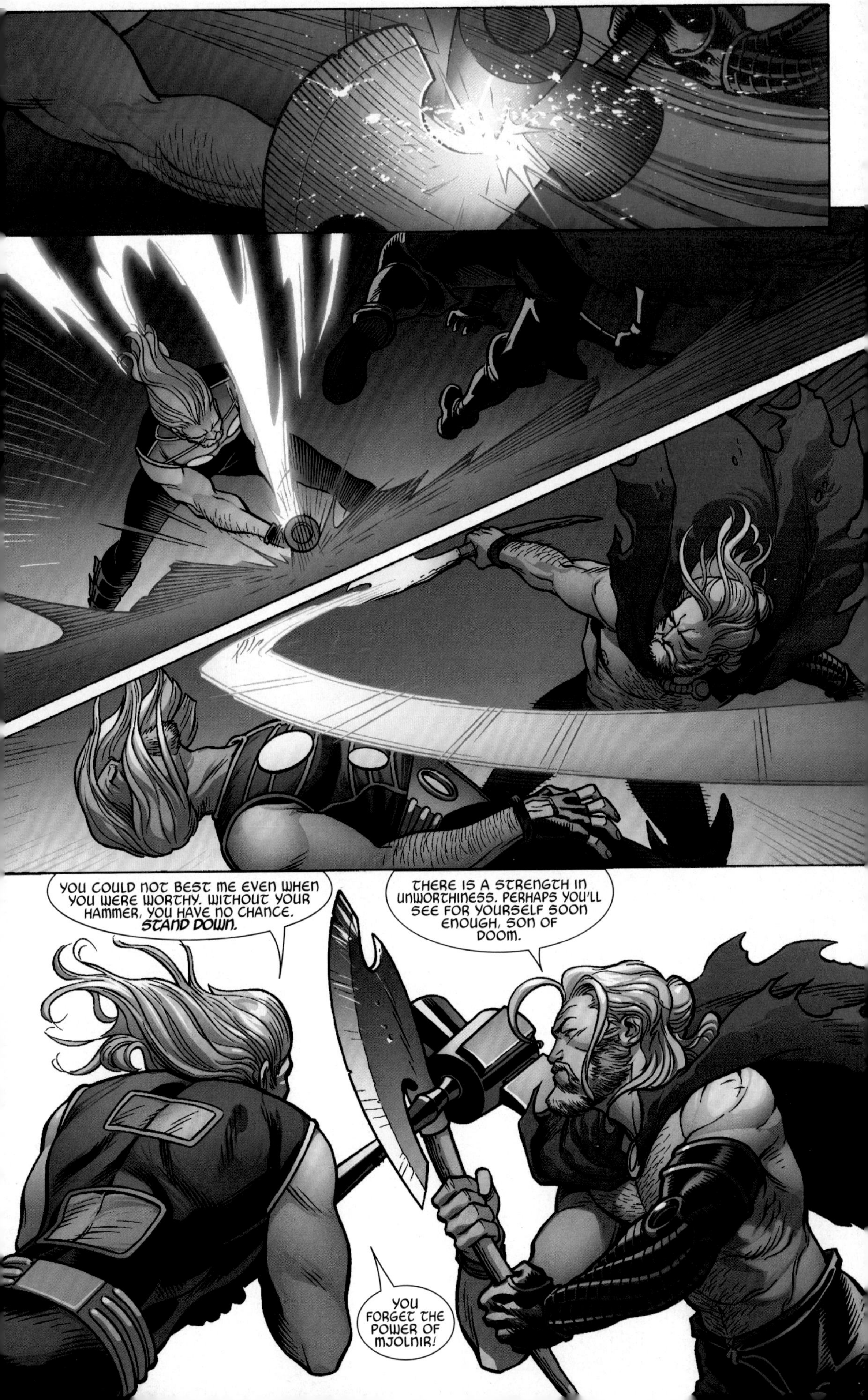
YOU COULD NOT BEST ME EVEN WHEN YOU WERE WORTHY. WITHOUT YOUR HAMMER, YOU HAVE NO CHANCE. STAND DOWN.
THERE IS A STRENGTH IN UNWORTHINESS. PERHAPS YOU'LL SEE FOR YOURSELF SOON ENOUGH, SON OF DOOM.
YOU FORGET THE POWER OF MJOLNIR!

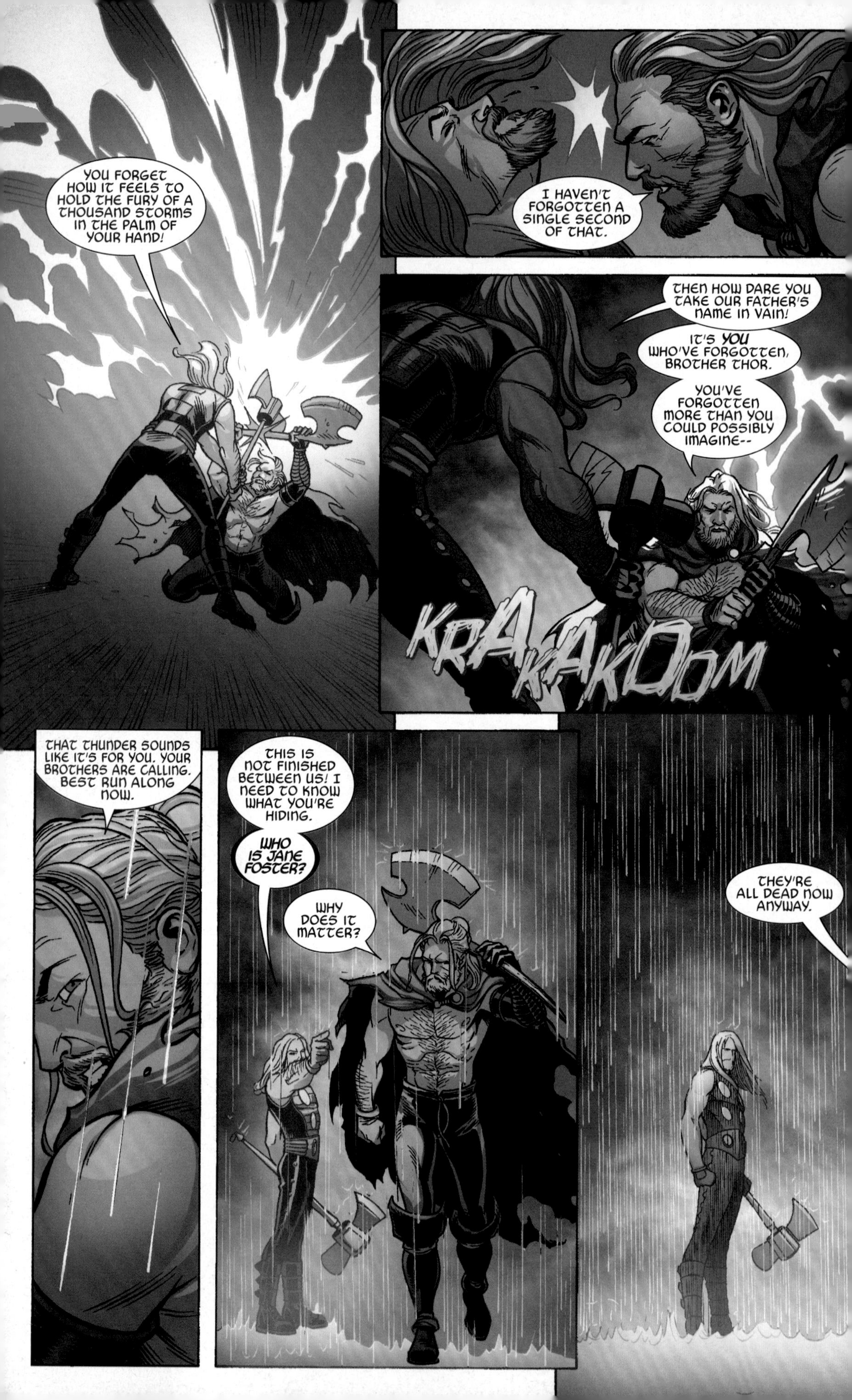

YOU FORGET HOW IT FEELS TO HOLD THE FURY OF A THOUSAND STORMS IN THE PALM OF YOUR HAND!
I HAVEN'T FORGOTTEN A SINGLE SECOND OF THAT.
THEN HOW DARE YOU TAKE OUR FATHER'S NAME IN VAIN!
IT'S YOU WHO'VE FORGOTTEN, BROTHER THOR.
YOU'VE FORGOTTEN MORE THAN YOU COULD POSSIBLY IMAGINE--
KRAKAKADOOM
THAT THUNDER SOUNDS LIKE IT'S FOR YOU. YOUR BROTHERS ARE CALLING. BEST RUN ALONG NOW.
THIS IS NOT FINISHED BETWEEN US! I NEED TO KNOW WHAT YOU'RE HIDING.
WHO IS JANE FOSTER?
WHY DOES IT MATTER?
THEY'RE ALL DEAD NOW ANYWAY.

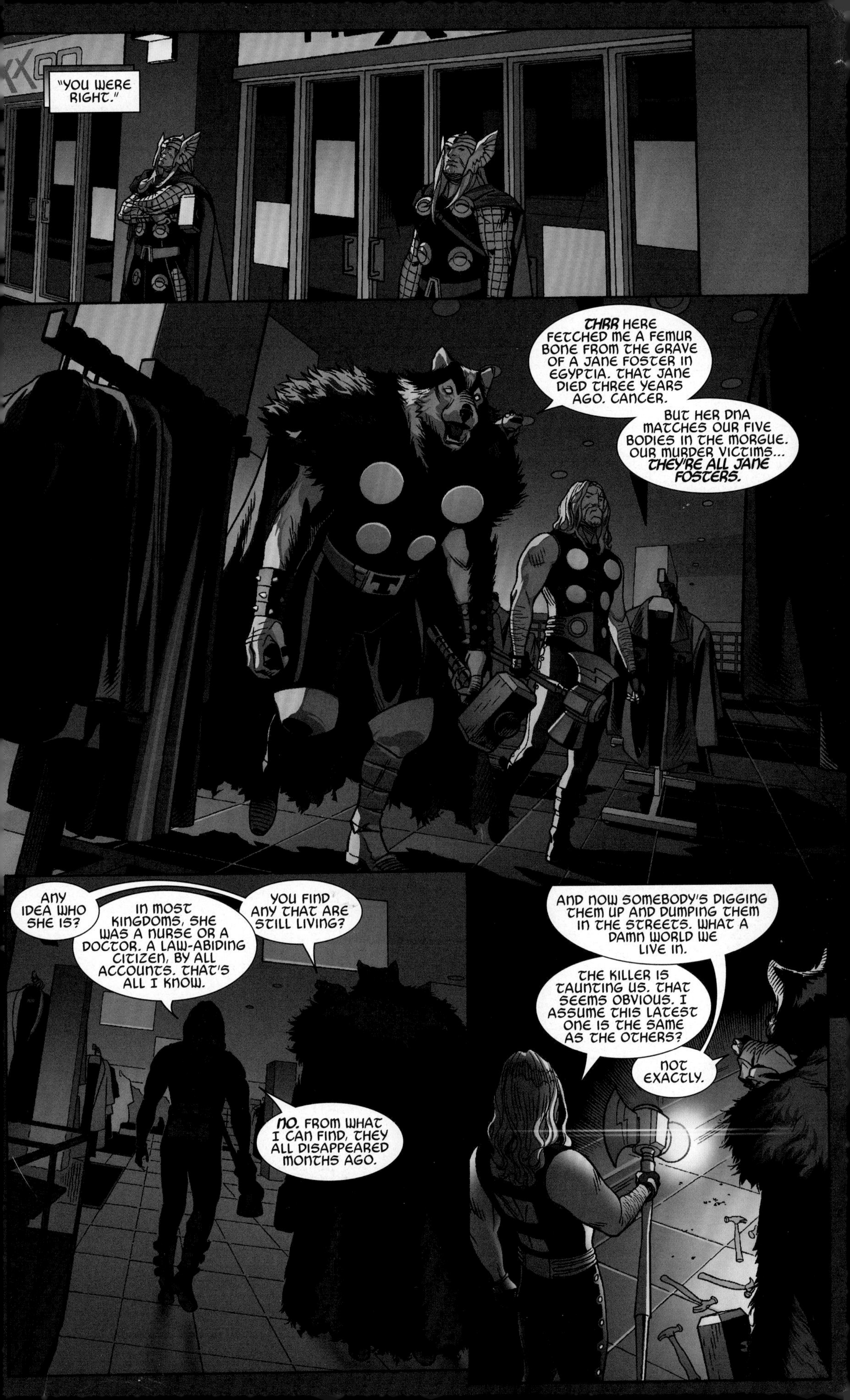
"YOU WERE RIGHT."
THRR HERE FETCHED ME A FEMUR BONE FROM THE GRAVE OF A JANE FOSTER IN EGYPTIA. THAT JANE DIED THREE YEARS AGO. CANCER.
BUT HER DNA MATCHES OUR FIVE BODIES IN THE MORGUE. OUR MURDER VICTIMS... THEY'RE ALL JANE FOSTERS.
ANY IDEA WHO SHE IS?
IN MOST KINGDOMS, SHE WAS A NURSE OR A DOCTOR. A LAW-ABIDING CITIZEN, BY ALL ACCOUNTS. THAT'S ALL I KNOW.
YOU FIND ANY THAT ARE STILL LIVING?
NO. FROM WHAT I CAN FIND, THEY ALL DISAPPEARED MONTHS AGO.
AND NOW SOMEBODY'S DIGGING THEM UP AND DUMPING THEM IN THE STREETS. WHAT A DAMN WORLD WE LIVE IN.
THE KILLER IS TAUNTING US. THAT SEEMS OBVIOUS. I ASSUME THIS LATEST ONE IS THE SAME AS THE OTHERS?
NOT EXACTLY.

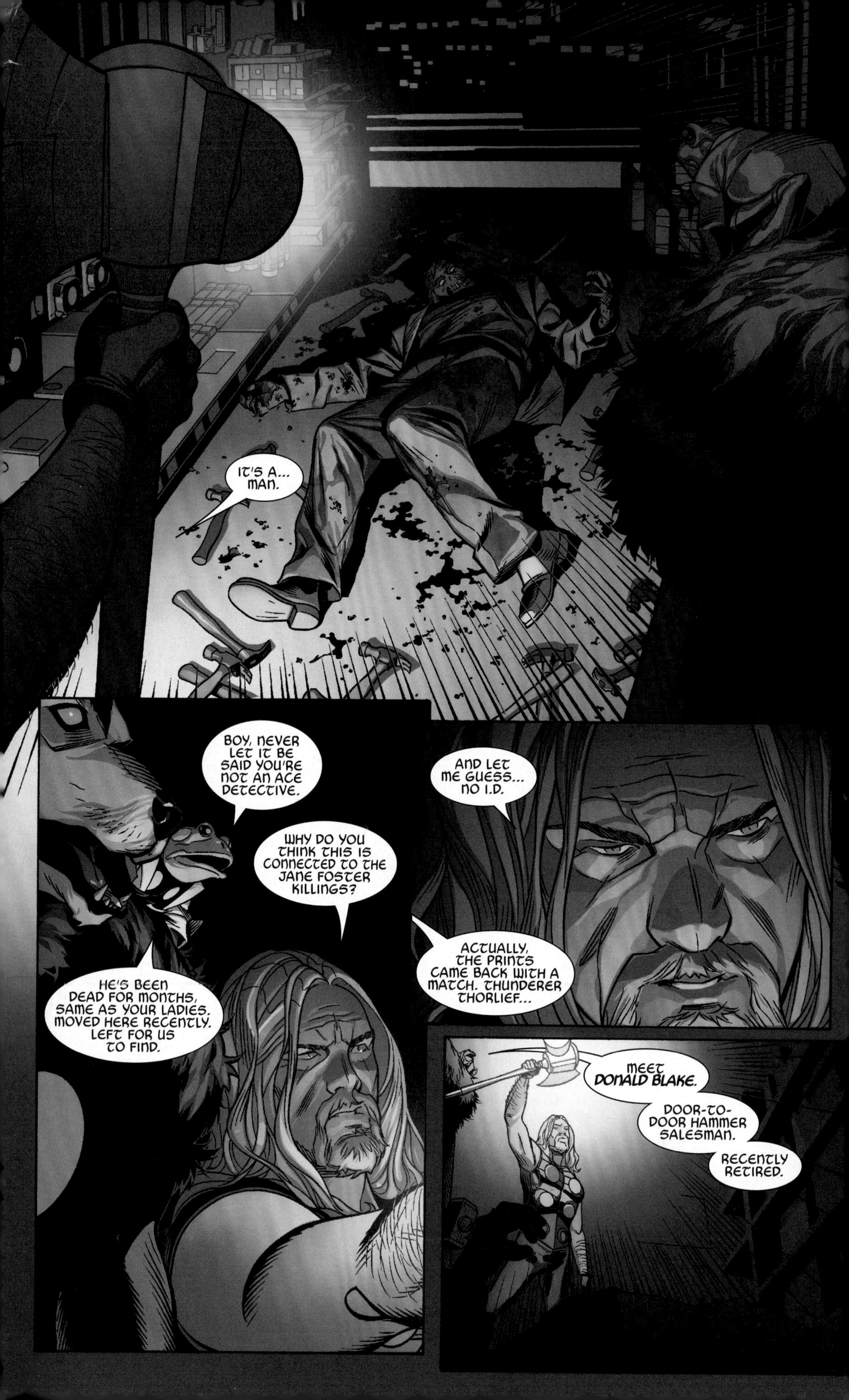
IT'S A... MAN.
BOY, NEVER LET IT BE SAID YOU'RE NOT AN ACE DETECTIVE.
WHY DO YOU THINK THIS IS CONNECTED TO THE JANE FOSTER KILLINGS?
HE'S BEEN DEAD FOR MONTHS, SAME AS YOUR LADIES. MOVED HERE RECENTLY. LEFT FOR US TO FIND.
AND LET ME GUESS... NO I.D.
ACTUALLY, THE PRINTS CAME BACK WITH A MATCH. THUNDERER THORLIEF...
MEET **DONALD BLAKE.**
DOOR-TO-DOOR HAMMER SALESMAN.
RECENTLY RETIRED.

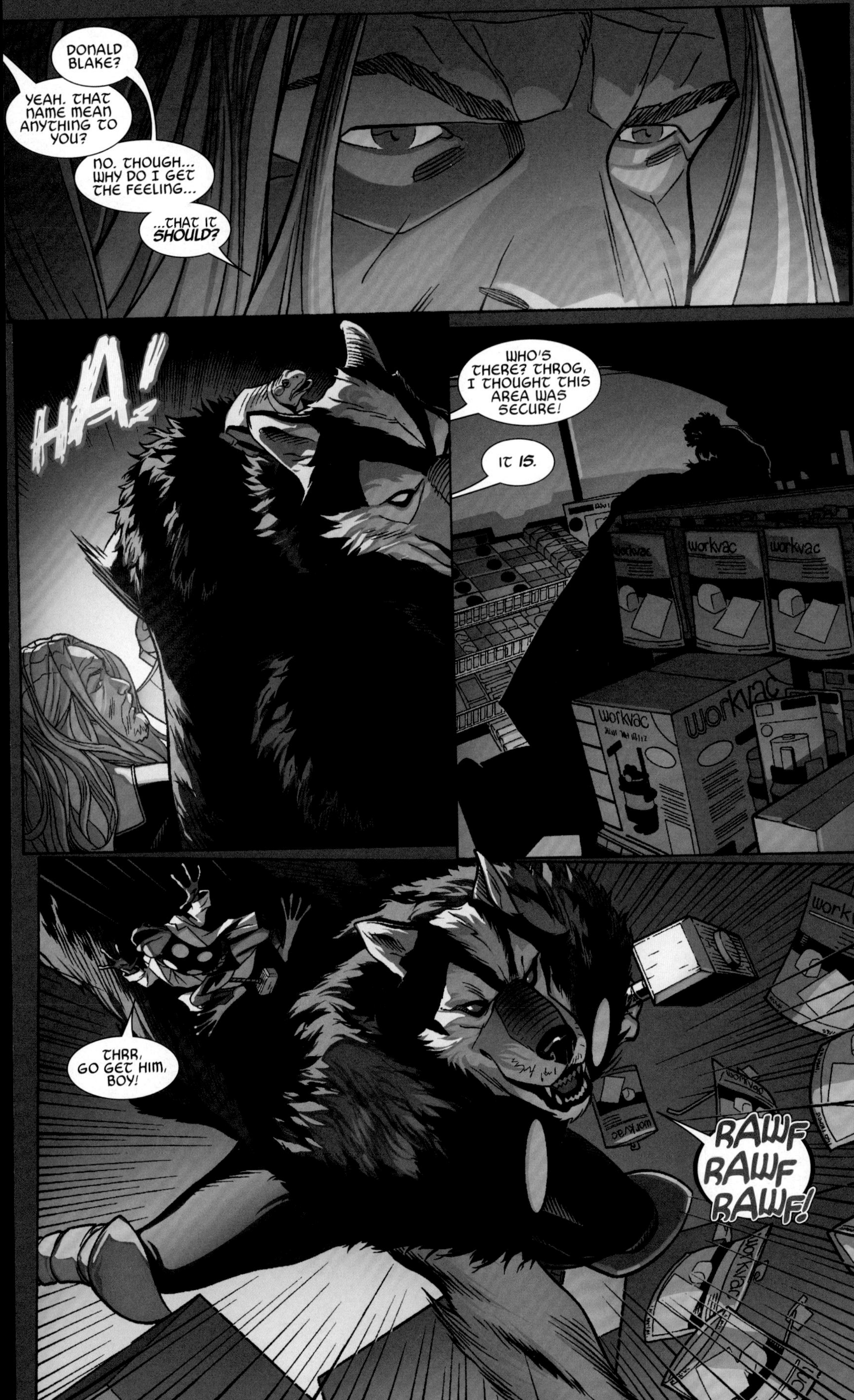
DONALD BLAKE?
YEAH. THAT NAME MEAN ANYTHING TO YOU?
NO. THOUGH... WHY DO I GET THE FEELING...
...THAT IT SHOULD?
HA!
WHO'S THERE? THROG, I THOUGHT THIS AREA WAS SECURE!
IT IS.
workvac
THRR, GO GET HIM, BOY!
RAWF RAWF RAWF!

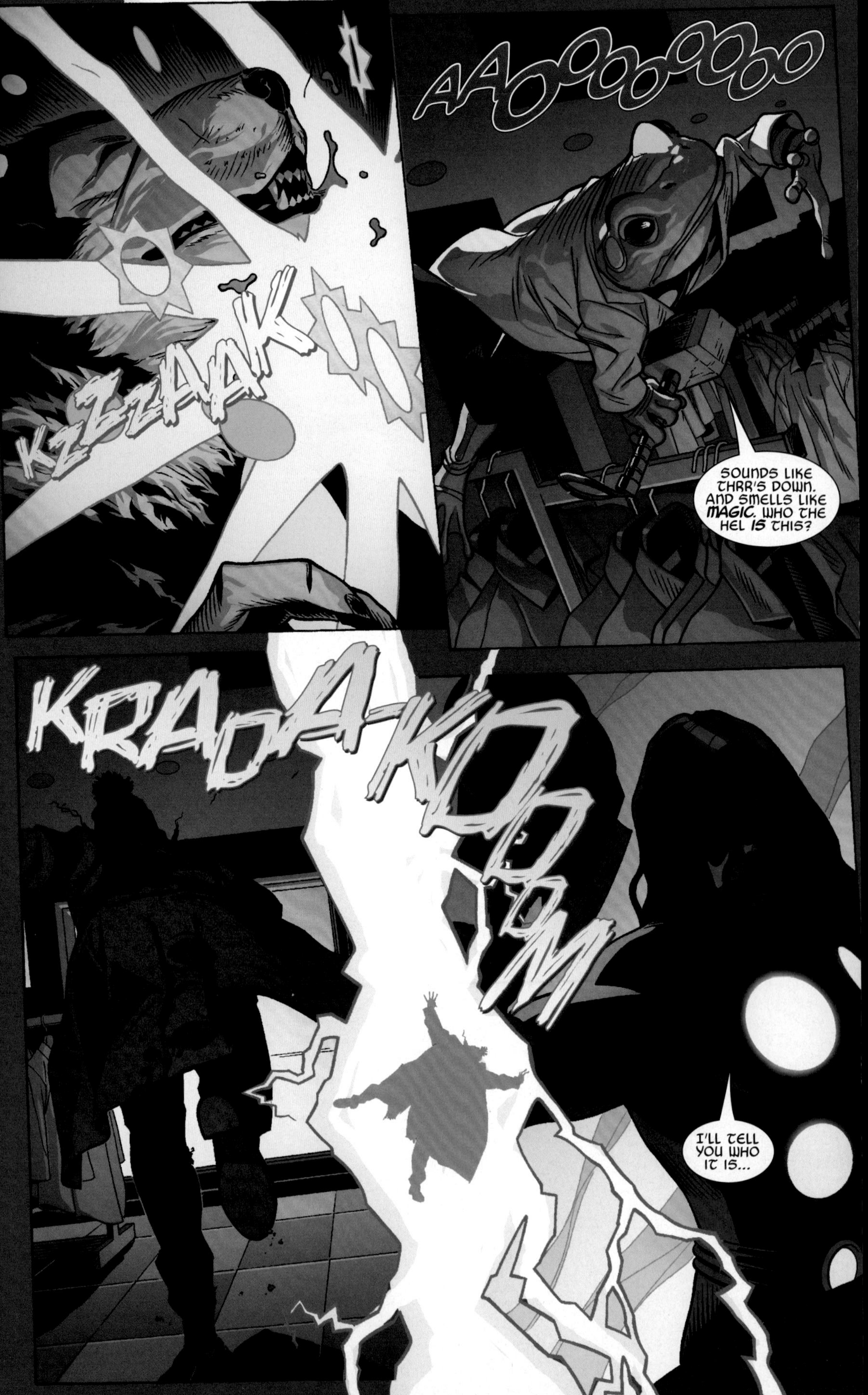
KZZZAAK
AAOOOOOOOO
SOUNDS LIKE THRR'S DOWN. AND SMELLS LIKE MAGIC. WHO THE HEL IS THIS?
KRADAKOOOOM
I'LL TELL YOU WHO IT IS...

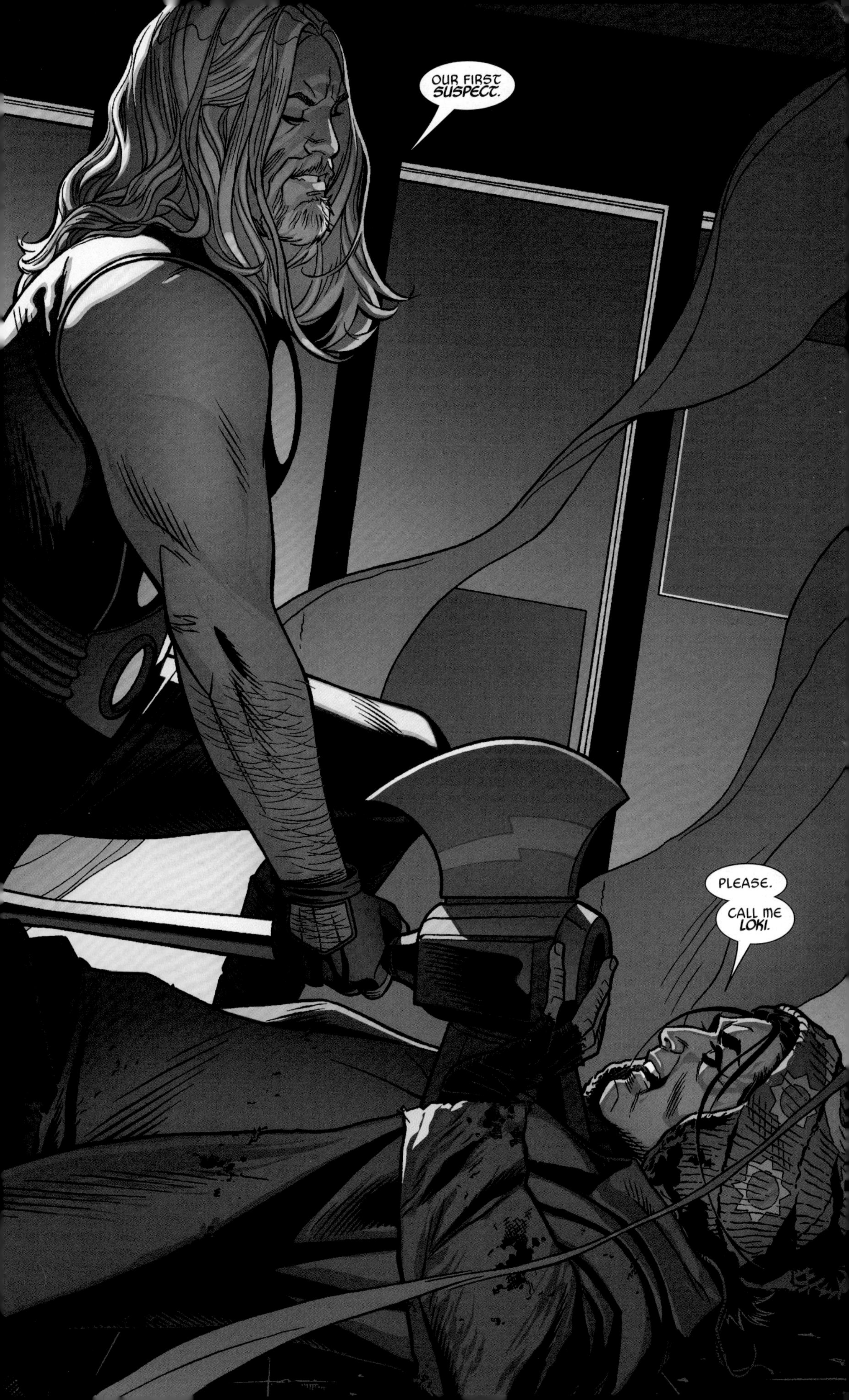
OUR FIRST SUSPECT.
PLEASE.
CALL ME LOKI.

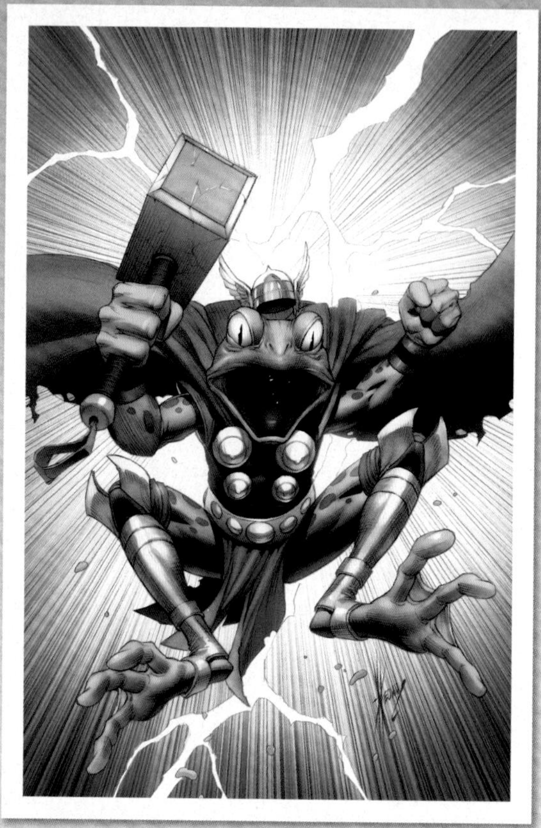

THORS No. 1 VARIANT BY
DALE KEOWN & JASON KEITH

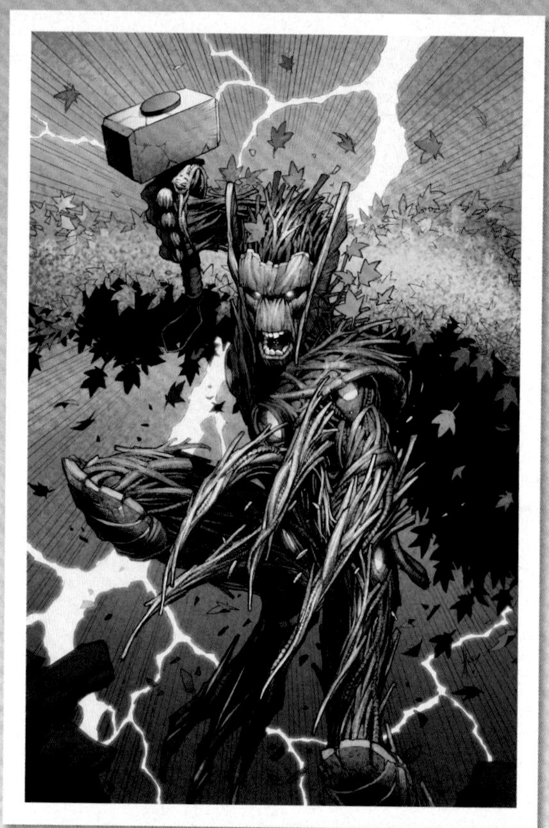

THORS No. 2 VARIANT BY
DALE KEOWN & JASON KEITH

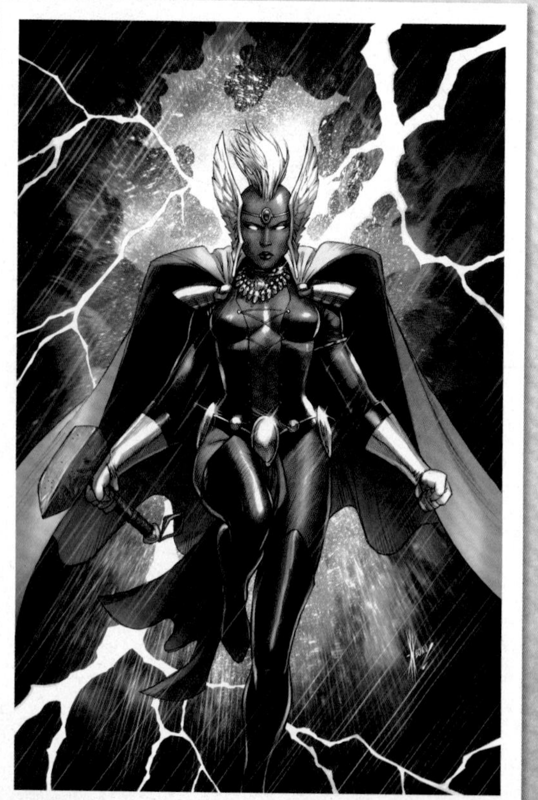

THORS No. 3 VARIANT BY
DALE KEOWN & JASON KEITH

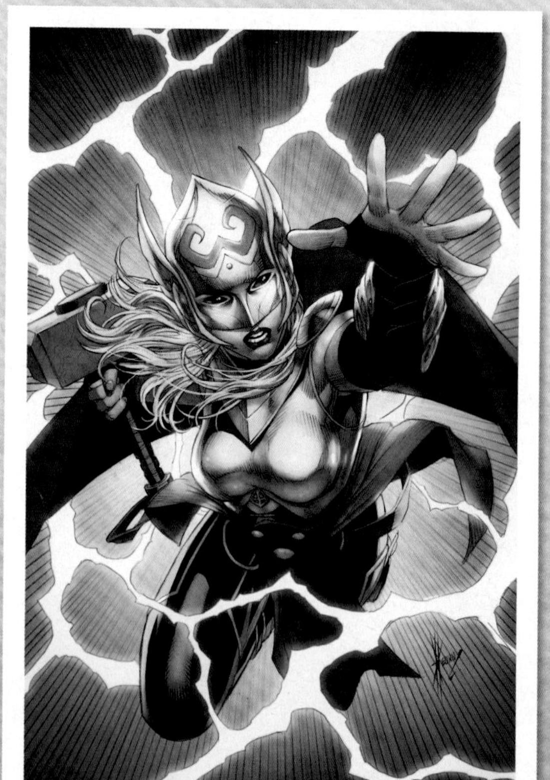

THORS No. 4 VARIANT BY
DALE KEOWN & JASON KEITH

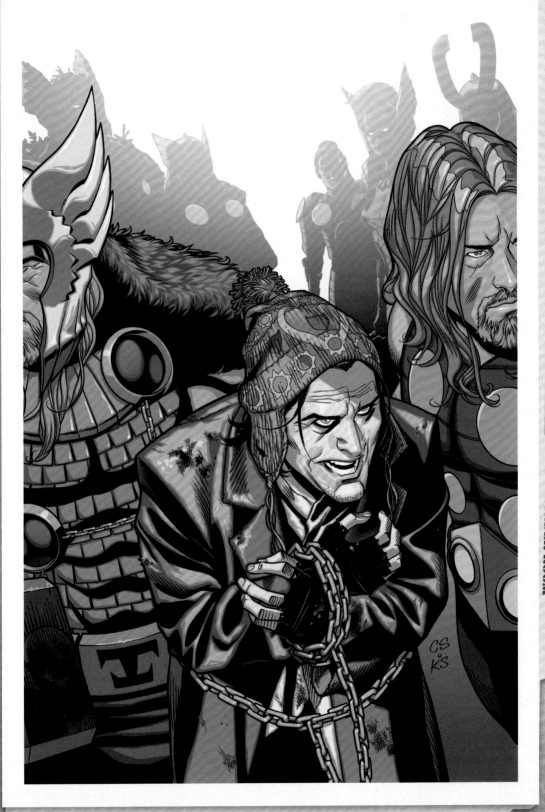

THORS No. 3
THE THUNDER ROOM

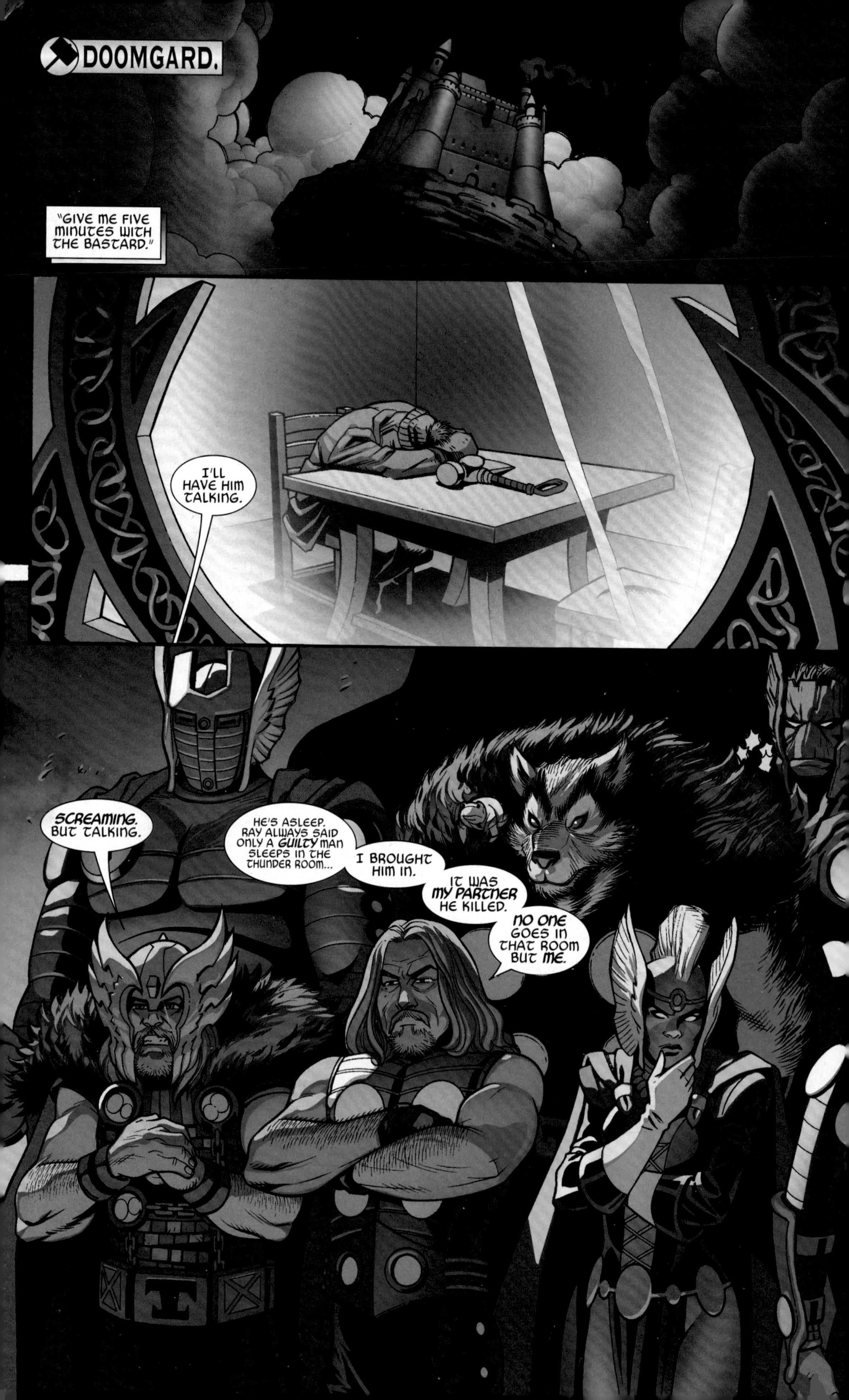
DOOMGARD.
"GIVE ME FIVE MINUTES WITH THE BASTARD."
I'LL HAVE HIM TALKING.
SCREAMING. BUT TALKING.
HE'S ASLEEP. RAY ALWAYS SAID ONLY A GUILTY MAN SLEEPS IN THE THUNDER ROOM...
I BROUGHT HIM IN.
IT WAS MY PARTNER HE KILLED.
NO ONE GOES IN THAT ROOM BUT ME.

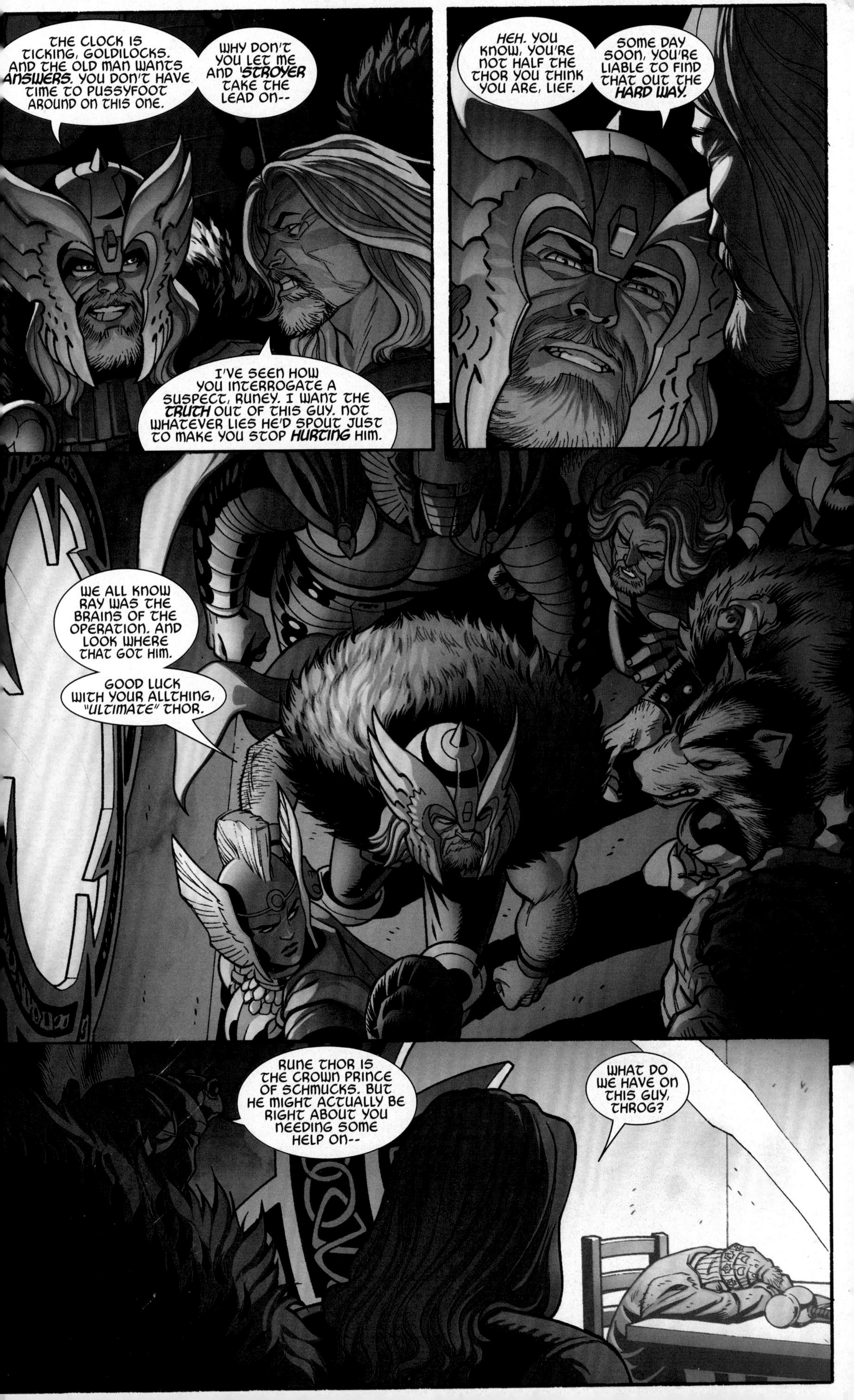
THE CLOCK IS TICKING, GOLDILOCKS. AND THE OLD MAN WANTS ANSWERS. YOU DON'T HAVE TIME TO PUSSYFOOT AROUND ON THIS ONE.
WHY DON'T YOU LET ME AND 'STROYER TAKE THE LEAD ON--
I'VE SEEN HOW YOU INTERROGATE A SUSPECT, RUNEY. I WANT THE TRUTH OUT OF THIS GUY. NOT WHATEVER LIES HE'D SPOUT JUST TO MAKE YOU STOP HURTING HIM.
HEH. YOU KNOW, YOU'RE NOT HALF THE THOR YOU THINK YOU ARE, LIEF.
SOME DAY SOON, YOU'RE LIABLE TO FIND THAT OUT THE HARD WAY.
WE ALL KNOW RAY WAS THE BRAINS OF THE OPERATION. AND LOOK WHERE THAT GOT HIM.
GOOD LUCK WITH YOUR ALLTHING, "ULTIMATE" THOR.
RUNE THOR IS THE CROWN PRINCE OF SCHMUCKS. BUT HE MIGHT ACTUALLY BE RIGHT ABOUT YOU NEEDING SOME HELP ON--
WHAT DO WE HAVE ON THIS GUY, THROG?

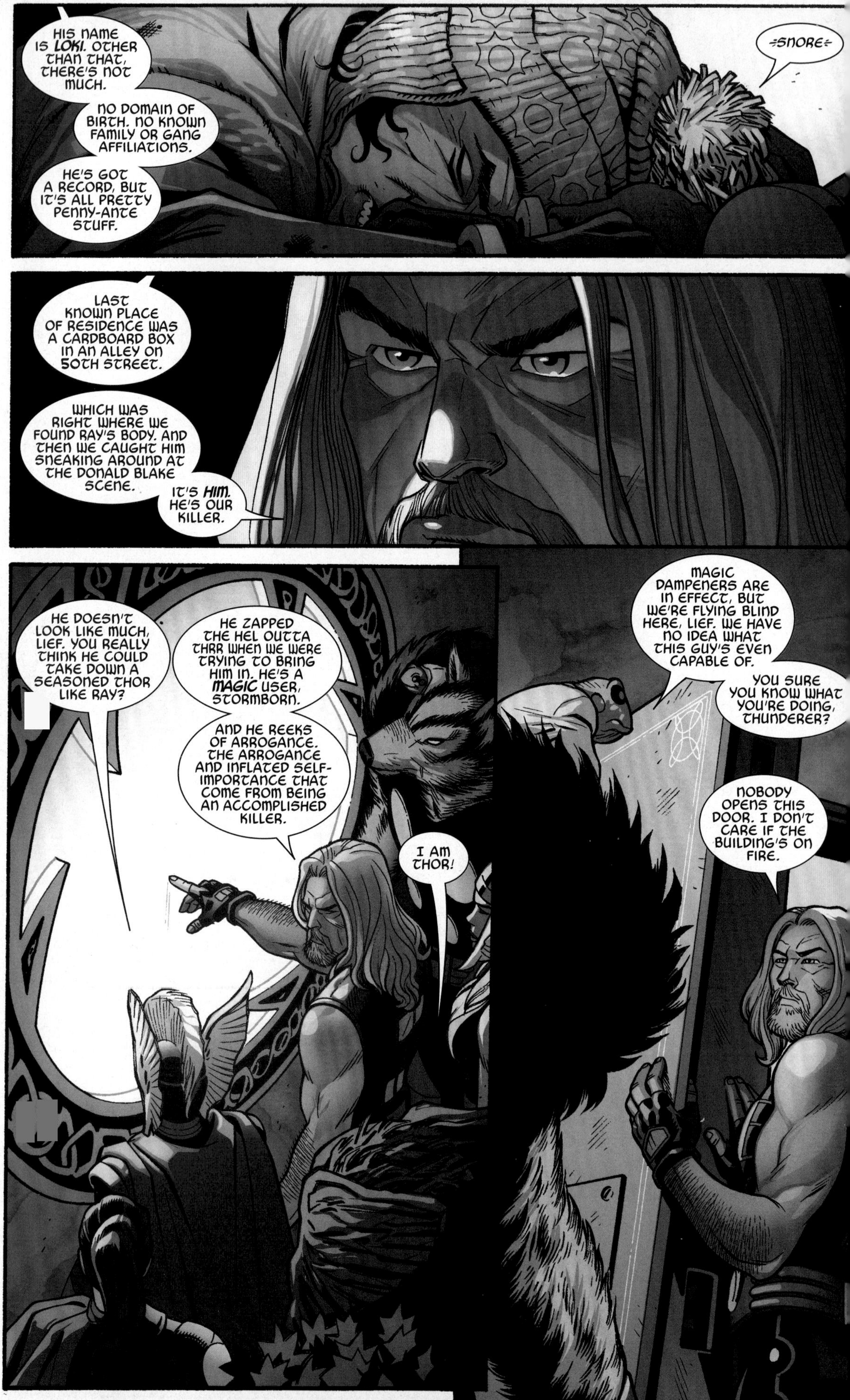
HIS NAME IS LOKI. OTHER THAN THAT, THERE'S NOT MUCH.
=SNORE=
NO DOMAIN OF BIRTH. NO KNOWN FAMILY OR GANG AFFILIATIONS.
HE'S GOT A RECORD, BUT IT'S ALL PRETTY PENNY-ANTE STUFF.
LAST KNOWN PLACE OF RESIDENCE WAS A CARDBOARD BOX IN AN ALLEY ON 50TH STREET.
WHICH WAS RIGHT WHERE WE FOUND RAY'S BODY. AND THEN WE CAUGHT HIM SNEAKING AROUND AT THE DONALD BLAKE SCENE.
IT'S HIM. HE'S OUR KILLER.
HE DOESN'T LOOK LIKE MUCH, LIEF. YOU REALLY THINK HE COULD TAKE DOWN A SEASONED THOR LIKE RAY?
HE ZAPPED THE HEL OUTTA THRR WHEN WE WERE TRYING TO BRING HIM IN. HE'S A MAGIC USER, STORMBORN.
AND HE REEKS OF ARROGANCE. THE ARROGANCE AND INFLATED SELF-IMPORTANCE THAT COME FROM BEING AN ACCOMPLISHED KILLER.
I AM THOR!
MAGIC DAMPENERS ARE IN EFFECT, BUT WE'RE FLYING BLIND HERE, LIEF. WE HAVE NO IDEA WHAT THIS GUY'S EVEN CAPABLE OF.
YOU SURE YOU KNOW WHAT YOU'RE DOING, THUNDERER?
NOBODY OPENS THIS DOOR. I DON'T CARE IF THE BUILDING'S ON FIRE.

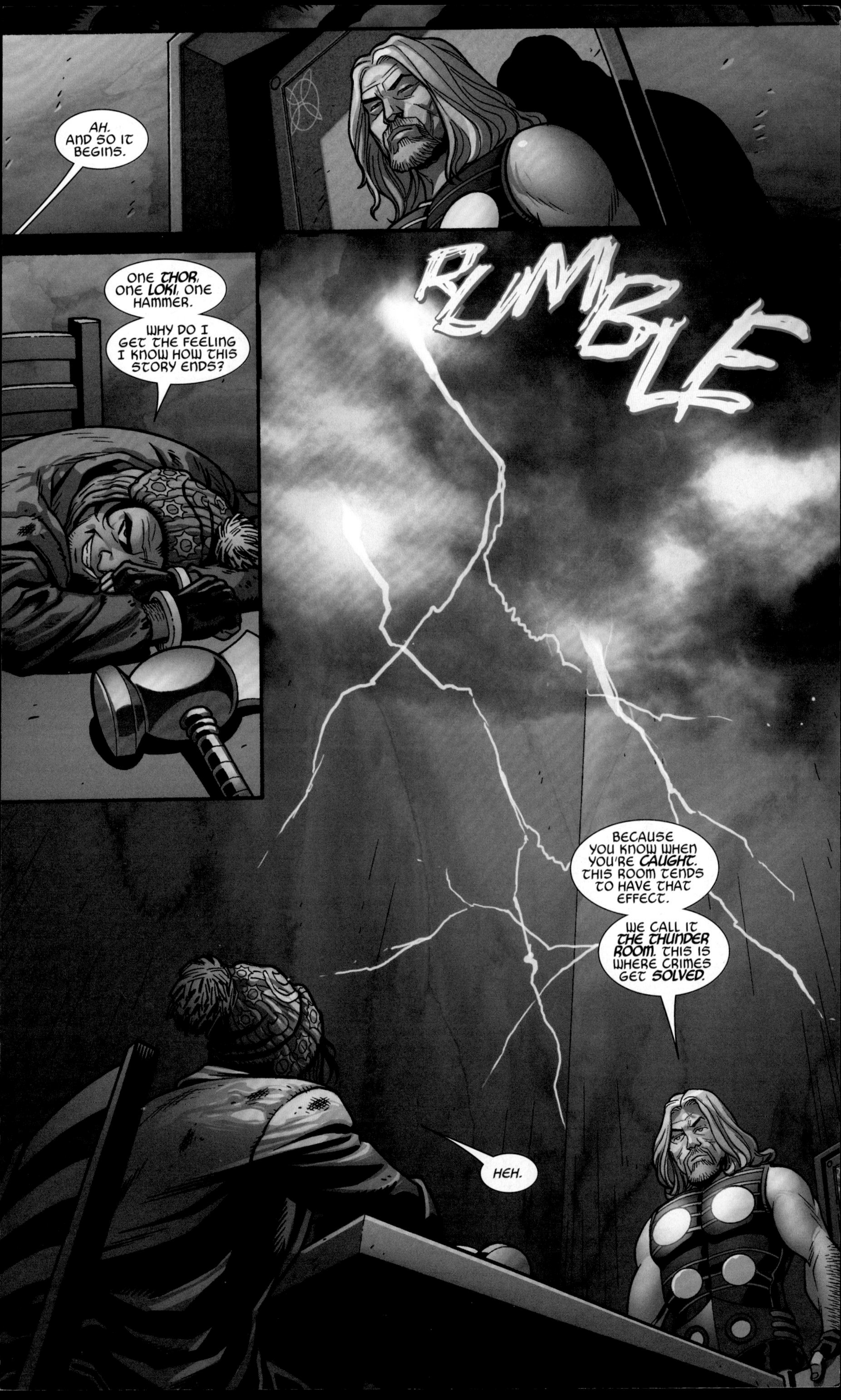

AH. AND SO IT BEGINS.
ONE THOR, ONE LOKI, ONE HAMMER.
WHY DO I GET THE FEELING I KNOW HOW THIS STORY ENDS?
RUMBLE
BECAUSE YOU KNOW WHEN YOU'RE CAUGHT. THIS ROOM TENDS TO HAVE THAT EFFECT.
WE CALL IT THE THUNDER ROOM. THIS IS WHERE CRIMES GET SOLVED.
HEH.

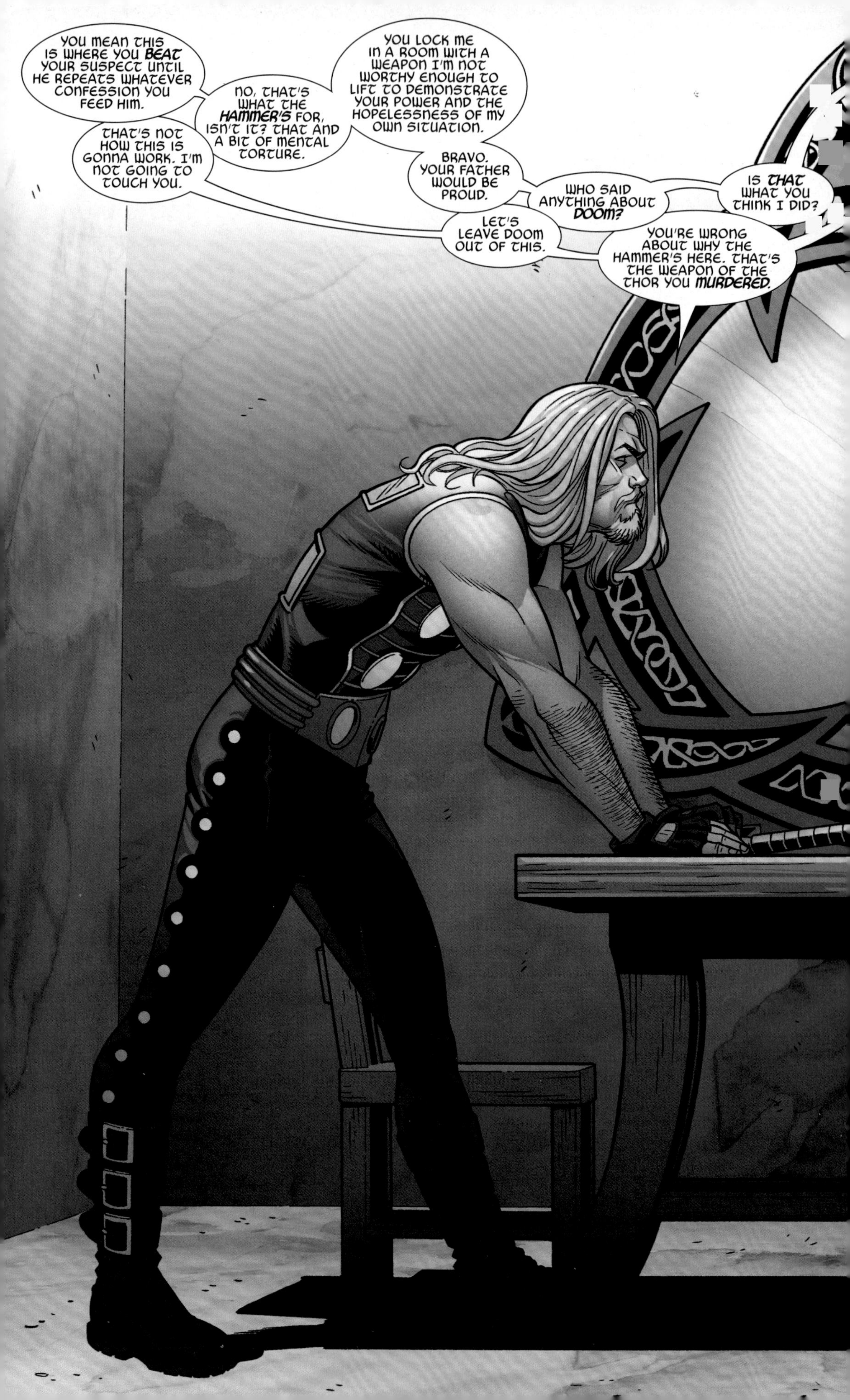
YOU MEAN THIS IS WHERE YOU BEAT YOUR SUSPECT UNTIL HE REPEATS WHATEVER CONFESSION YOU FEED HIM.
THAT'S NOT HOW THIS IS GONNA WORK. I'M NOT GOING TO TOUCH YOU.
NO, THAT'S WHAT THE HAMMER'S FOR, ISN'T IT? THAT AND A BIT OF MENTAL TORTURE.
YOU LOCK ME IN A ROOM WITH A WEAPON I'M NOT WORTHY ENOUGH TO LIFT TO DEMONSTRATE YOUR POWER AND THE HOPELESSNESS OF MY OWN SITUATION.
BRAVO. YOUR FATHER WOULD BE PROUD.
LET'S LEAVE DOOM OUT OF THIS.
WHO SAID ANYTHING ABOUT DOOM?
IS THAT WHAT YOU THINK I DID?
YOU'RE WRONG ABOUT WHY THE HAMMER'S HERE. THAT'S THE WEAPON OF THE THOR YOU MURDERED.

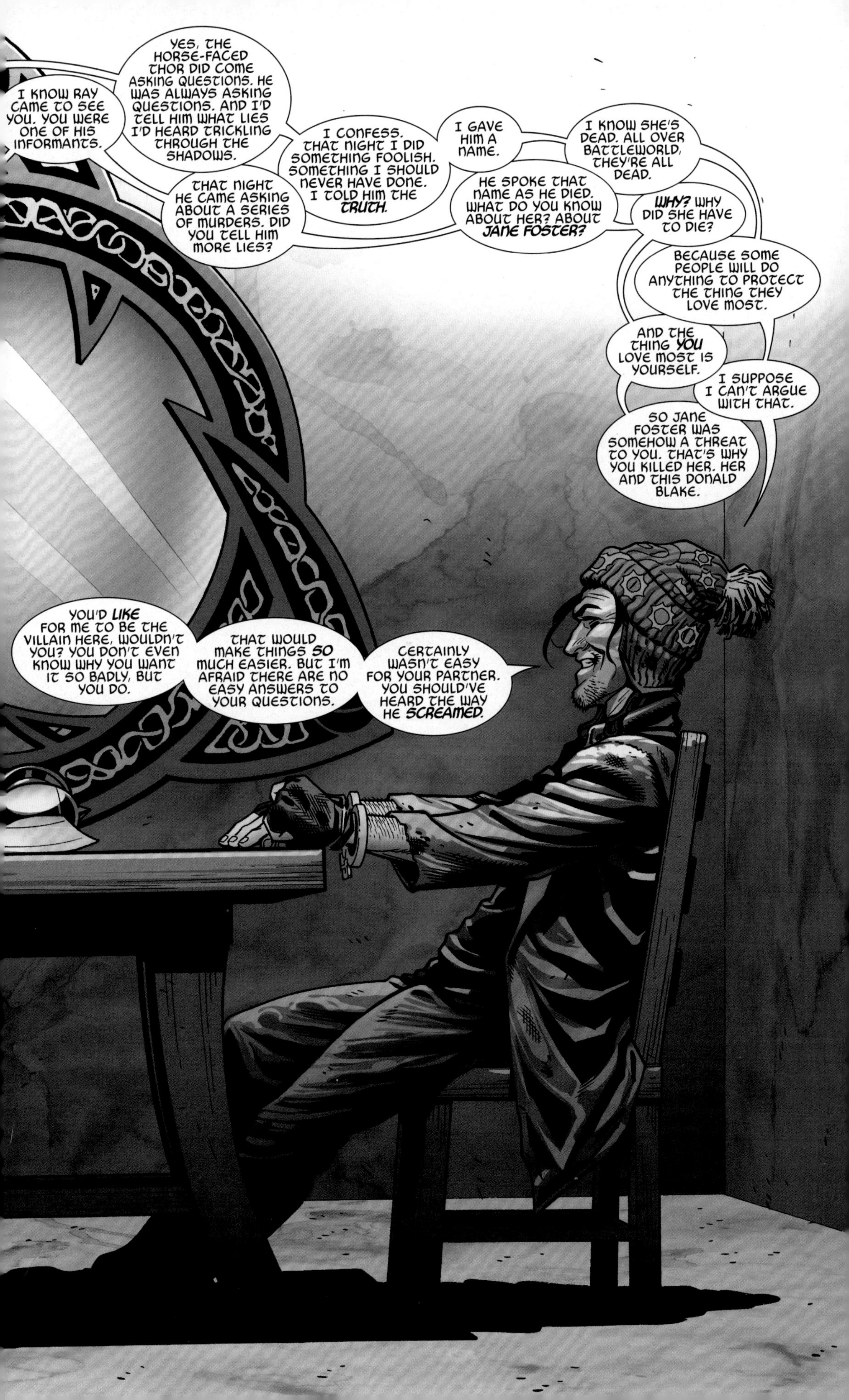
I KNOW RAY CAME TO SEE YOU. YOU WERE ONE OF HIS INFORMANTS.
YES, THE HORSE-FACED THOR DID COME ASKING QUESTIONS. HE WAS ALWAYS ASKING QUESTIONS. AND I'D TELL HIM WHAT LIES I'D HEARD TRICKLING THROUGH THE SHADOWS.
THAT NIGHT HE CAME ASKING ABOUT A SERIES OF MURDERS. DID YOU TELL HIM MORE LIES?
I CONFESS. THAT NIGHT I DID SOMETHING FOOLISH. SOMETHING I SHOULD NEVER HAVE DONE. I TOLD HIM THE TRUTH.
I GAVE HIM A NAME.
HE SPOKE THAT NAME AS HE DIED. WHAT DO YOU KNOW ABOUT HER? ABOUT JANE FOSTER?
I KNOW SHE'S DEAD. ALL OVER BATTLEWORLD, THEY'RE ALL DEAD.
WHY? WHY DID SHE HAVE TO DIE?
BECAUSE SOME PEOPLE WILL DO ANYTHING TO PROTECT THE THING THEY LOVE MOST.
AND THE THING YOU LOVE MOST IS YOURSELF.
I SUPPOSE I CAN'T ARGUE WITH THAT.
SO JANE FOSTER WAS SOMEHOW A THREAT TO YOU. THAT'S WHY YOU KILLED HER. HER AND THIS DONALD BLAKE.
YOU'D LIKE FOR ME TO BE THE VILLAIN HERE, WOULDN'T YOU? YOU DON'T EVEN KNOW WHY YOU WANT IT SO BADLY, BUT YOU DO.
THAT WOULD MAKE THINGS SO MUCH EASIER. BUT I'M AFRAID THERE ARE NO EASY ANSWERS TO YOUR QUESTIONS.
CERTAINLY WASN'T EASY FOR YOUR PARTNER. YOU SHOULD'VE HEARD THE WAY HE SCREAMED.

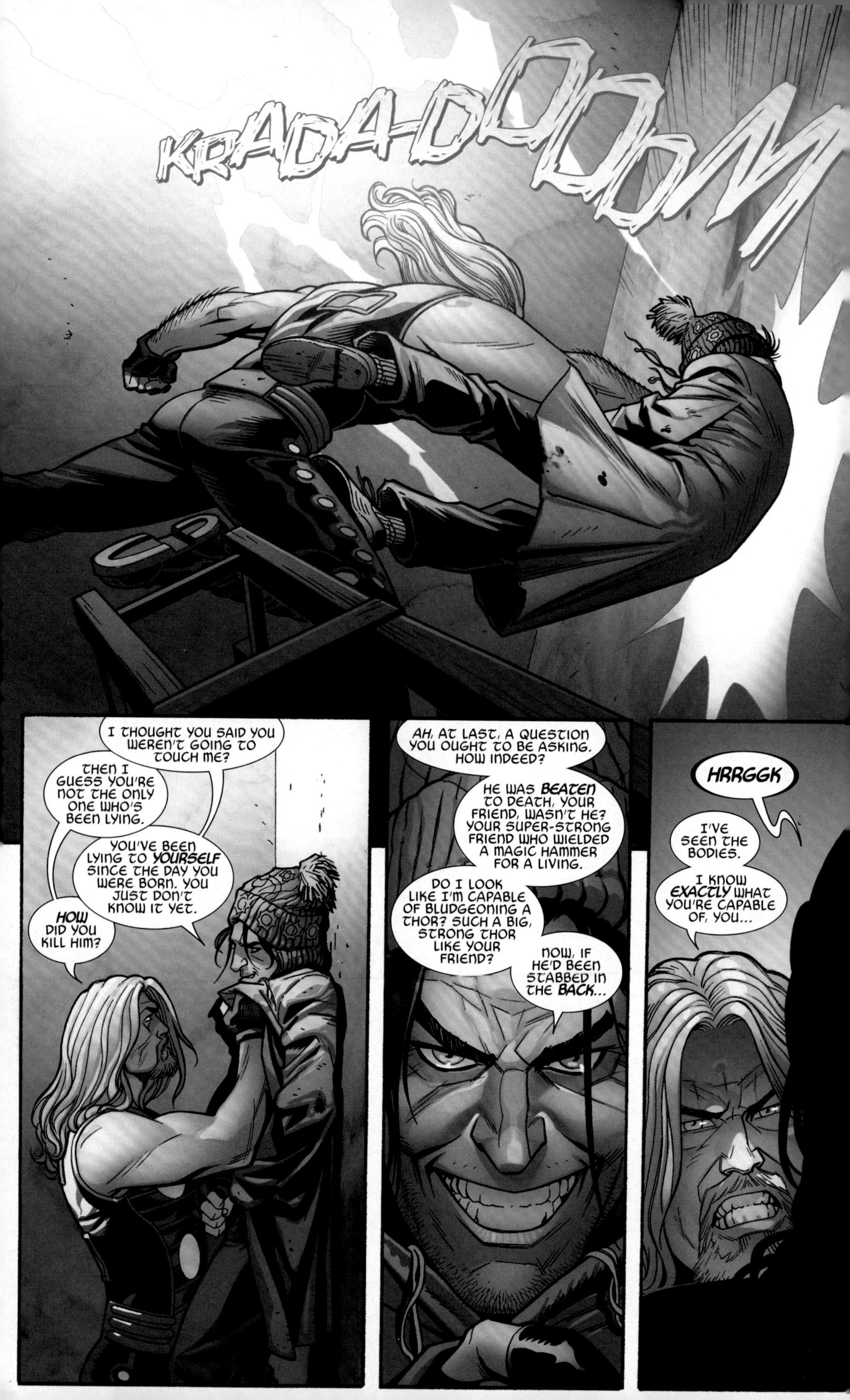
KRADA-DOOOM
I THOUGHT YOU SAID YOU WEREN'T GOING TO TOUCH ME?
THEN I GUESS YOU'RE NOT THE ONLY ONE WHO'S BEEN LYING.
YOU'VE BEEN LYING TO YOURSELF SINCE THE DAY YOU WERE BORN. YOU JUST DON'T KNOW IT YET.
HOW DID YOU KILL HIM?
AH, AT LAST, A QUESTION YOU OUGHT TO BE ASKING. HOW INDEED?
HE WAS BEATEN TO DEATH, YOUR FRIEND, WASN'T HE? YOUR SUPER-STRONG FRIEND WHO WIELDED A MAGIC HAMMER FOR A LIVING.
DO I LOOK LIKE I'M CAPABLE OF BLUDGEONING A THOR? SUCH A BIG, STRONG THOR LIKE YOUR FRIEND?
NOW, IF HE'D BEEN STABBED IN THE BACK...
HRRGGK
I'VE SEEN THE BODIES.
I KNOW EXACTLY WHAT YOU'RE CAPABLE OF, YOU...

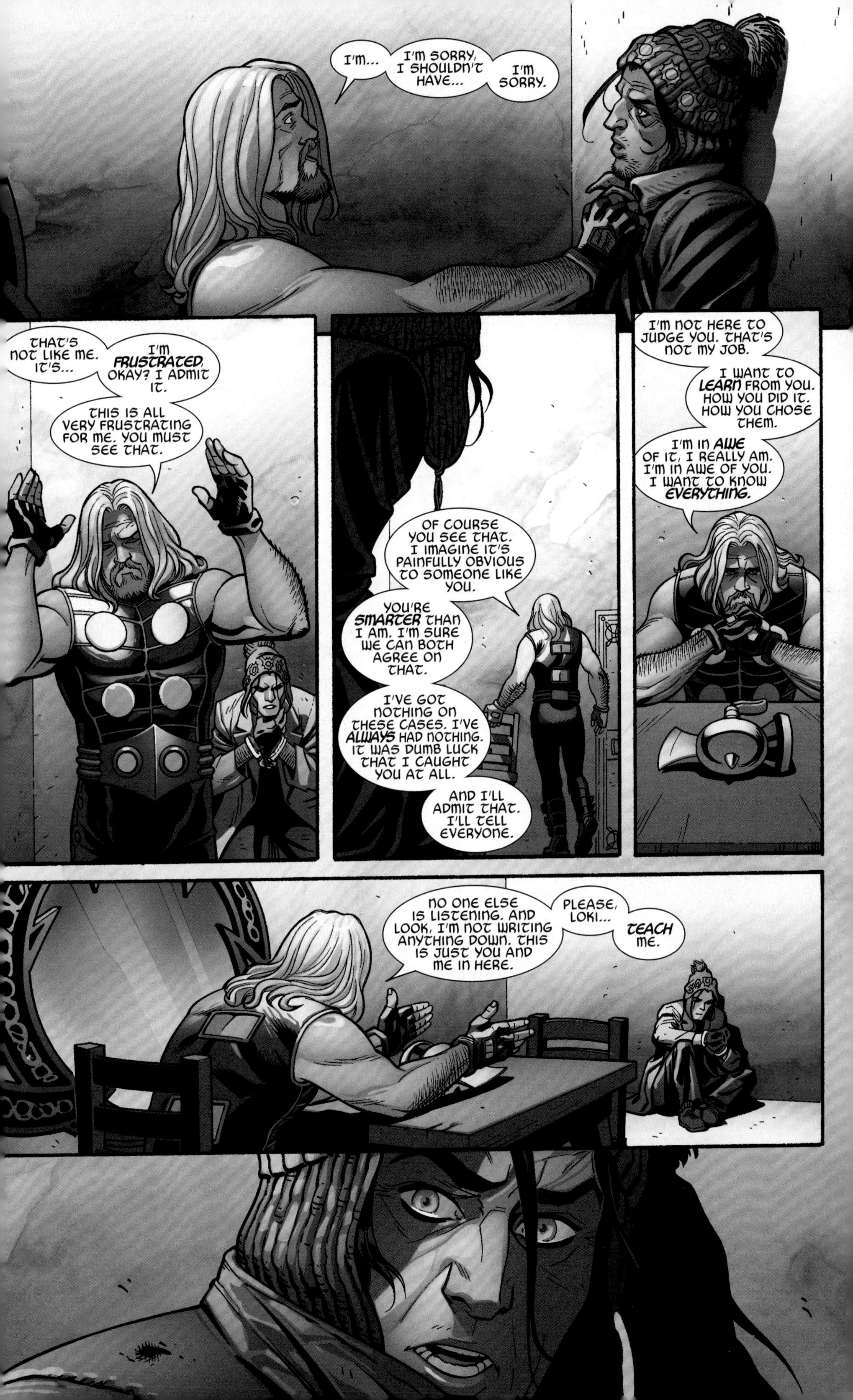
I'M...
I'M SORRY, I SHOULDN'T HAVE...
I'M SORRY.
THAT'S NOT LIKE ME. IT'S...
I'M FRUSTRATED, OKAY? I ADMIT IT.
THIS IS ALL VERY FRUSTRATING FOR ME. YOU MUST SEE THAT.
OF COURSE YOU SEE THAT. I IMAGINE IT'S PAINFULLY OBVIOUS TO SOMEONE LIKE YOU.
YOU'RE SMARTER THAN I AM. I'M SURE WE CAN BOTH AGREE ON THAT.
I'VE GOT NOTHING ON THESE CASES. I'VE ALWAYS HAD NOTHING. IT WAS DUMB LUCK THAT I CAUGHT YOU AT ALL.
AND I'LL ADMIT THAT. I'LL TELL EVERYONE.
I'M NOT HERE TO JUDGE YOU. THAT'S NOT MY JOB.
I WANT TO LEARN FROM YOU. HOW YOU DID IT. HOW YOU CHOSE THEM.
I'M IN AWE OF IT, I REALLY AM. I'M IN AWE OF YOU. I WANT TO KNOW EVERYTHING.
NO ONE ELSE IS LISTENING. AND LOOK, I'M NOT WRITING ANYTHING DOWN. THIS IS JUST YOU AND ME IN HERE.
PLEASE, LOKI...
TEACH ME.

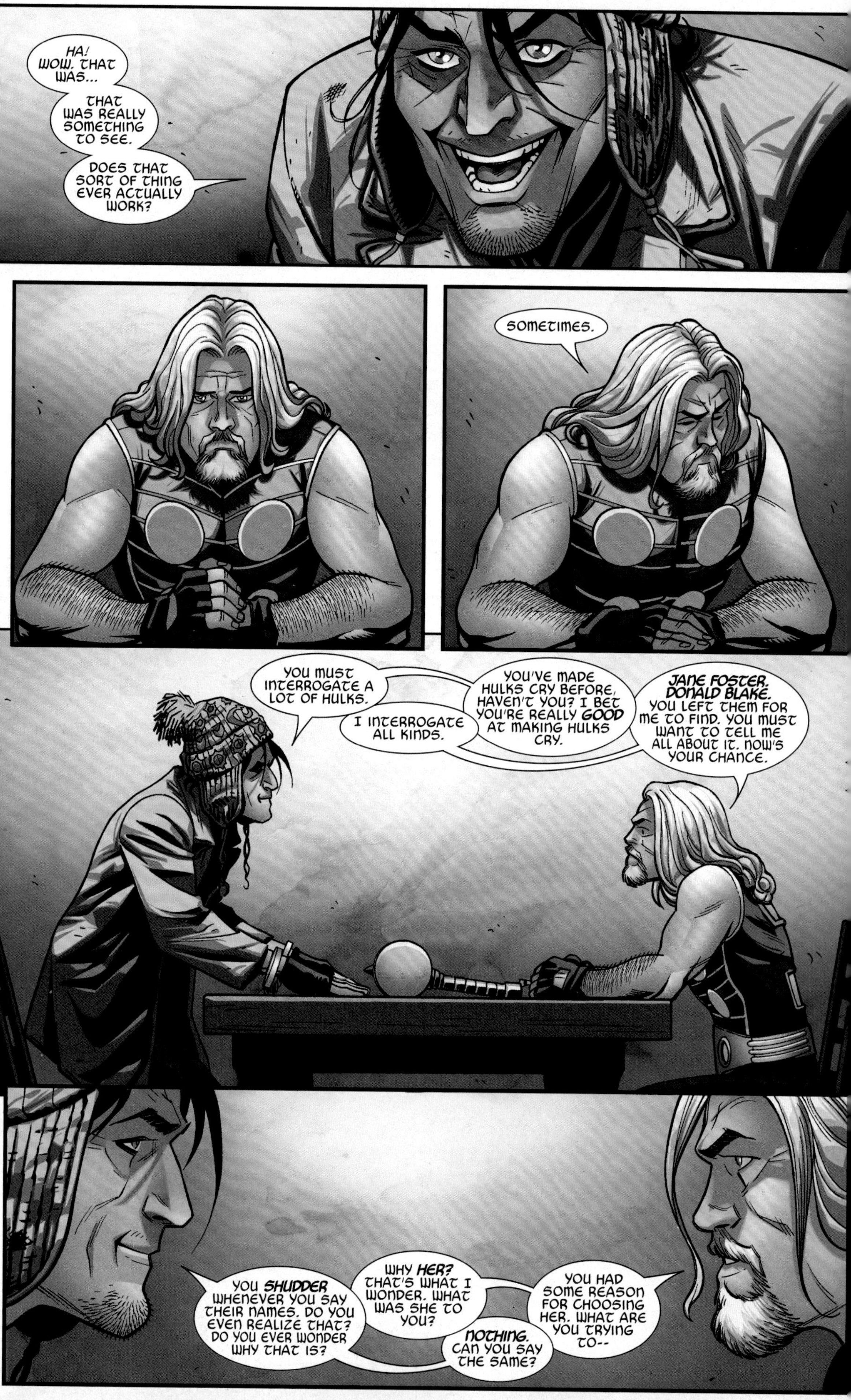
HA! WOW. THAT WAS...
THAT WAS REALLY SOMETHING TO SEE.
DOES THAT SORT OF THING EVER ACTUALLY WORK?
SOMETIMES.
YOU MUST INTERROGATE A LOT OF HULKS.
I INTERROGATE ALL KINDS.
YOU'VE MADE HULKS CRY BEFORE, HAVEN'T YOU? I BET YOU'RE REALLY GOOD AT MAKING HULKS CRY.
JANE FOSTER. DONALD BLAKE. YOU LEFT THEM FOR ME TO FIND. YOU MUST WANT TO TELL ME ALL ABOUT IT. NOW'S YOUR CHANCE.
YOU SHUDDER WHENEVER YOU SAY THEIR NAMES. DO YOU EVEN REALIZE THAT? DO YOU EVER WONDER WHY THAT IS?
NOTHING. CAN YOU SAY THE SAME?
WHY HER? THAT'S WHAT I WONDER. WHAT WAS SHE TO YOU?
YOU HAD SOME REASON FOR CHOOSING HER. WHAT ARE YOU TRYING TO--

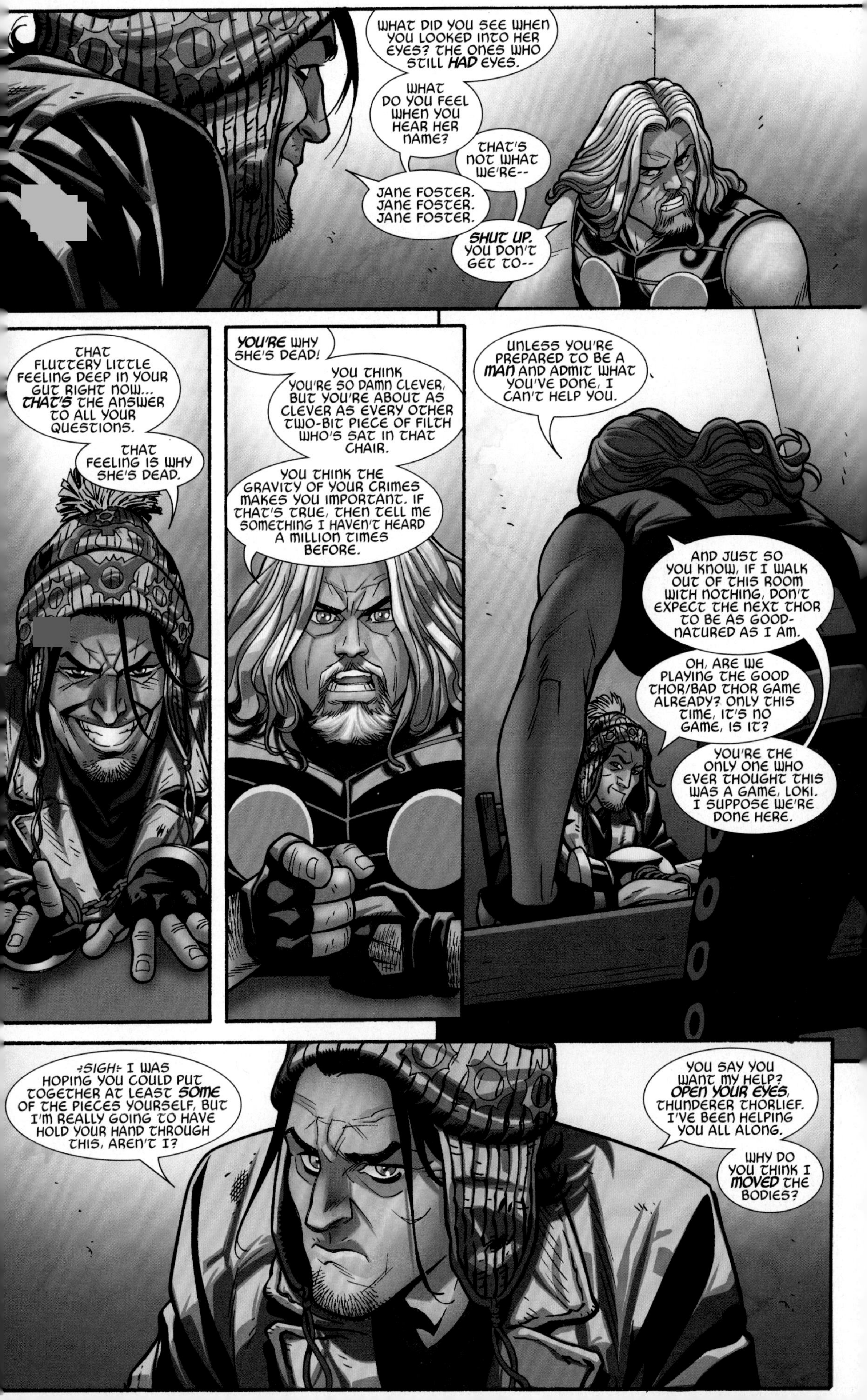
WHAT DID YOU SEE WHEN YOU LOOKED INTO HER EYES? THE ONES WHO STILL *HAD* EYES.
WHAT DO YOU FEEL WHEN YOU HEAR HER NAME?
THAT'S NOT WHAT WE'RE--
JANE FOSTER. JANE FOSTER. JANE FOSTER.
SHUT UP. YOU DON'T GET TO--
THAT FLUTTERY LITTLE FEELING DEEP IN YOUR GUT RIGHT NOW... *THAT'S* THE ANSWER TO ALL YOUR QUESTIONS.
THAT FEELING IS WHY SHE'S DEAD.
YOU'RE WHY SHE'S DEAD!
YOU THINK YOU'RE SO DAMN CLEVER, BUT YOU'RE ABOUT AS CLEVER AS EVERY OTHER TWO-BIT PIECE OF FILTH WHO'S SAT IN THAT CHAIR.
YOU THINK THE GRAVITY OF YOUR CRIMES MAKES YOU IMPORTANT. IF THAT'S TRUE, THEN TELL ME SOMETHING I HAVEN'T HEARD A MILLION TIMES BEFORE.
UNLESS YOU'RE PREPARED TO BE A *MAN* AND ADMIT WHAT YOU'VE DONE, I CAN'T HELP YOU.
AND JUST SO YOU KNOW, IF I WALK OUT OF THIS ROOM WITH NOTHING, DON'T EXPECT THE NEXT THOR TO BE AS GOOD-NATURED AS I AM.
OH, ARE WE PLAYING THE GOOD THOR/BAD THOR GAME ALREADY? ONLY THIS TIME, IT'S NO GAME, IS IT?
YOU'RE THE ONLY ONE WHO EVER THOUGHT THIS WAS A GAME, LOKI. I SUPPOSE WE'RE DONE HERE.
÷SIGH÷ I WAS HOPING YOU COULD PUT TOGETHER AT LEAST *SOME* OF THE PIECES YOURSELF, BUT I'M REALLY GOING TO HAVE HOLD YOUR HAND THROUGH THIS, AREN'T I?
YOU SAY YOU WANT MY HELP? *OPEN YOUR EYES*, THUNDERER THORLIEF. I'VE BEEN HELPING YOU ALL ALONG.
WHY DO YOU THINK I *MOVED* THE BODIES?

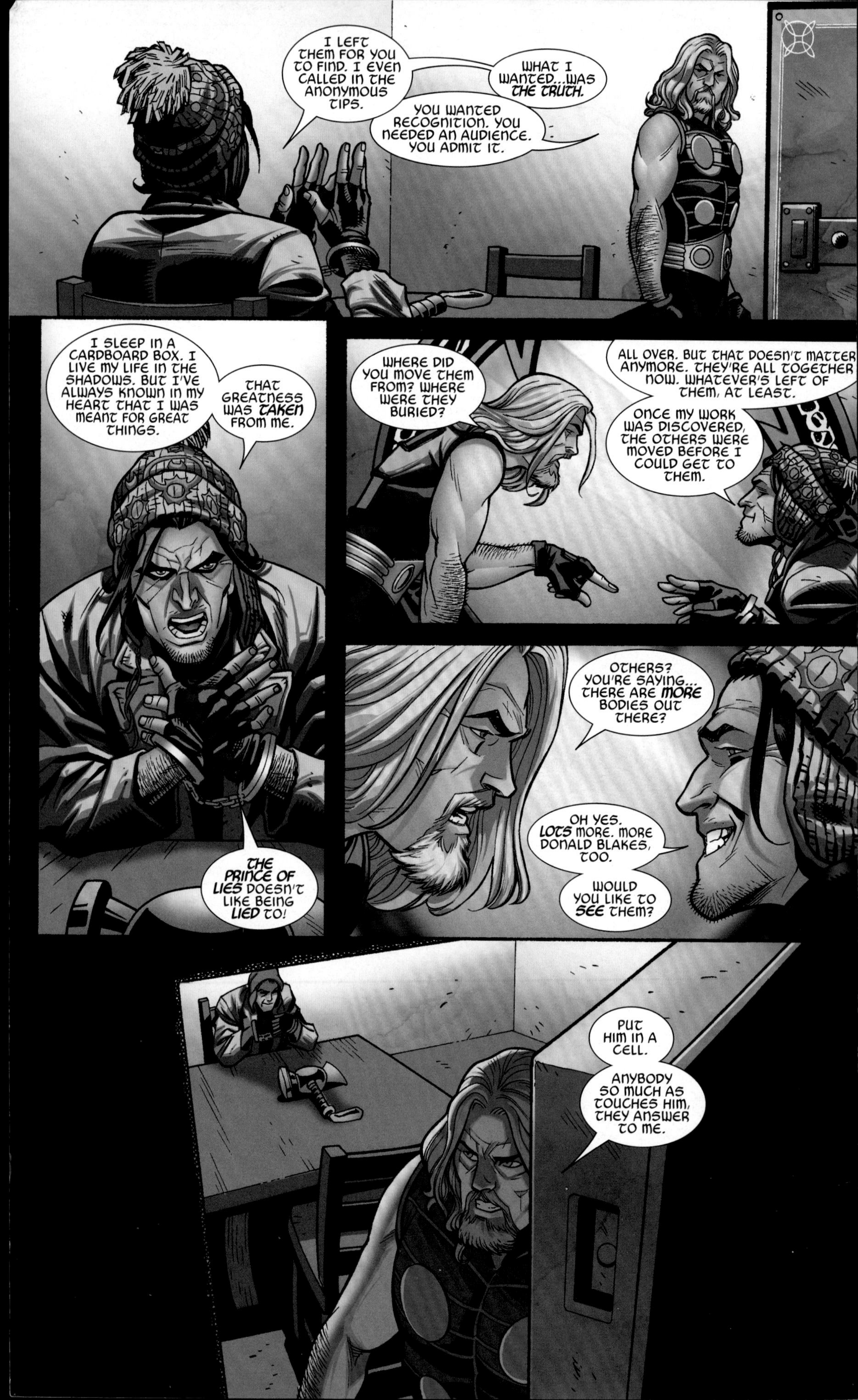
I LEFT THEM FOR YOU TO FIND. I EVEN CALLED IN THE ANONYMOUS TIPS.
WHAT I WANTED...WAS THE TRUTH.
YOU WANTED RECOGNITION. YOU NEEDED AN AUDIENCE. YOU ADMIT IT.
I SLEEP IN A CARDBOARD BOX. I LIVE MY LIFE IN THE SHADOWS. BUT I'VE ALWAYS KNOWN IN MY HEART THAT I WAS MEANT FOR GREAT THINGS.
THAT GREATNESS WAS TAKEN FROM ME.
THE PRINCE OF LIES DOESN'T LIKE BEING LIED TO!
WHERE DID YOU MOVE THEM FROM? WHERE WERE THEY BURIED?
ALL OVER. BUT THAT DOESN'T MATTER ANYMORE. THEY'RE ALL TOGETHER NOW. WHATEVER'S LEFT OF THEM, AT LEAST.
ONCE MY WORK WAS DISCOVERED, THE OTHERS WERE MOVED BEFORE I COULD GET TO THEM.
OTHERS? YOU'RE SAYING... THERE ARE MORE BODIES OUT THERE?
OH YES. LOTS MORE. MORE DONALD BLAKES, TOO.
WOULD YOU LIKE TO SEE THEM?
PUT HIM IN A CELL.
ANYBODY SO MUCH AS TOUCHES HIM, THEY ANSWER TO ME.

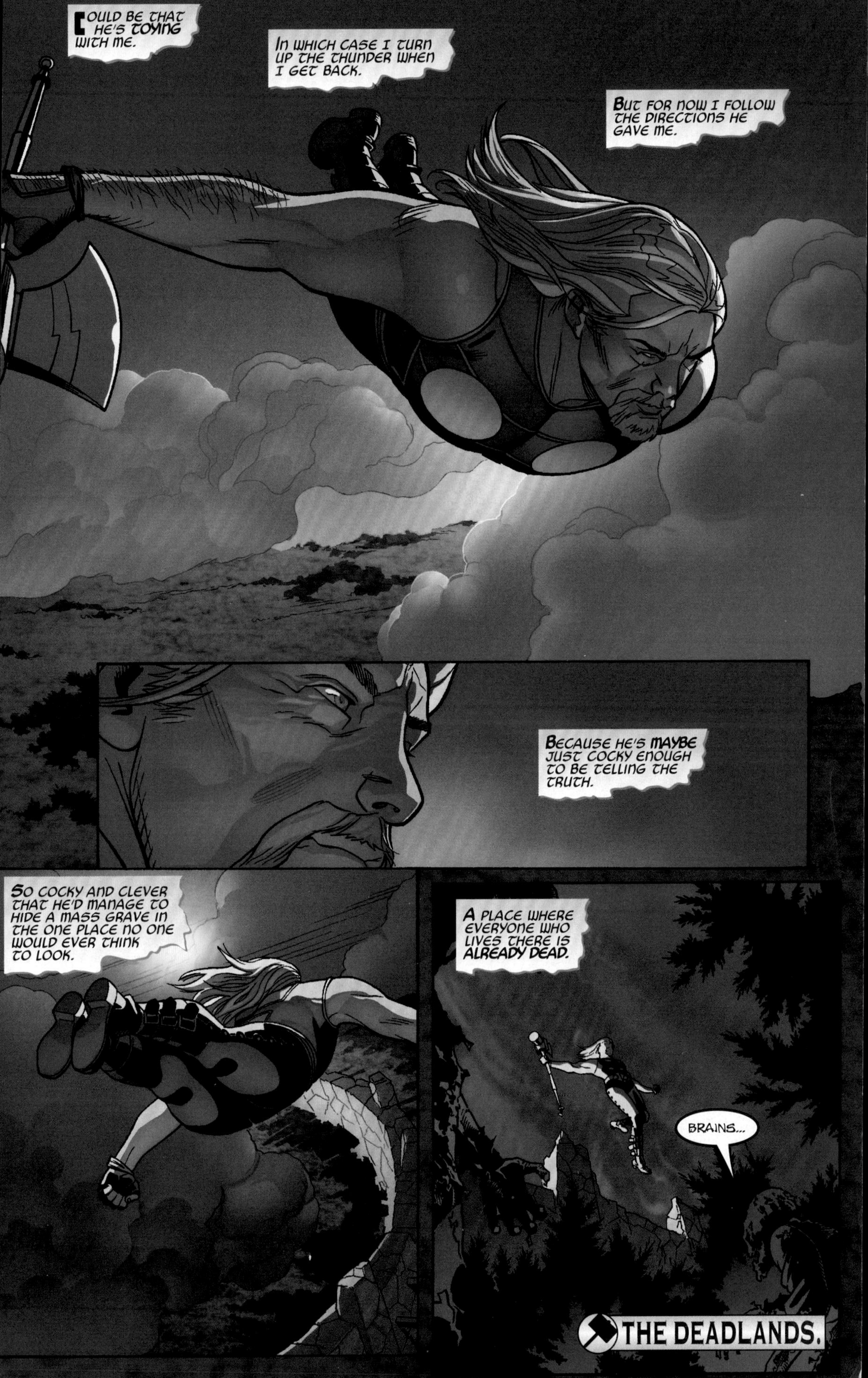
COULD BE THAT HE'S TOYING WITH ME.
IN WHICH CASE I TURN UP THE THUNDER WHEN I GET BACK.
BUT FOR NOW I FOLLOW THE DIRECTIONS HE GAVE ME.
BECAUSE HE'S MAYBE JUST COCKY ENOUGH TO BE TELLING THE TRUTH.
SO COCKY AND CLEVER THAT HE'D MANAGE TO HIDE A MASS GRAVE IN THE ONE PLACE NO ONE WOULD EVER THINK TO LOOK.
A PLACE WHERE EVERYONE WHO LIVES THERE IS ALREADY DEAD.
BRAINS...
THE DEADLANDS.

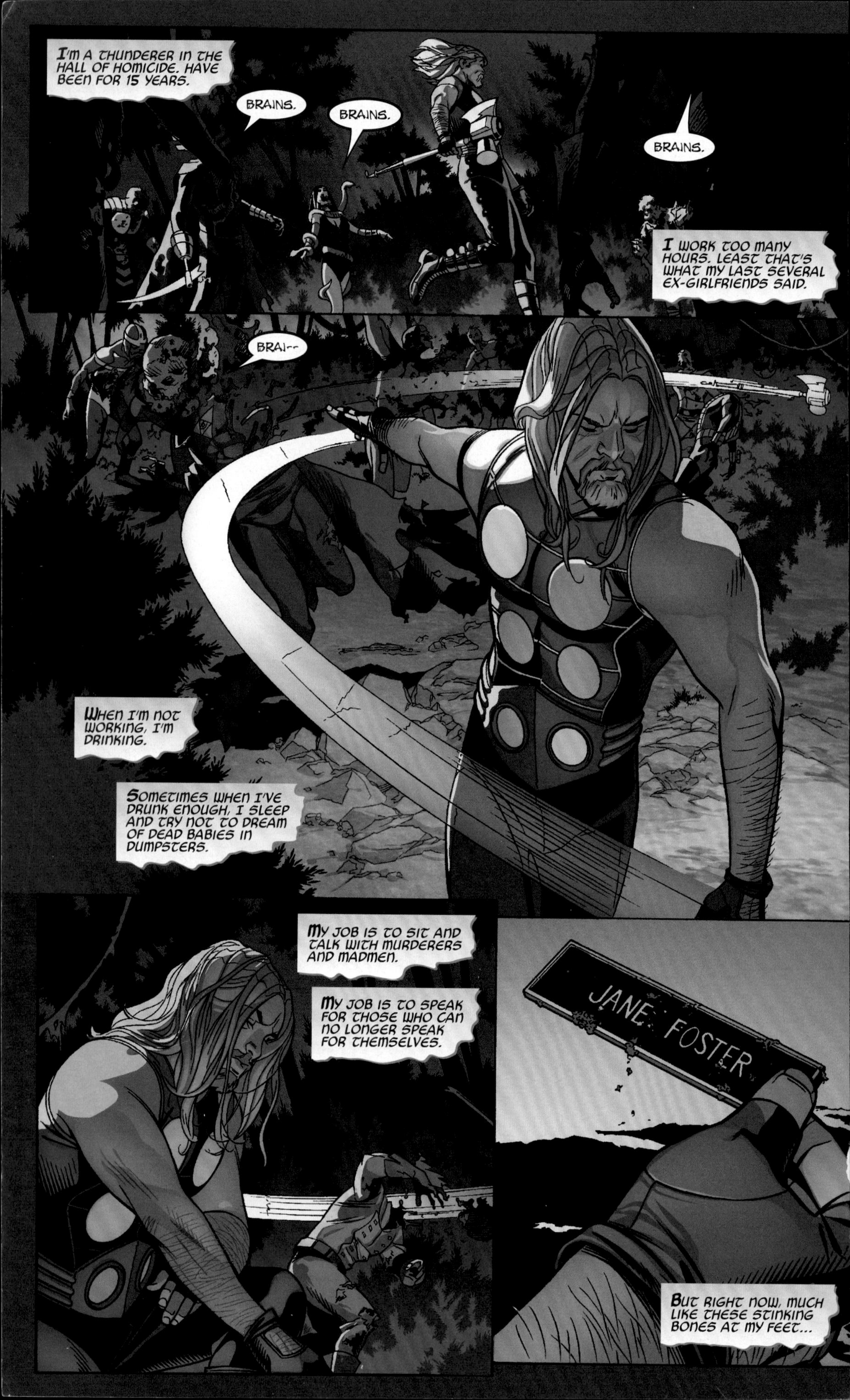
I'M A THUNDERER IN THE HALL OF HOMICIDE. HAVE BEEN FOR 15 YEARS.
BRAINS.
BRAINS.
BRAINS.
I WORK TOO MANY HOURS. LEAST THAT'S WHAT MY LAST SEVERAL EX-GIRLFRIENDS SAID.
BRAI--
WHEN I'M NOT WORKING, I'M DRINKING.
SOMETIMES WHEN I'VE DRUNK ENOUGH, I SLEEP AND TRY NOT TO DREAM OF DEAD BABIES IN DUMPSTERS.
MY JOB IS TO SIT AND TALK WITH MURDERERS AND MADMEN.
MY JOB IS TO SPEAK FOR THOSE WHO CAN NO LONGER SPEAK FOR THEMSELVES.
JANE FOSTER
BUT RIGHT NOW, MUCH LIKE THESE STINKING BONES AT MY FEET...

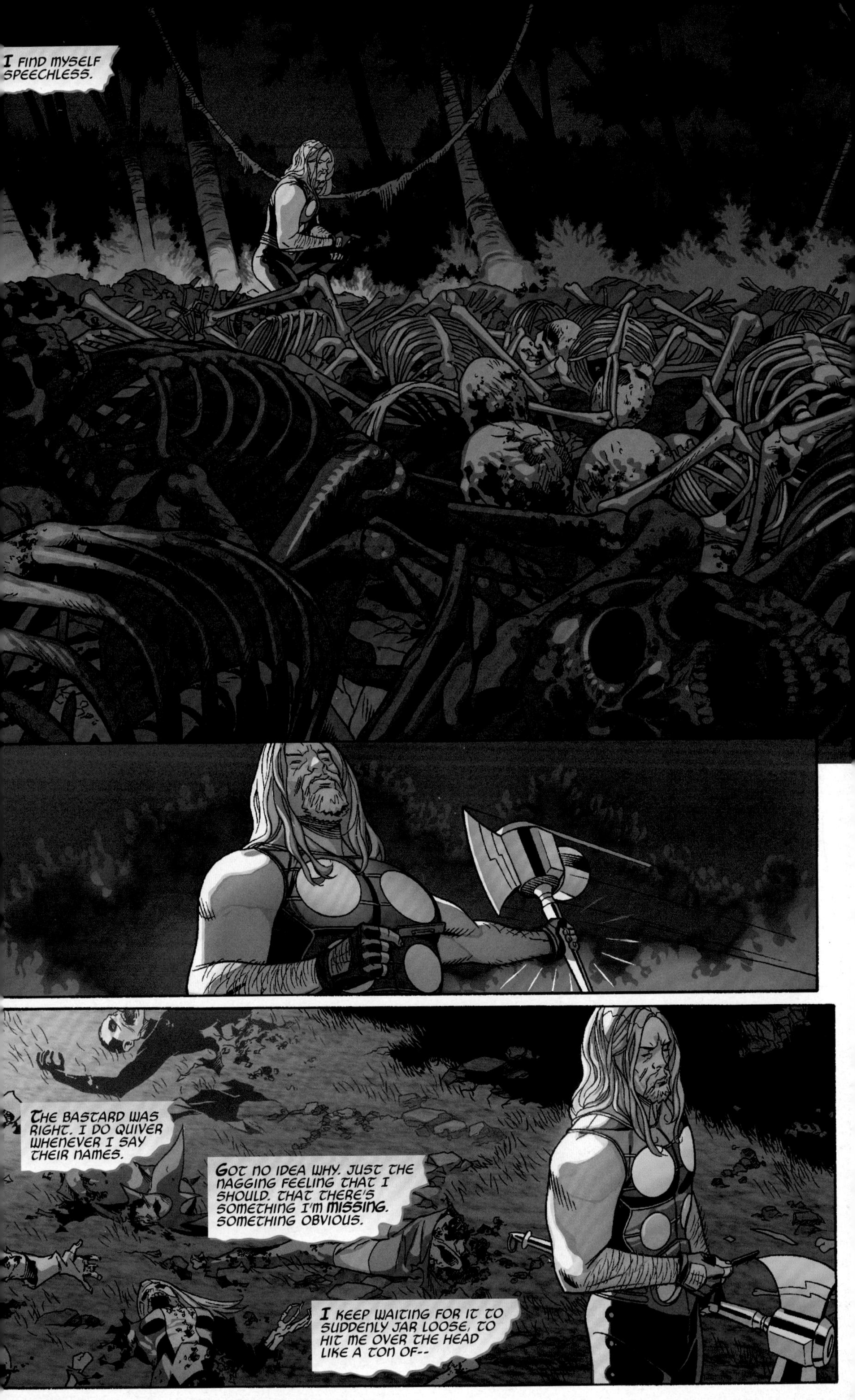
I FIND MYSELF SPEECHLESS.
THE BASTARD WAS RIGHT. I DO QUIVER WHENEVER I SAY THEIR NAMES.
GOT NO IDEA WHY. JUST THE NAGGING FEELING THAT I SHOULD. THAT THERE'S SOMETHING I'M **MISSING**. SOMETHING OBVIOUS.
I KEEP WAITING FOR IT TO SUDDENLY JAR LOOSE, TO HIT ME OVER THE HEAD LIKE A TON OF--

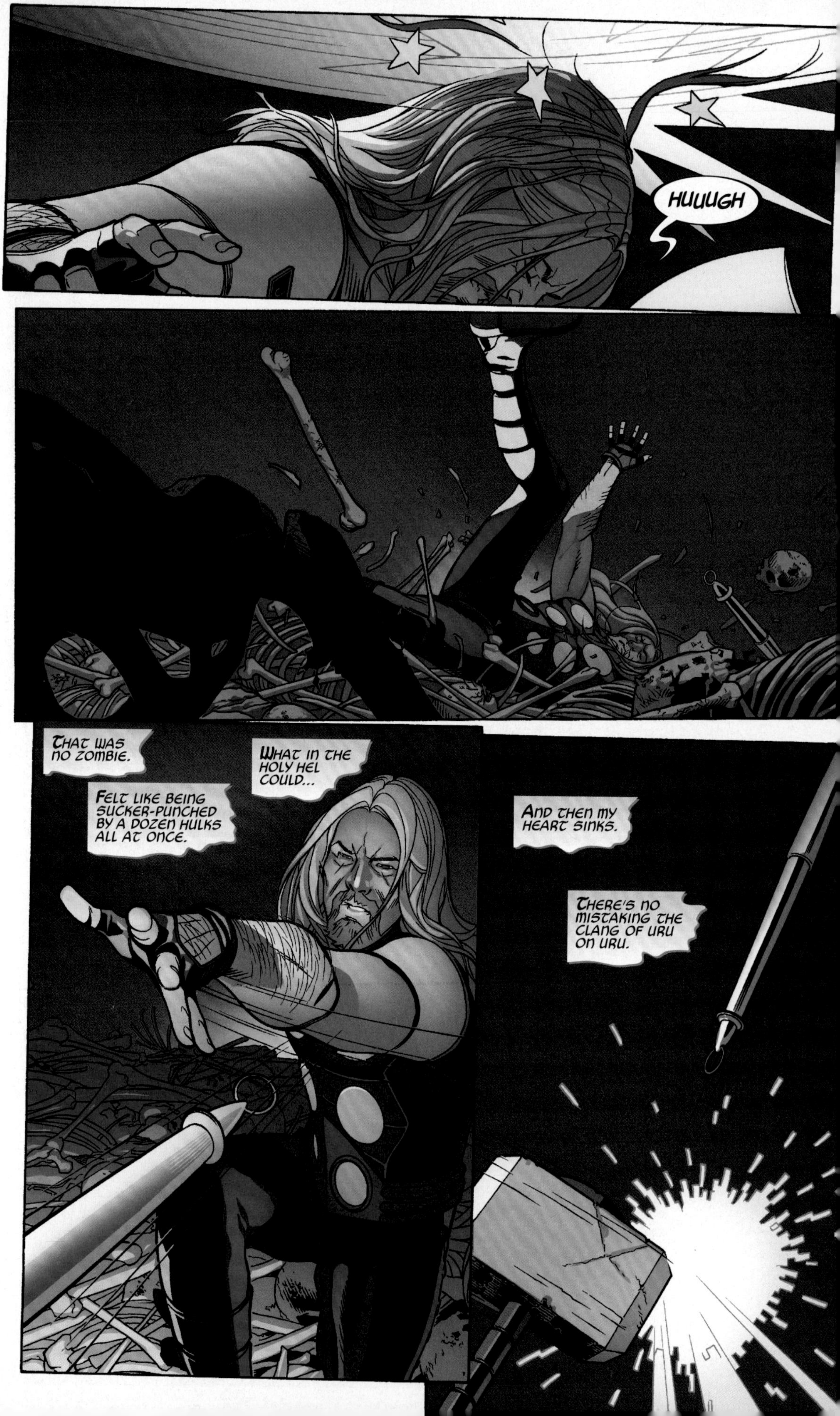
HUUUGH
THAT WAS NO ZOMBIE.
FELT LIKE BEING SUCKER-PUNCHED BY A DOZEN HULKS ALL AT ONCE.
WHAT IN THE HOLY HEL COULD...
AND THEN MY HEART SINKS.
THERE'S NO MISTAKING THE CLANG OF URU ON URU.

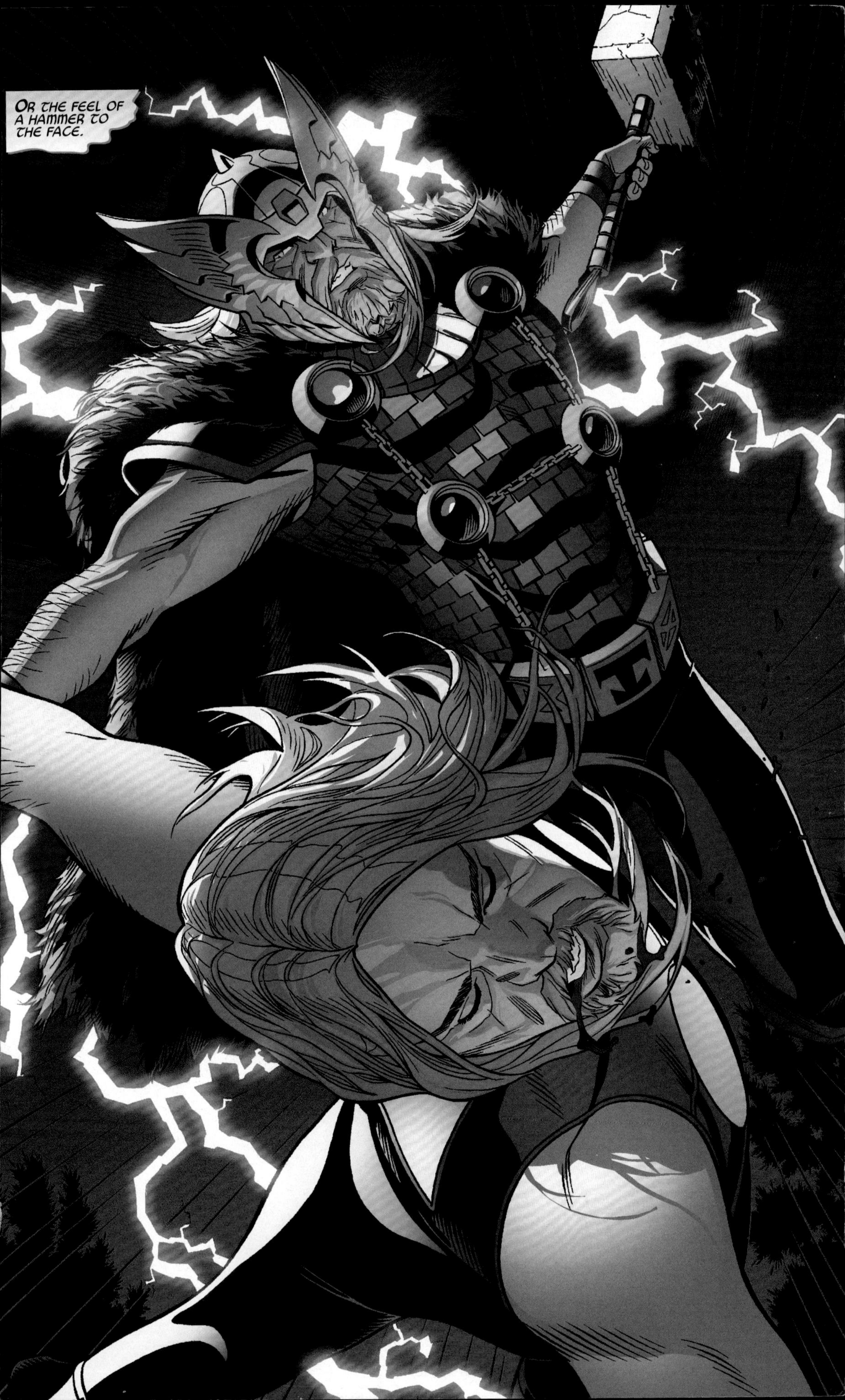
OR THE FEEL OF A HAMMER TO THE FACE.

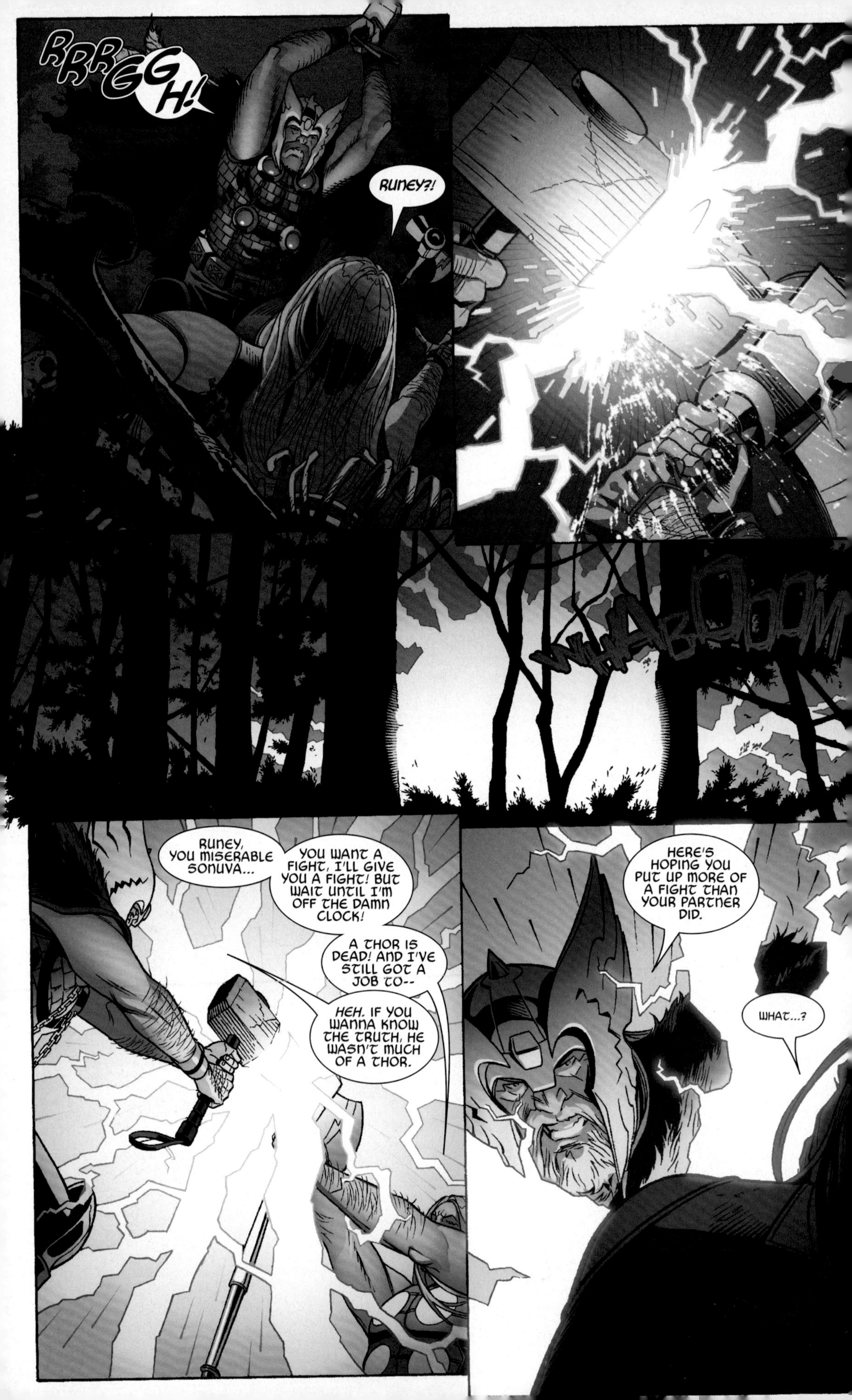
RRRGGH!
RUNEY?!
WHABOOOM
RUNEY, YOU MISERABLE SONUVA...
YOU WANT A FIGHT, I'LL GIVE YOU A FIGHT! BUT WAIT UNTIL I'M OFF THE DAMN CLOCK!
A THOR IS DEAD! AND I'VE STILL GOT A JOB TO--
HEH. IF YOU WANNA KNOW THE TRUTH, HE WASN'T MUCH OF A THOR.
HERE'S HOPING YOU PUT UP MORE OF A FIGHT THAN YOUR PARTNER DID.
WHAT...?

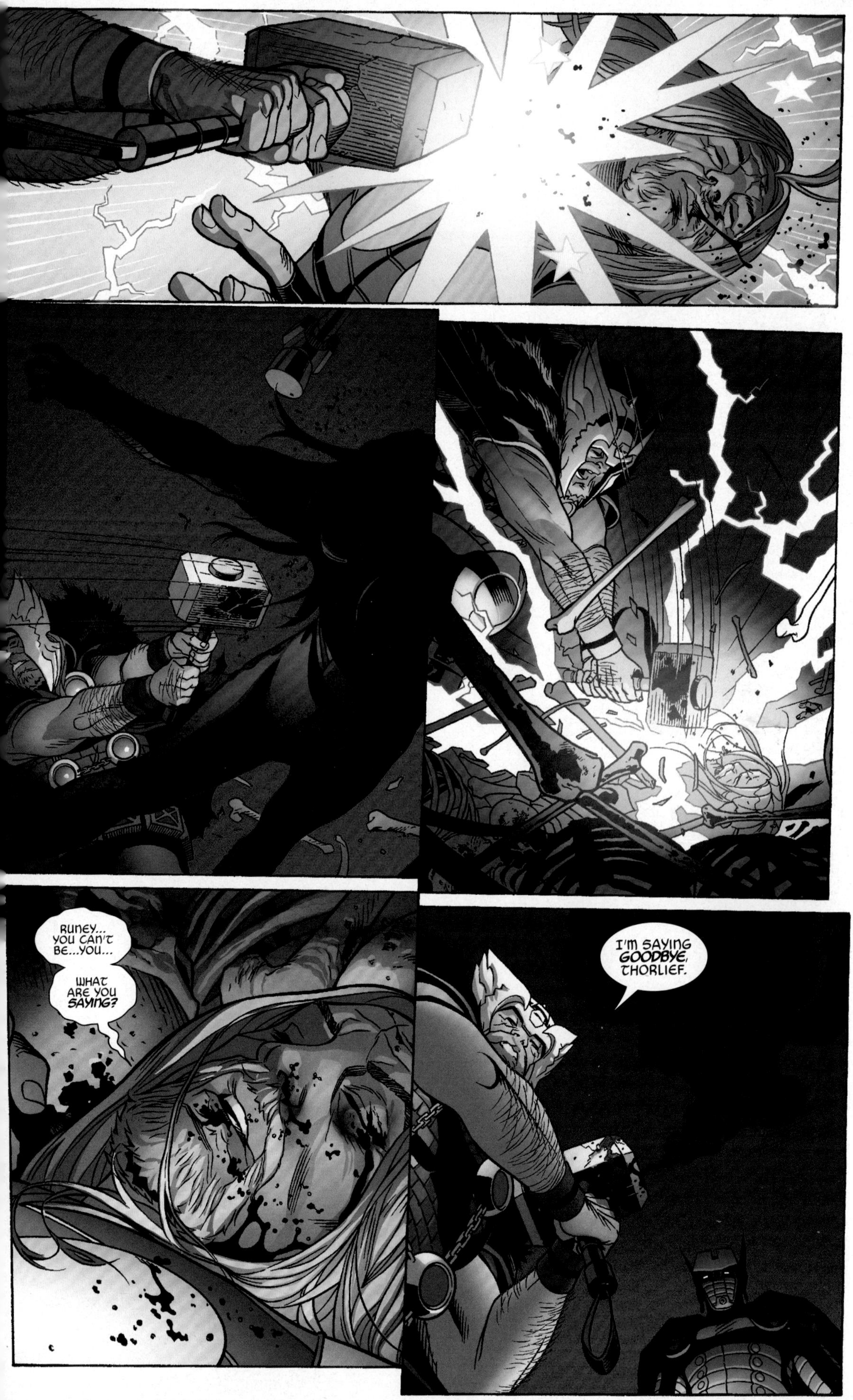
RUNEY... YOU CAN'T BE...YOU...
WHAT ARE YOU *SAYING?*
I'M SAYING *GOODBYE*, THORLIEF.

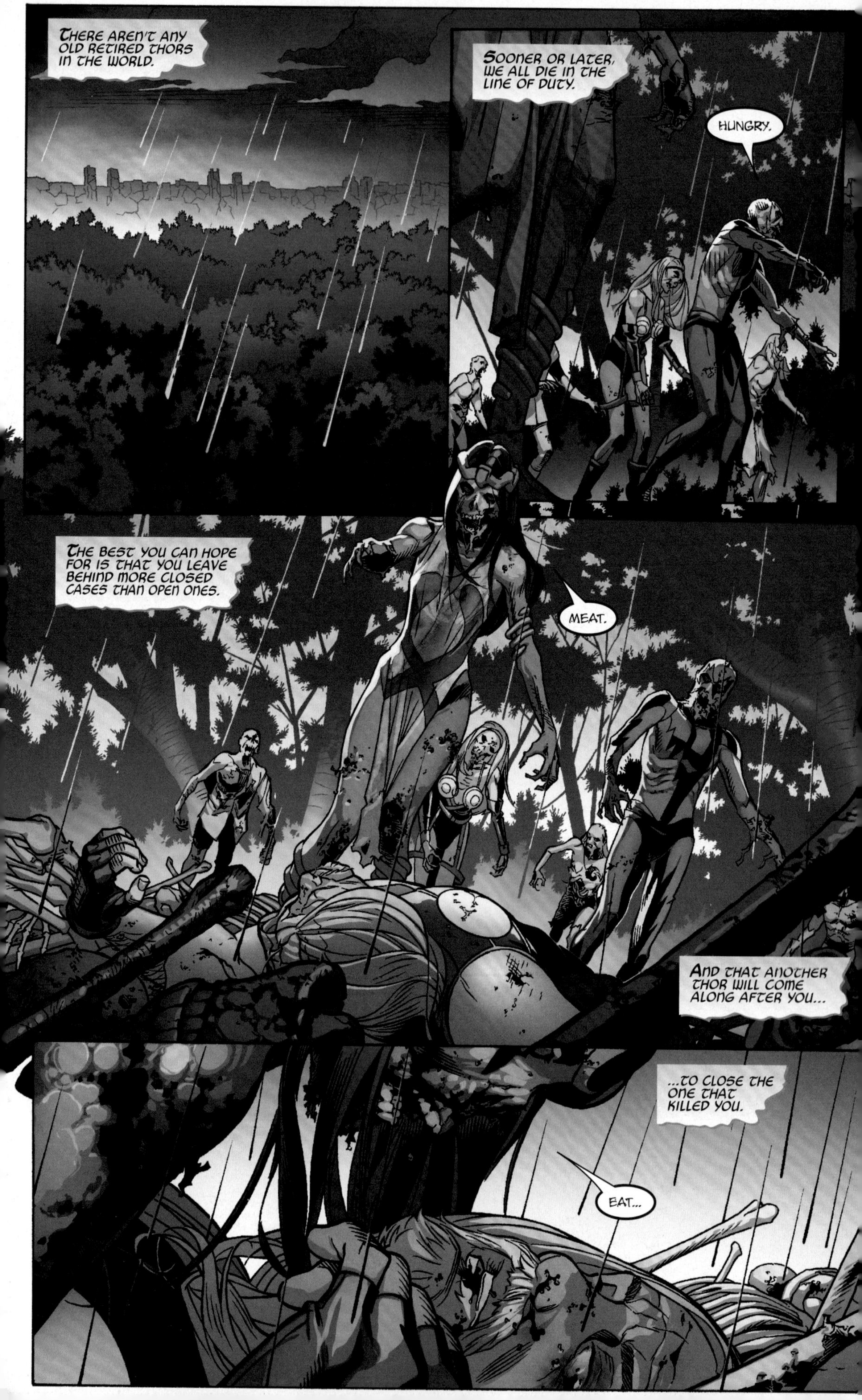
There aren't any old retired Thors in the world.
Sooner or later, we all die in the line of duty.
Hungry.
The best you can hope for is that you leave behind more closed cases than open ones.
Meat.
And that another Thor will come along after you...
...to close the one that killed you.
Eat...

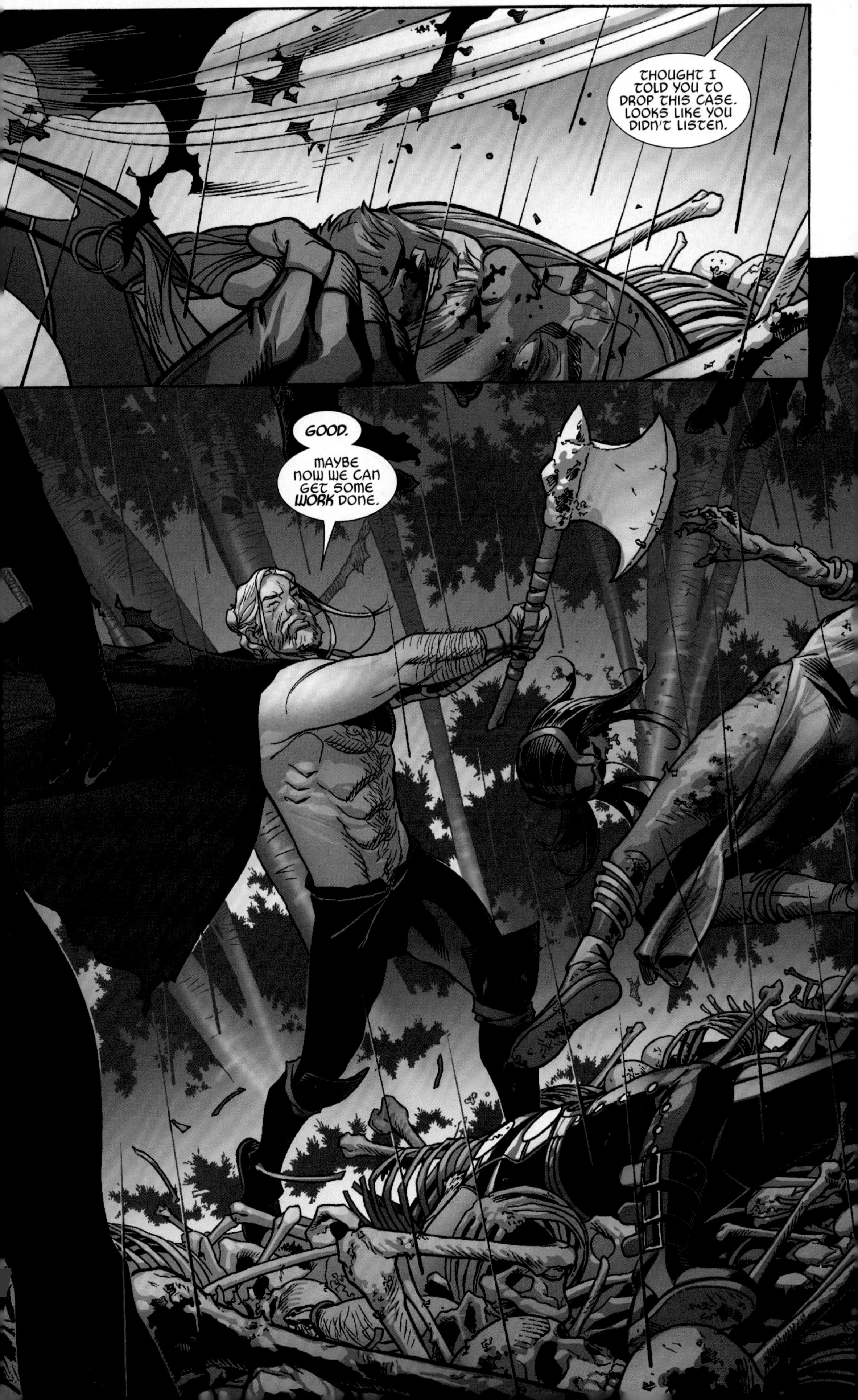
THOUGHT I TOLD YOU TO DROP THIS CASE. LOOKS LIKE YOU DIDN'T LISTEN.
GOOD.
MAYBE NOW WE CAN GET SOME **WORK** DONE.

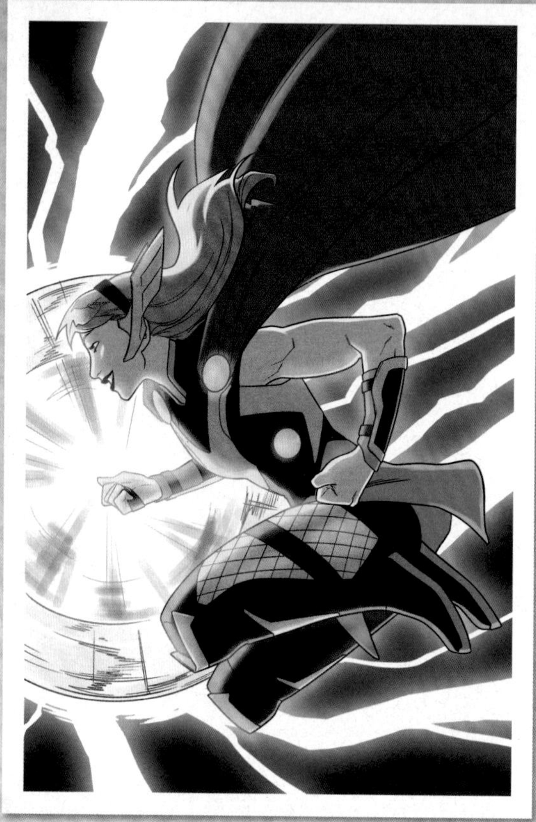

THORS No. 1 GWEN OF THUNDER VARIANT BY
KRIS ANKA

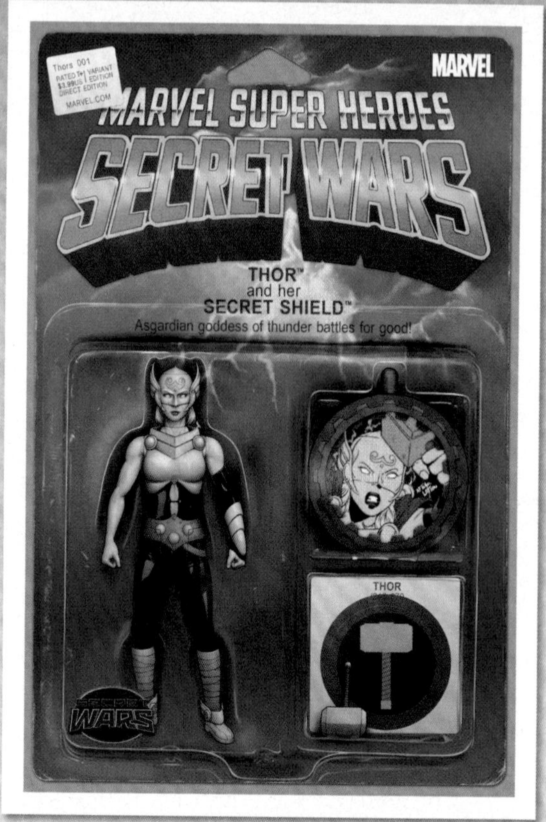
MARVEL
MARVEL SUPER HEROES
SECRET WARS
THOR™
and her
SECRET SHIELD™
Asgardian goddess of thunder battles for good!
WARS
THOR

THORS No. 1 ACTION FIGURE VARIANT BY
JOHN TYLER CHRISTOPHER

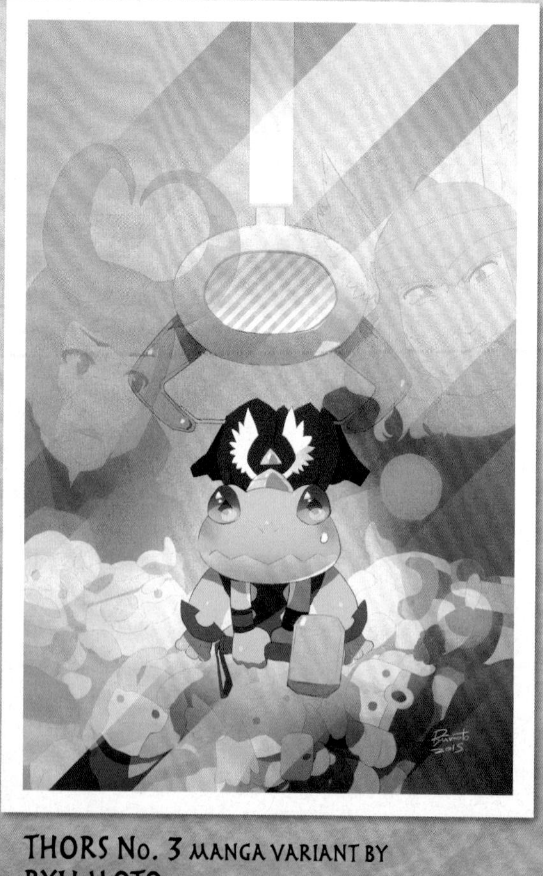

THORS No. 3 MANGA VARIANT BY
RYU MOTO

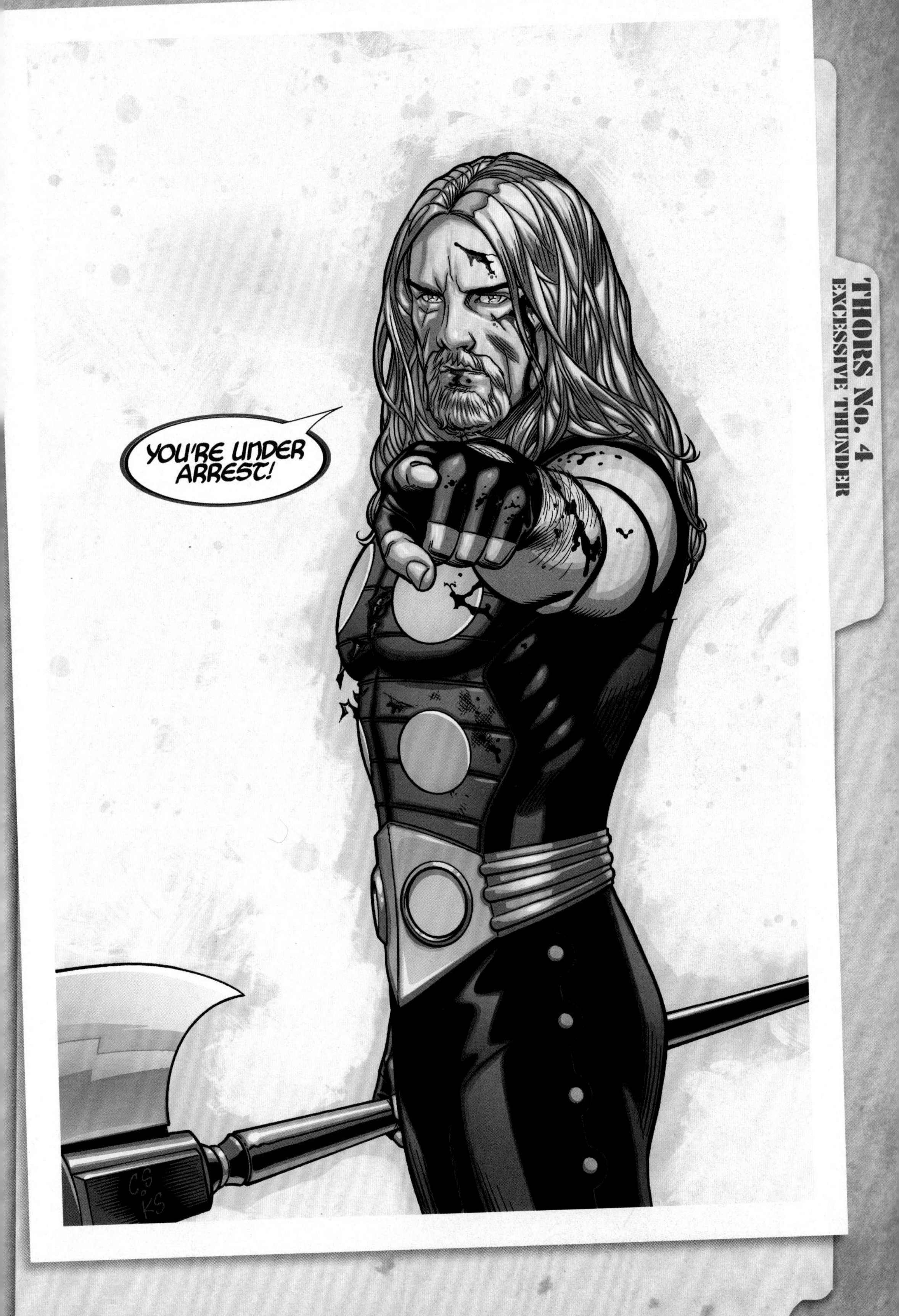
YOU'RE UNDER ARREST!
THORS No. 4
EXCESSIVE THUNDER

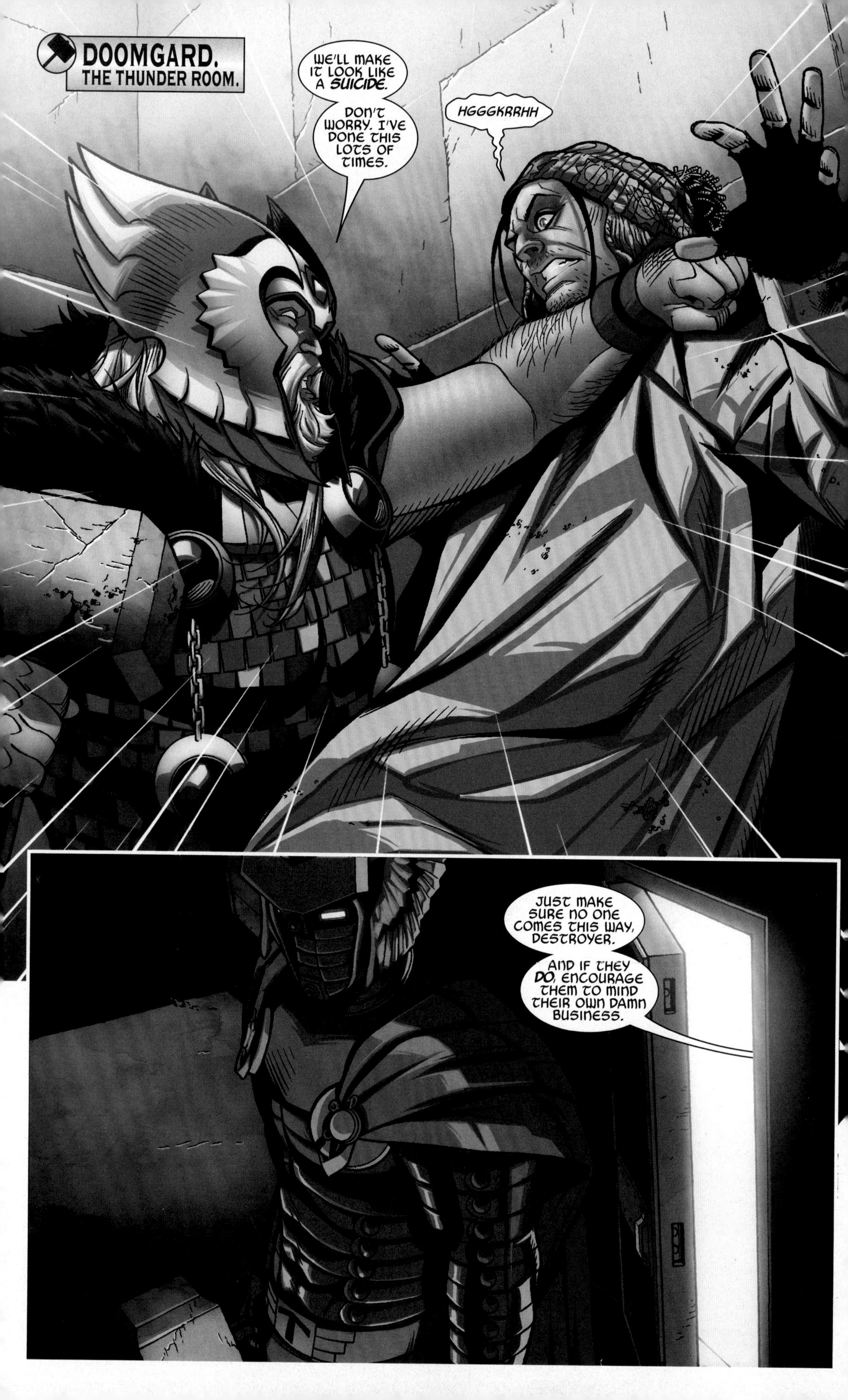
DOOMGARD.
THE THUNDER ROOM.
WE'LL MAKE IT LOOK LIKE A SUICIDE.
DON'T WORRY. I'VE DONE THIS LOTS OF TIMES.
HGGGKRRHH
JUST MAKE SURE NO ONE COMES THIS WAY, DESTROYER.
AND IF THEY DO, ENCOURAGE THEM TO MIND THEIR OWN DAMN BUSINESS.

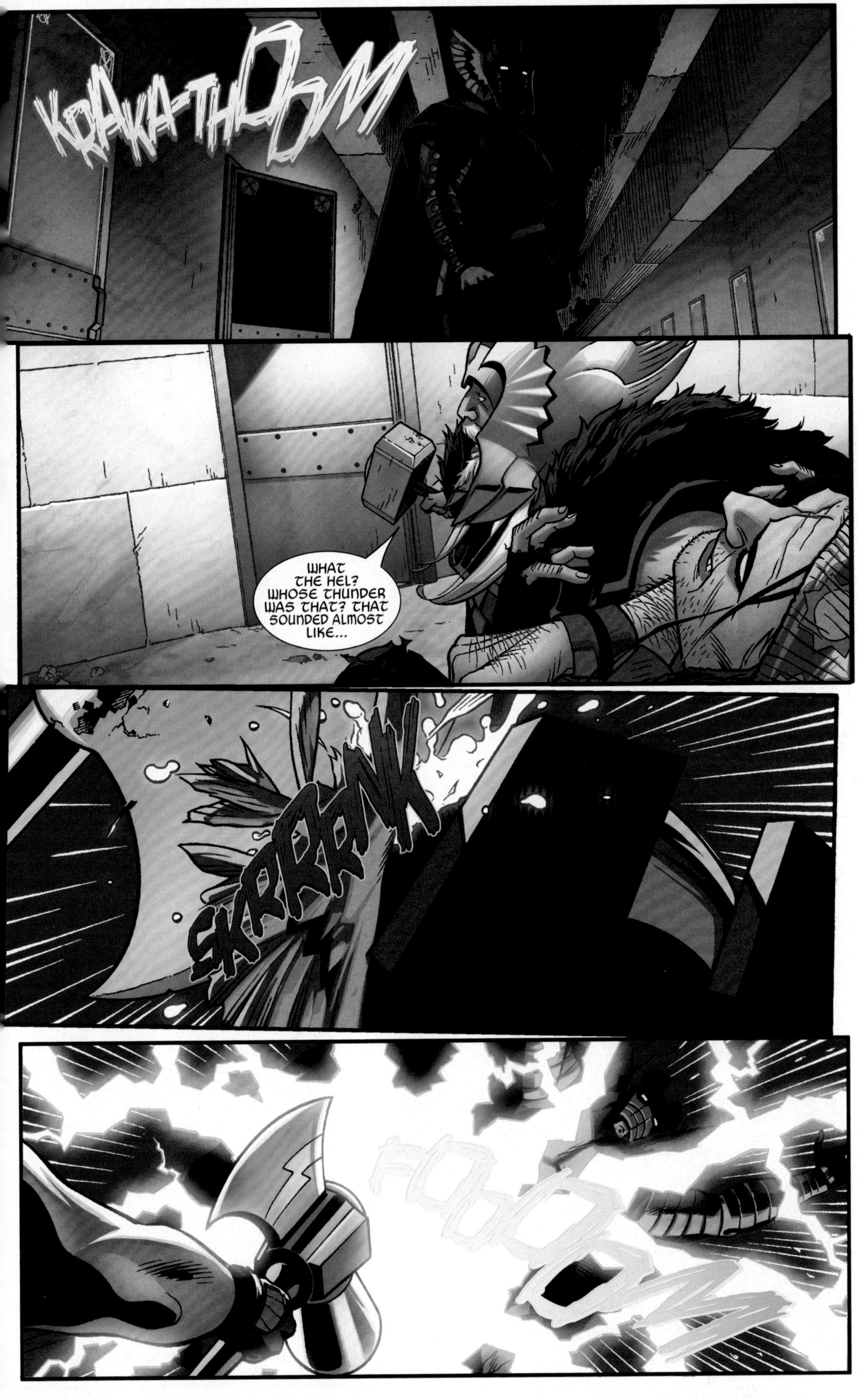
KRAKA-THOOM
WHAT THE HEL? WHOSE THUNDER WAS THAT? THAT SOUNDED ALMOST LIKE...
SKRRRNK
FOOOOM

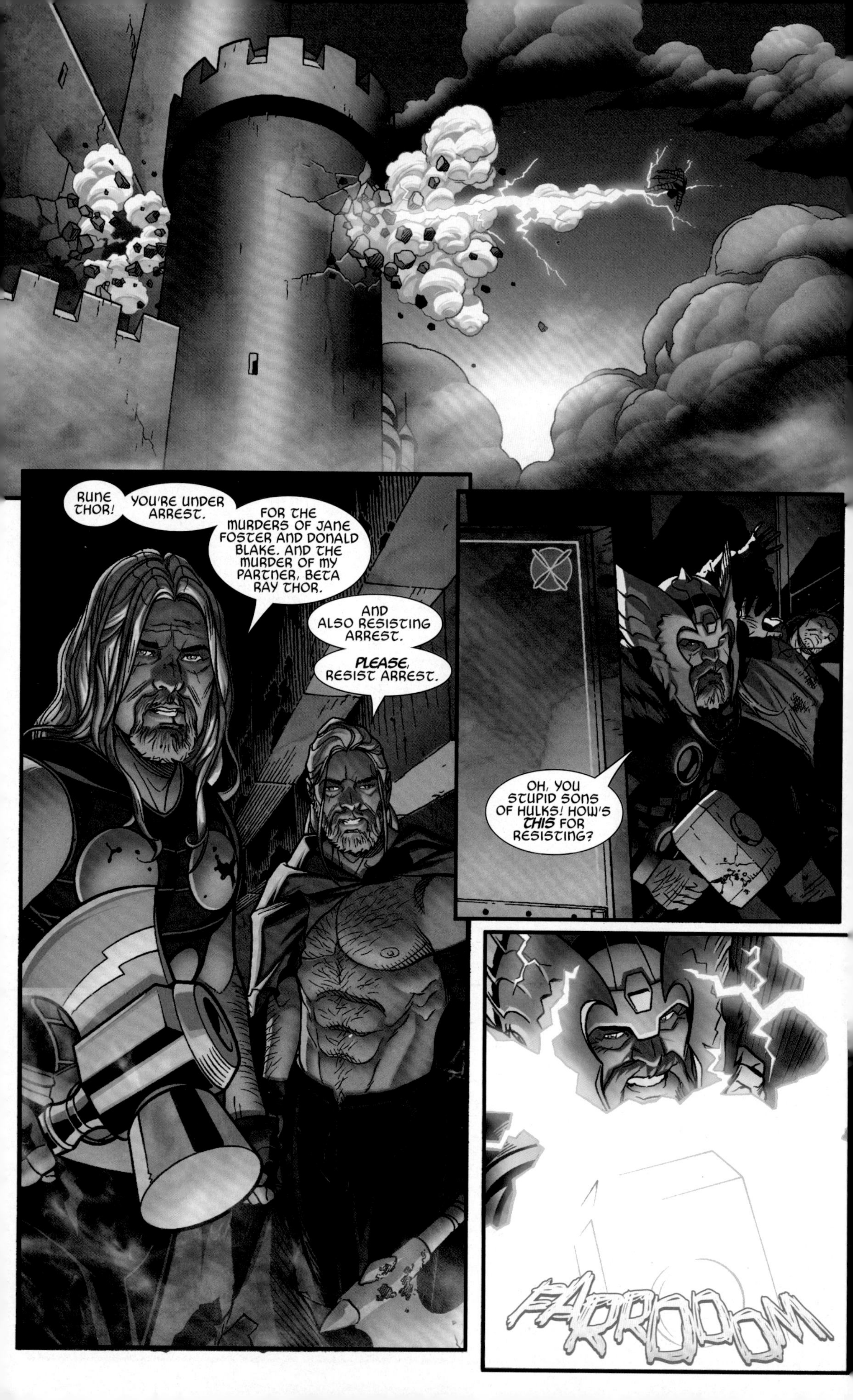

RUNE THOR!
YOU'RE UNDER ARREST.
FOR THE MURDERS OF JANE FOSTER AND DONALD BLAKE. AND THE MURDER OF MY PARTNER, BETA RAY THOR.
AND ALSO RESISTING ARREST.
PLEASE, RESIST ARREST.
OH, YOU STUPID SONS OF HULKS! HOW'S THIS FOR RESISTING?
FADROOOM

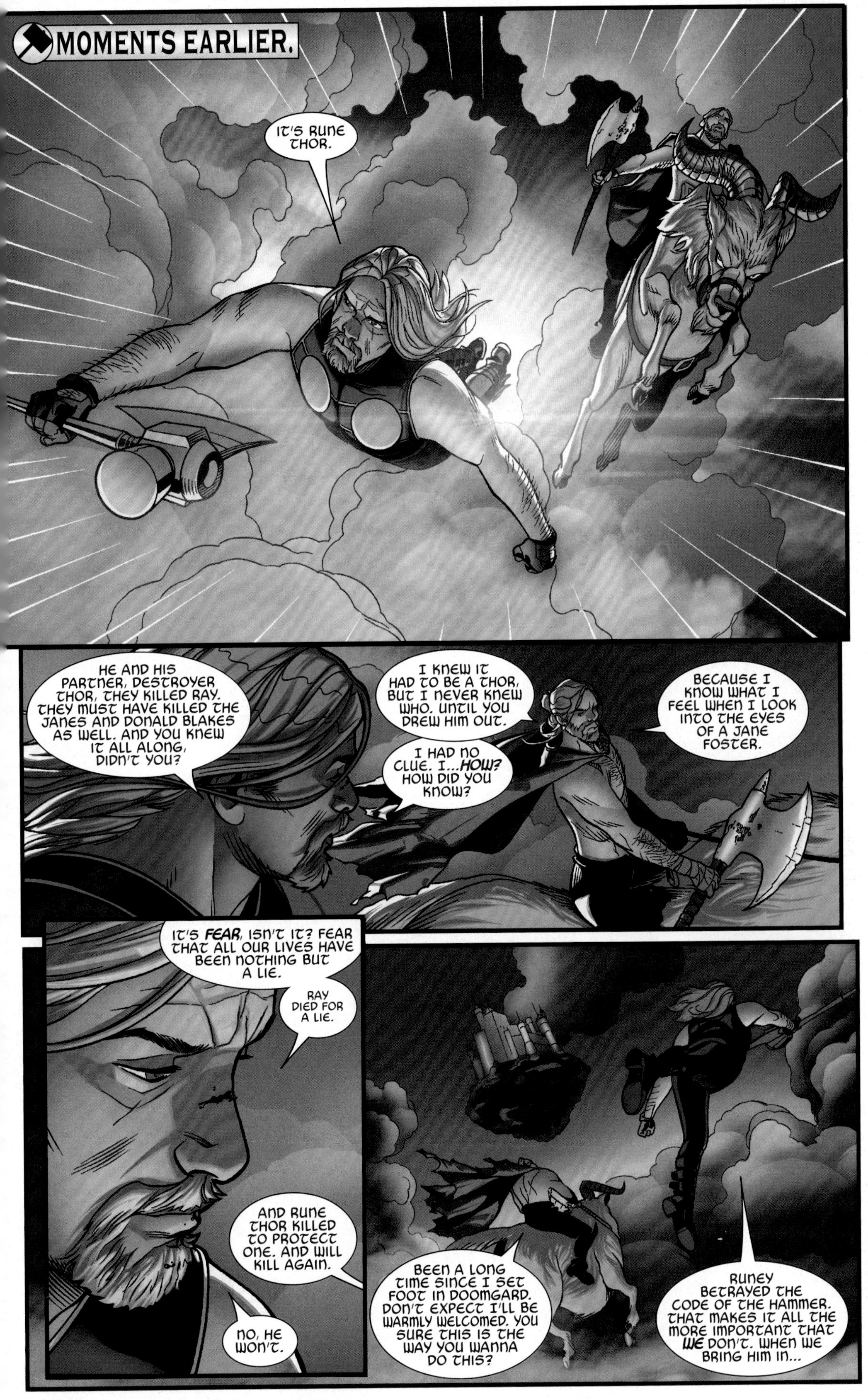
MOMENTS EARLIER.
IT'S RUNE THOR.
HE AND HIS PARTNER, DESTROYER THOR, THEY KILLED RAY. THEY MUST HAVE KILLED THE JANES AND DONALD BLAKES AS WELL. AND YOU KNEW IT ALL ALONG, DIDN'T YOU?
I KNEW IT HAD TO BE A THOR, BUT I NEVER KNEW WHO. UNTIL YOU DREW HIM OUT.
I HAD NO CLUE. I...HOW? HOW DID YOU KNOW?
BECAUSE I KNOW WHAT I FEEL WHEN I LOOK INTO THE EYES OF A JANE FOSTER.
IT'S FEAR, ISN'T IT? FEAR THAT ALL OUR LIVES HAVE BEEN NOTHING BUT A LIE.
RAY DIED FOR A LIE.
AND RUNE THOR KILLED TO PROTECT ONE. AND WILL KILL AGAIN.
NO, HE WON'T.
BEEN A LONG TIME SINCE I SET FOOT IN DOOMGARD. DON'T EXPECT I'LL BE WARMLY WELCOMED. YOU SURE THIS IS THE WAY YOU WANNA DO THIS?
RUNEY BETRAYED THE CODE OF THE HAMMER. THAT MAKES IT ALL THE MORE IMPORTANT THAT WE DON'T. WHEN WE BRING HIM IN...

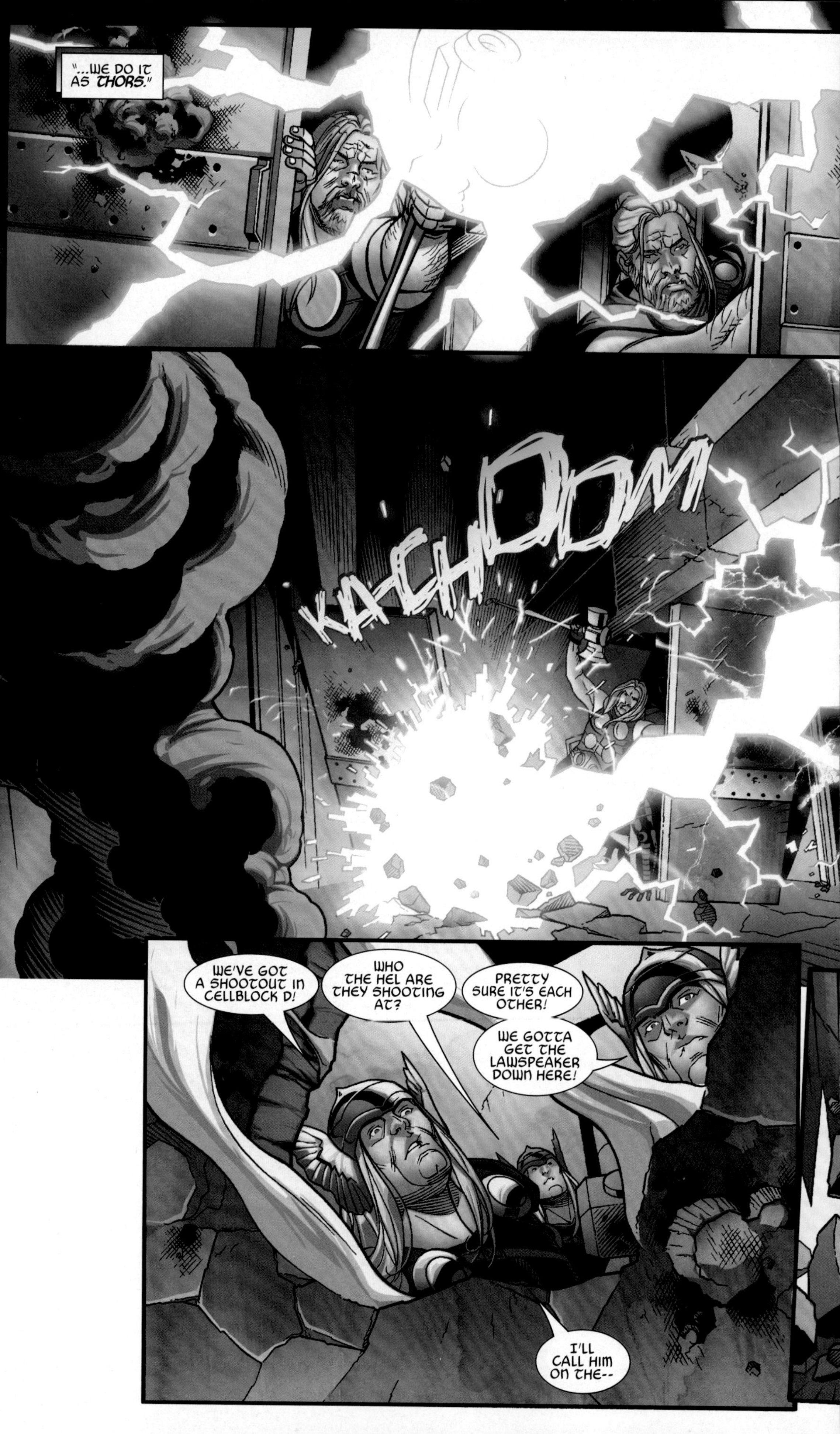
"...WE DO IT AS THORS."
KA-CHOOM
WE'VE GOT A SHOOTOUT IN CELLBLOCK D!
WHO THE HEL ARE THEY SHOOTING AT?
PRETTY SURE IT'S EACH OTHER!
WE GOTTA GET THE LAWSPEAKER DOWN HERE!
I'LL CALL HIM ON THE--

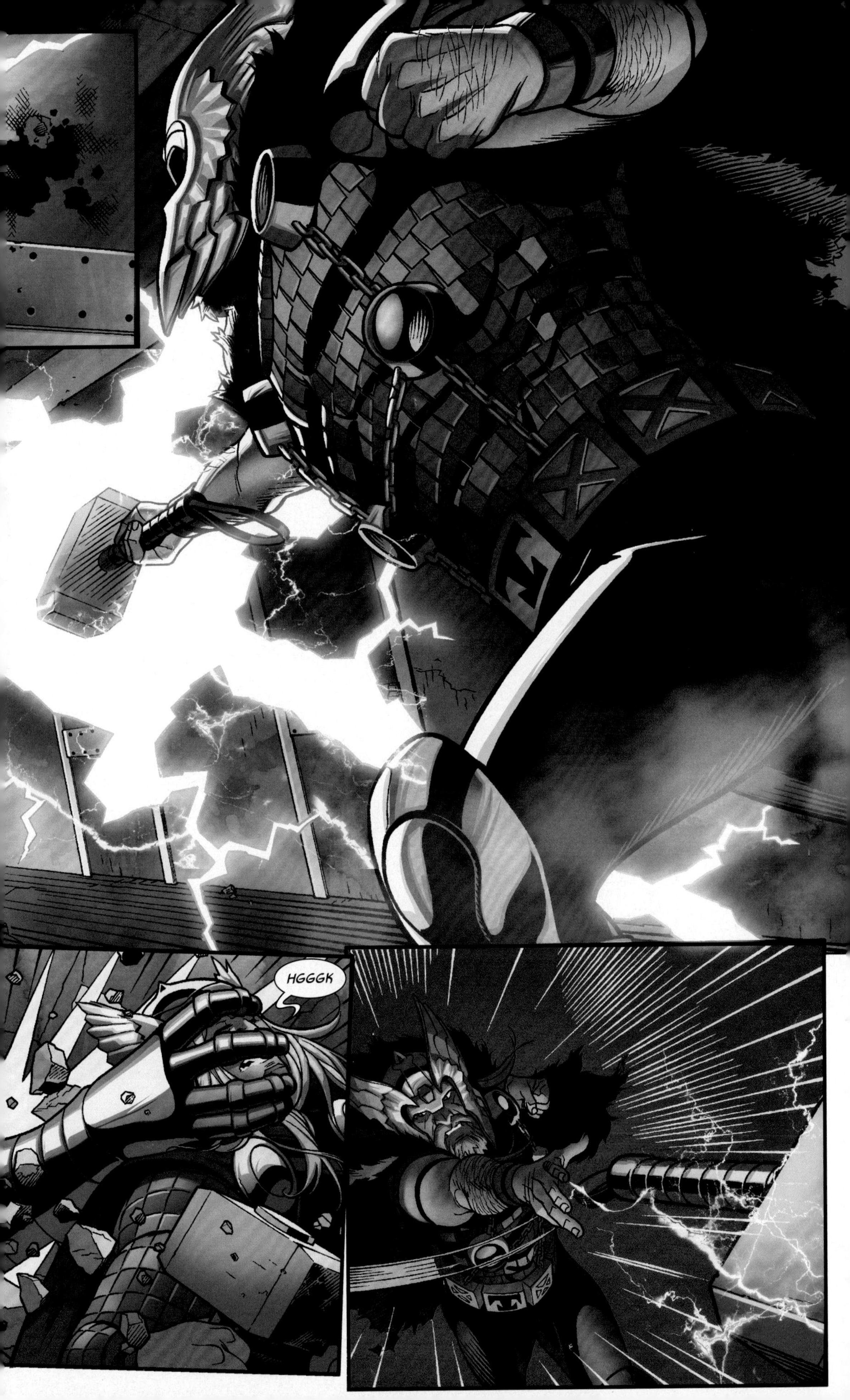
HGGGK

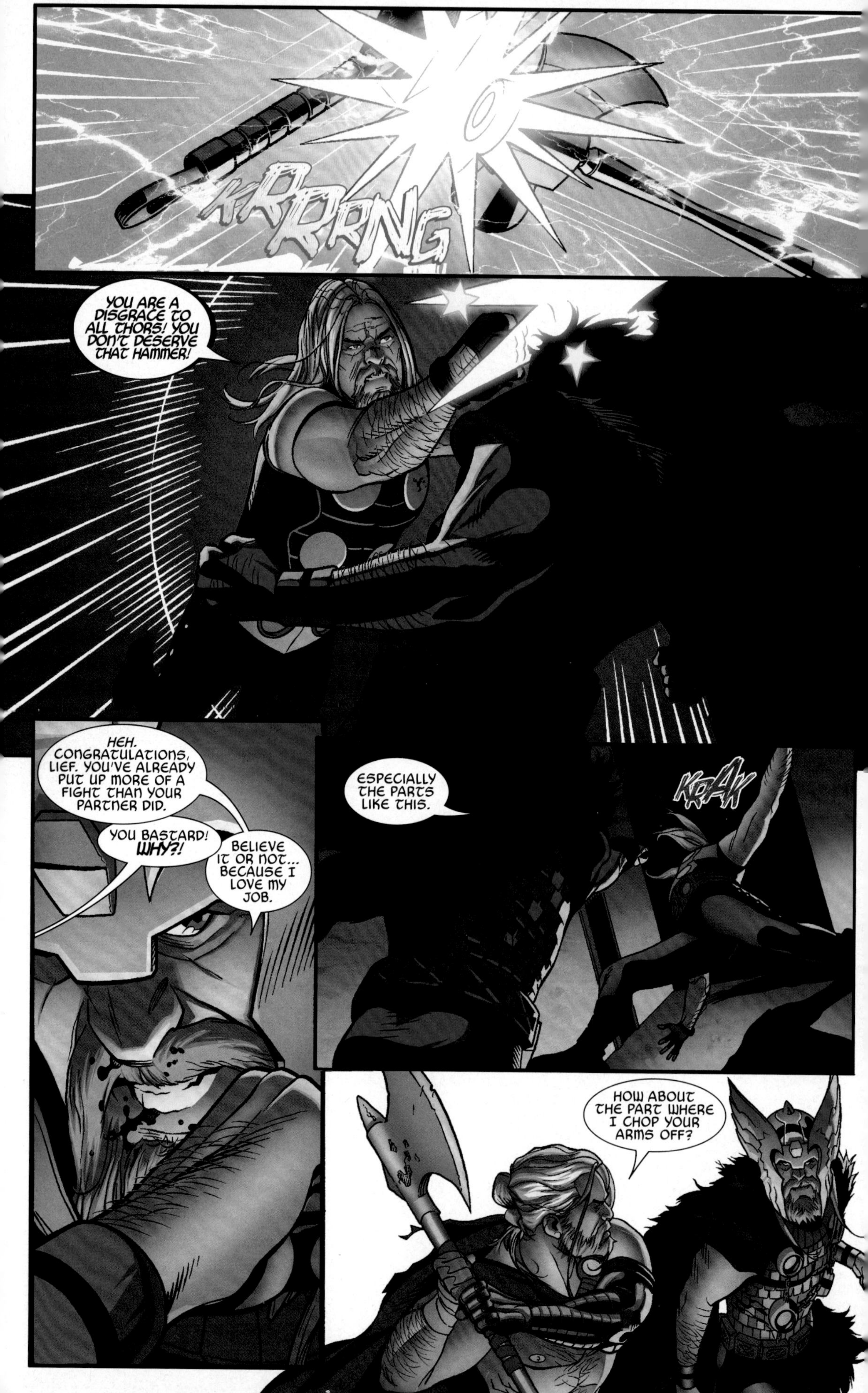
KRRRNG
YOU ARE A DISGRACE TO ALL THORS! YOU DON'T DESERVE THAT HAMMER!
HEH. CONGRATULATIONS, LIEF. YOU'VE ALREADY PUT UP MORE OF A FIGHT THAN YOUR PARTNER DID.
YOU BASTARD! WHY?!
BELIEVE IT OR NOT... BECAUSE I LOVE MY JOB.
ESPECIALLY THE PARTS LIKE THIS.
KRAK
HOW ABOUT THE PART WHERE I CHOP YOUR ARMS OFF?

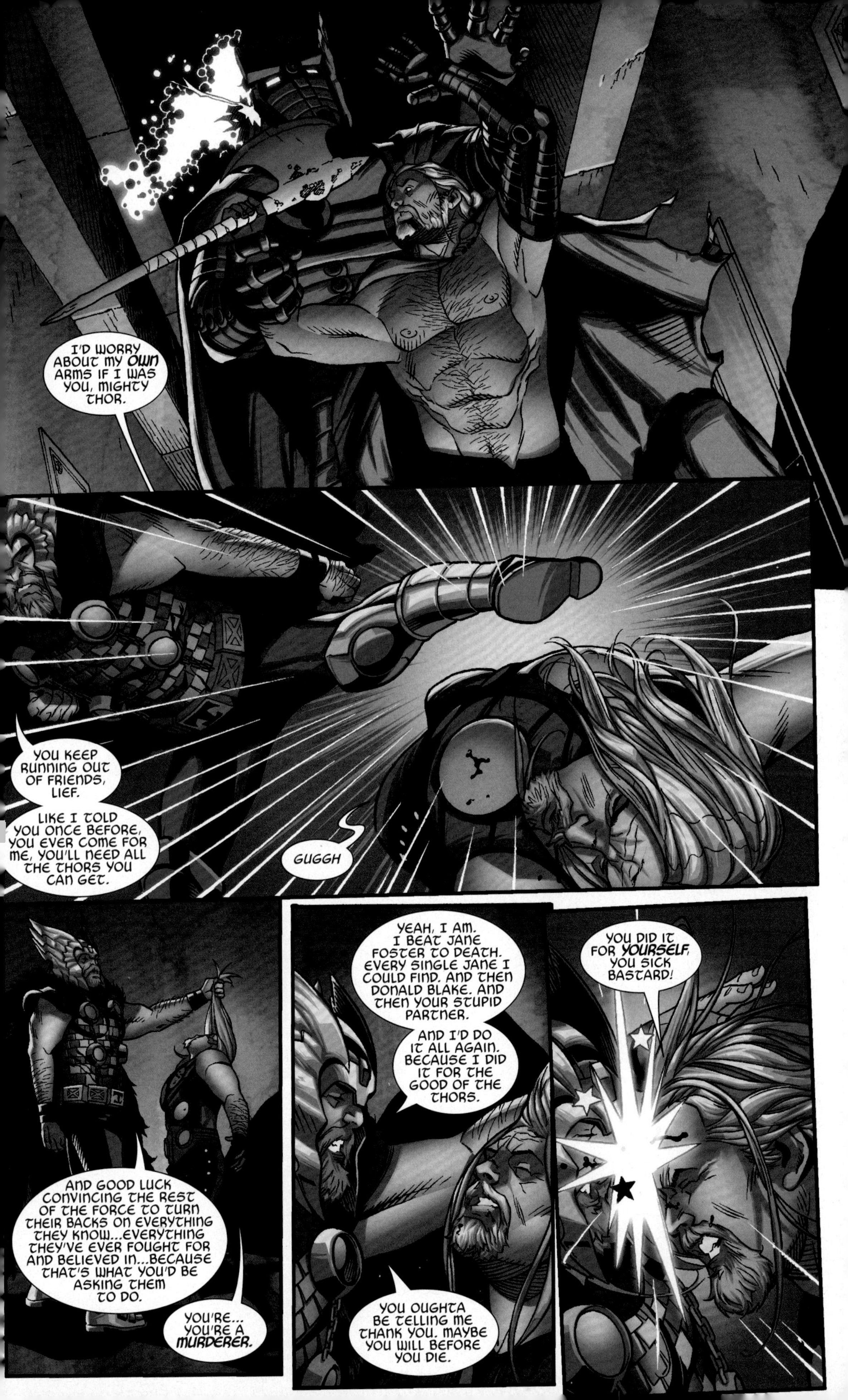
I'D WORRY ABOUT MY OWN ARMS IF I WAS YOU, MIGHTY THOR.
YOU KEEP RUNNING OUT OF FRIENDS, LIEF.
LIKE I TOLD YOU ONCE BEFORE, YOU EVER COME FOR ME, YOU'LL NEED ALL THE THORS YOU CAN GET.
GUGGH
AND GOOD LUCK CONVINCING THE REST OF THE FORCE TO TURN THEIR BACKS ON EVERYTHING THEY KNOW...EVERYTHING THEY'VE EVER FOUGHT FOR AND BELIEVED IN...BECAUSE THAT'S WHAT YOU'D BE ASKING THEM TO DO.
YOU'RE... YOU'RE A MURDERER.
YEAH, I AM. I BEAT JANE FOSTER TO DEATH. EVERY SINGLE JANE I COULD FIND. AND THEN DONALD BLAKE. AND THEN YOUR STUPID PARTNER.
AND I'D DO IT ALL AGAIN. BECAUSE I DID IT FOR THE GOOD OF THE THORS.
YOU OUGHTA BE TELLING ME THANK YOU. MAYBE YOU WILL BEFORE YOU DIE.
YOU DID IT FOR YOURSELF, YOU SICK BASTARD!

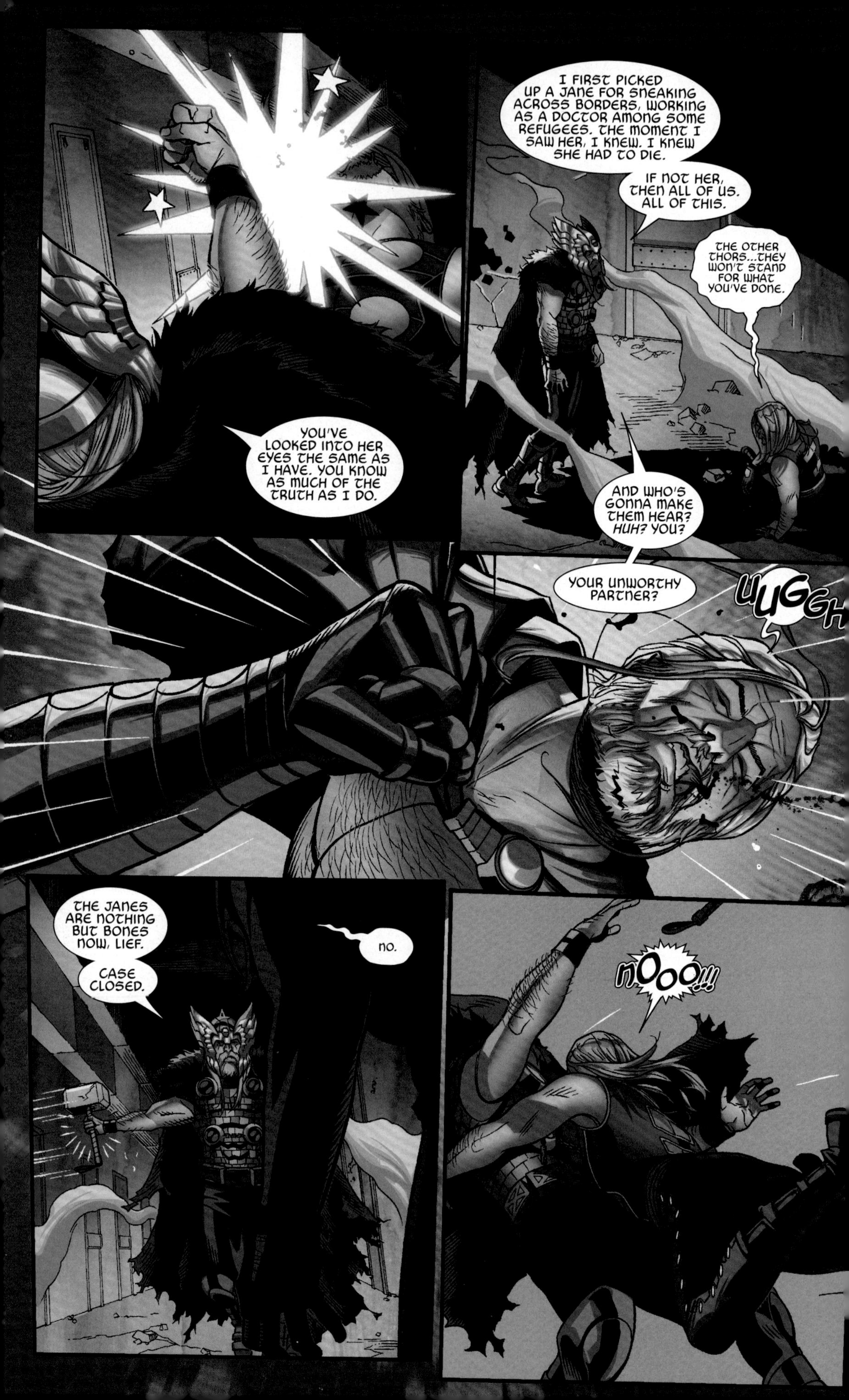
YOU'VE LOOKED INTO HER EYES THE SAME AS I HAVE. YOU KNOW AS MUCH OF THE TRUTH AS I DO.
I FIRST PICKED UP A JANE FOR SNEAKING ACROSS BORDERS, WORKING AS A DOCTOR AMONG SOME REFUGEES. THE MOMENT I SAW HER, I KNEW. I KNEW SHE HAD TO DIE.
IF NOT HER, THEN ALL OF US. ALL OF THIS.
THE OTHER THORS...THEY WON'T STAND FOR WHAT YOU'VE DONE.
AND WHO'S GONNA MAKE THEM HEAR? *HUH?* YOU?
YOUR UNWORTHY PARTNER?
UUGGH
THE JANES ARE NOTHING BUT BONES NOW, LIEF.
CASE CLOSED.
no.
nOOO!!!

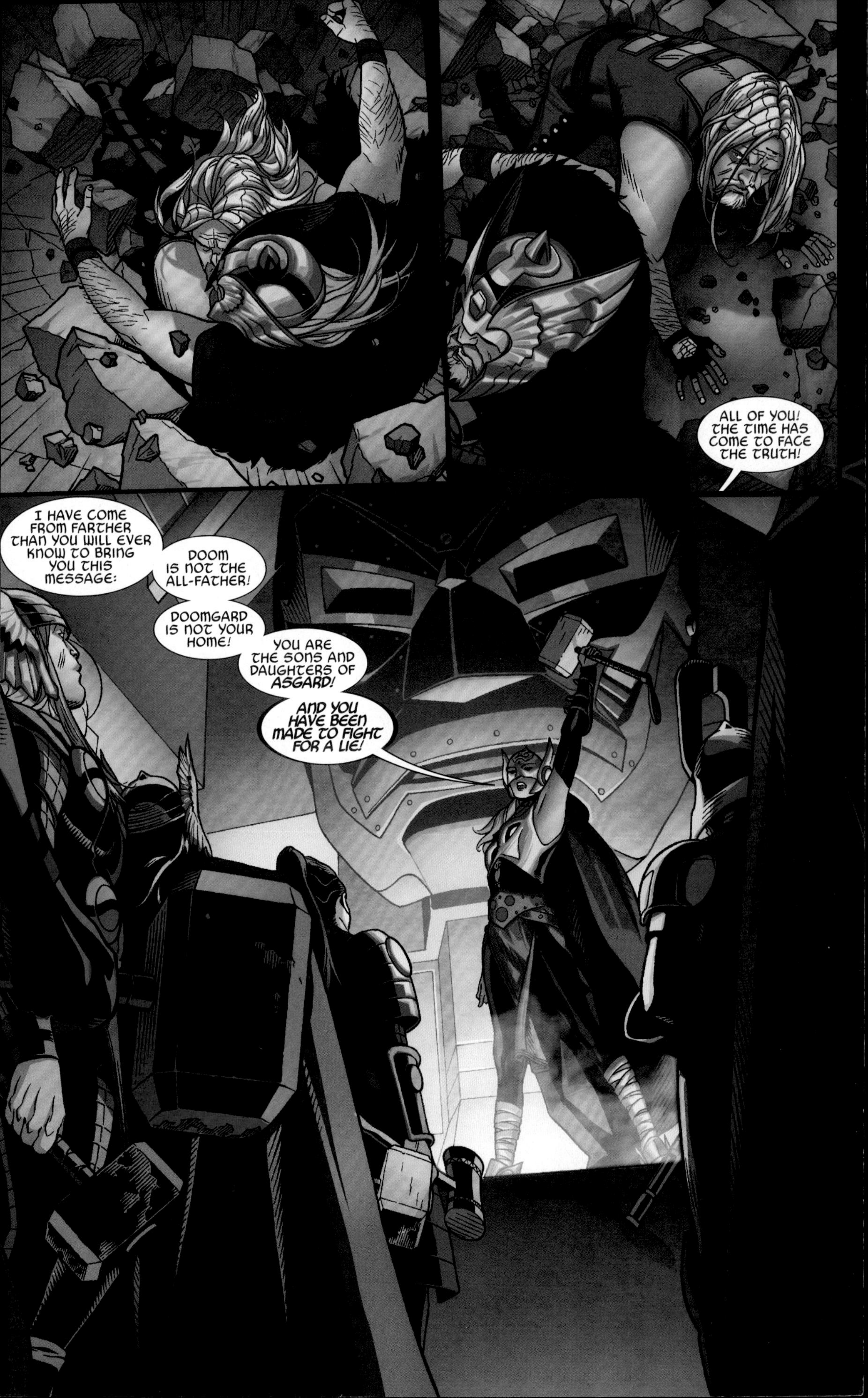
ALL OF YOU! THE TIME HAS COME TO FACE THE TRUTH!
I HAVE COME FROM FARTHER THAN YOU WILL EVER KNOW TO BRING YOU THIS MESSAGE:
DOOM IS NOT THE ALL-FATHER!
DOOMGARD IS NOT YOUR HOME!
YOU ARE THE SONS AND DAUGHTERS OF ASGARD!
AND YOU HAVE BEEN MADE TO FIGHT FOR A LIE!

BLASPHEMY!

NO! **DOOM** IS THE BLASPHEMY!

HE REMADE THE WORLD IN HIS OWN IMAGE! HE REMADE ALL OF YOU! AFTER HE HELPED MURDER THE OLD WORLD!

LIES!

DO NOT CLOSE YOUR EARS TO THE THUNDER IN MY WORDS, BROTHERS AND SISTERS! DO NOT TURN AWAY FROM THE TRUTH, EVEN THOUGH IT HURTS!

THE HOUR OF RECKONING IS AT HAND! THE FINAL BATTLE IS NOW! AND SO IT MUST BE DECIDED, ONCE AND FOR ALL...

ARE THESE THE CHILDREN OF DOOM I SEE BEFORE ME?

OR ARE YOU TRULY WORTHY TO CARRY THOSE HAMMERS?!

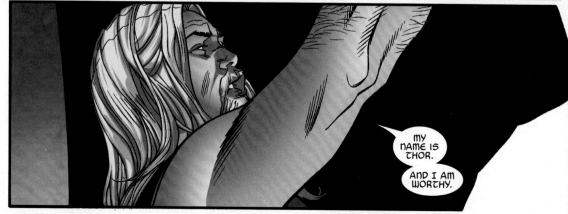

MY NAME IS THOR.

AND I AM WORTHY.

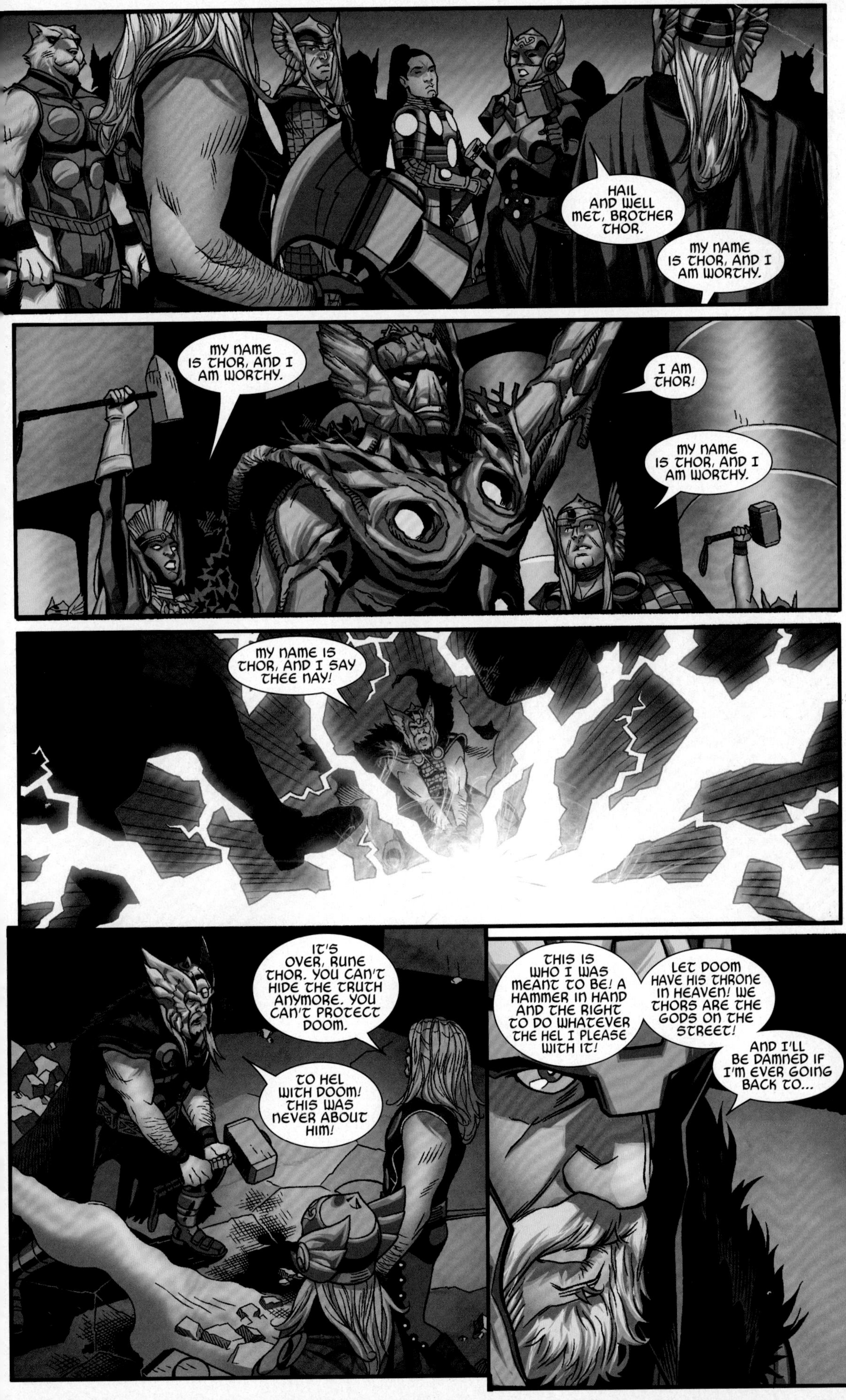

HAIL AND WELL MET, BROTHER THOR.
MY NAME IS THOR, AND I AM WORTHY.
MY NAME IS THOR, AND I AM WORTHY.
I AM THOR!
MY NAME IS THOR, AND I AM WORTHY.
MY NAME IS THOR, AND I SAY THEE NAY!
IT'S OVER, RUNE THOR. YOU CAN'T HIDE THE TRUTH ANYMORE. YOU CAN'T PROTECT DOOM.
TO HEL WITH DOOM! THIS WAS NEVER ABOUT HIM!
THIS IS WHO I WAS MEANT TO BE! A HAMMER IN HAND AND THE RIGHT TO DO WHATEVER THE HEL I PLEASE WITH IT!
LET DOOM HAVE HIS THRONE IN HEAVEN! WE THORS ARE THE GODS ON THE STREET!
AND I'LL BE DAMNED IF I'M EVER GOING BACK TO...

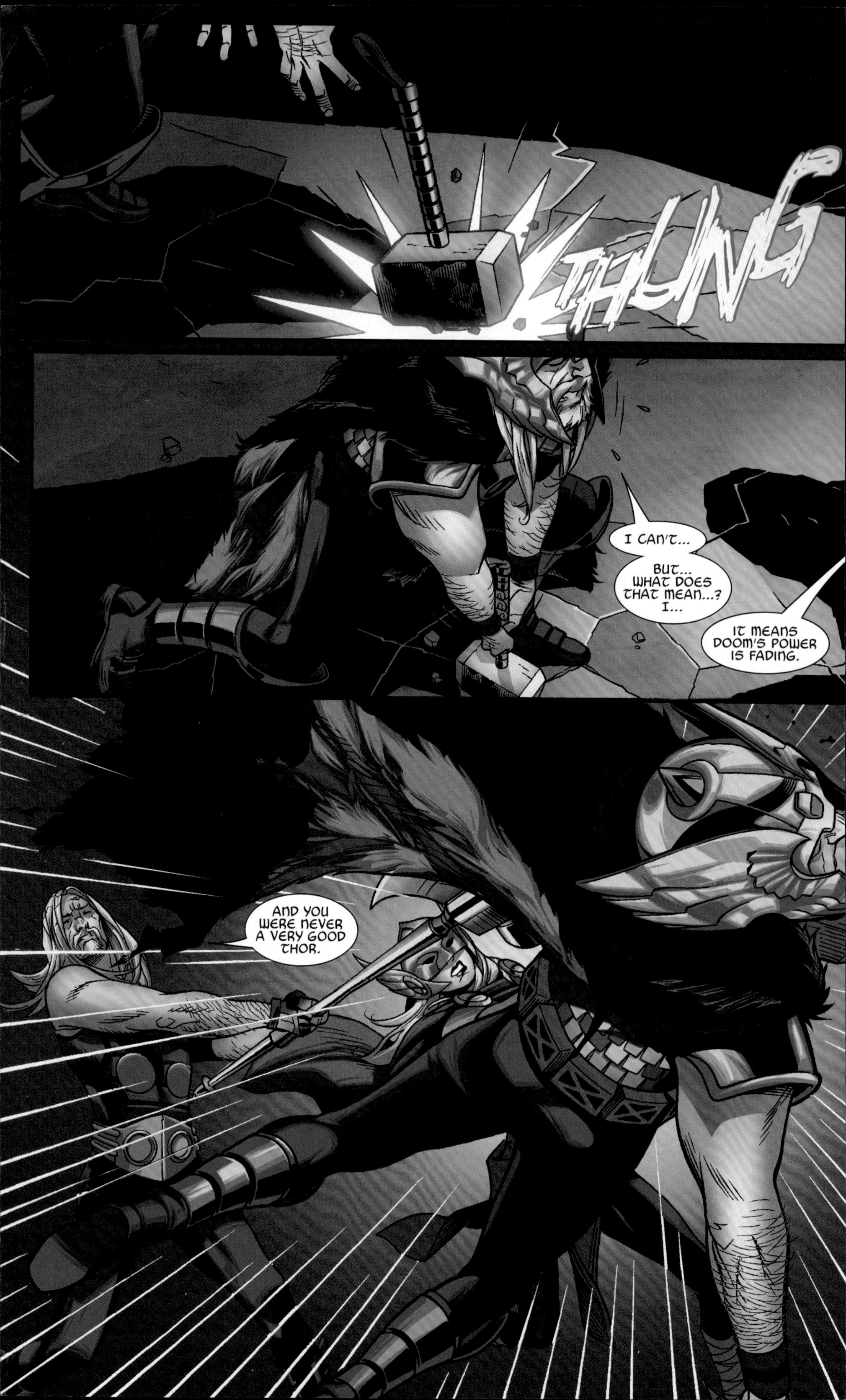
THUNG
I CAN'T...
BUT... WHAT DOES THAT MEAN...? I...
IT MEANS DOOM'S POWER IS FADING.
AND YOU WERE NEVER A VERY GOOD THOR.

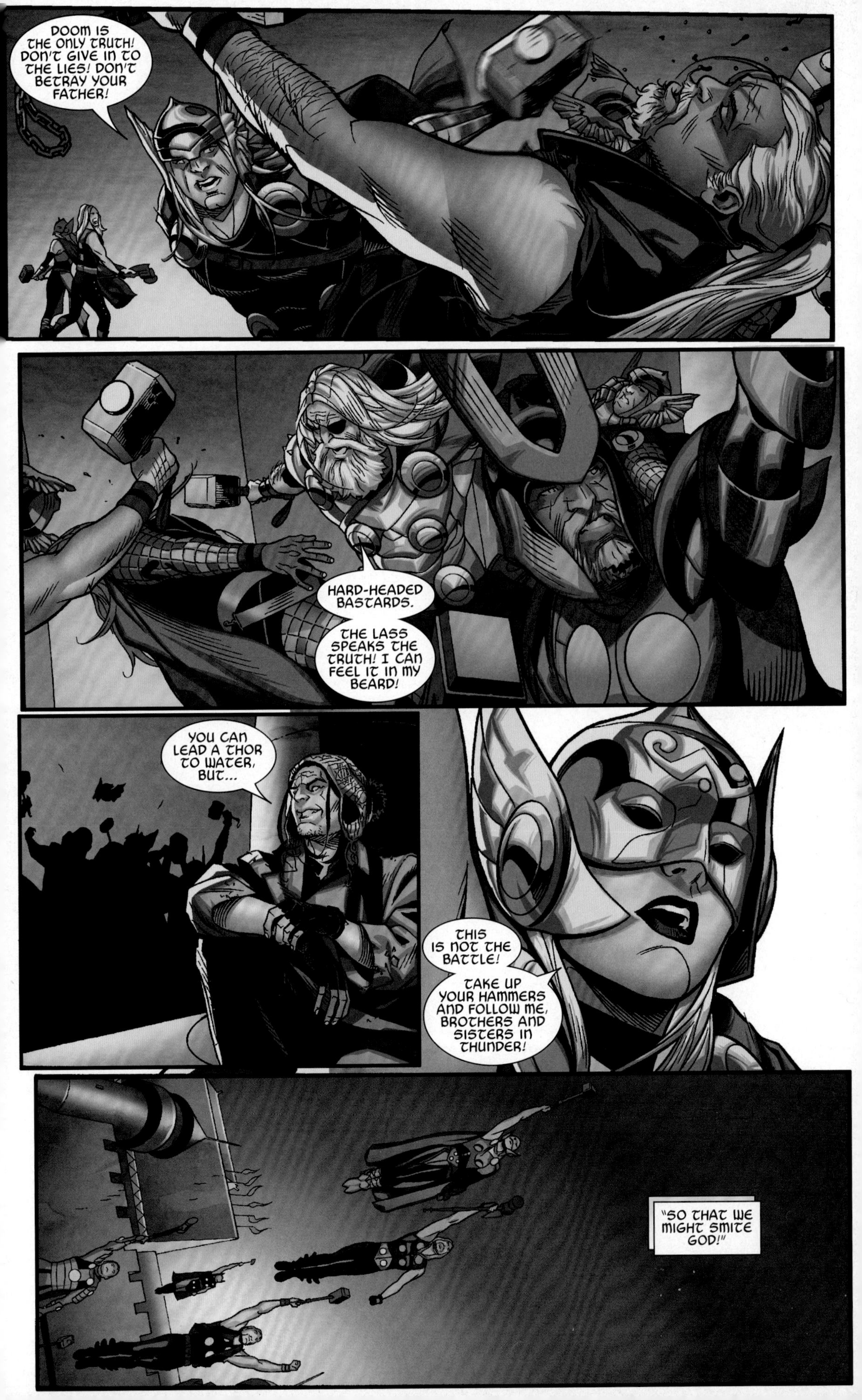
DOOM IS THE ONLY TRUTH! DON'T GIVE IN TO THE LIES! DON'T BETRAY YOUR FATHER!
HARD-HEADED BASTARDS.
THE LASS SPEAKS THE TRUTH! I CAN FEEL IT IN MY BEARD!
YOU CAN LEAD A THOR TO WATER, BUT...
THIS IS NOT THE BATTLE!
TAKE UP YOUR HAMMERS AND FOLLOW ME, BROTHERS AND SISTERS IN THUNDER!
"SO THAT WE MIGHT SMITE GOD!"

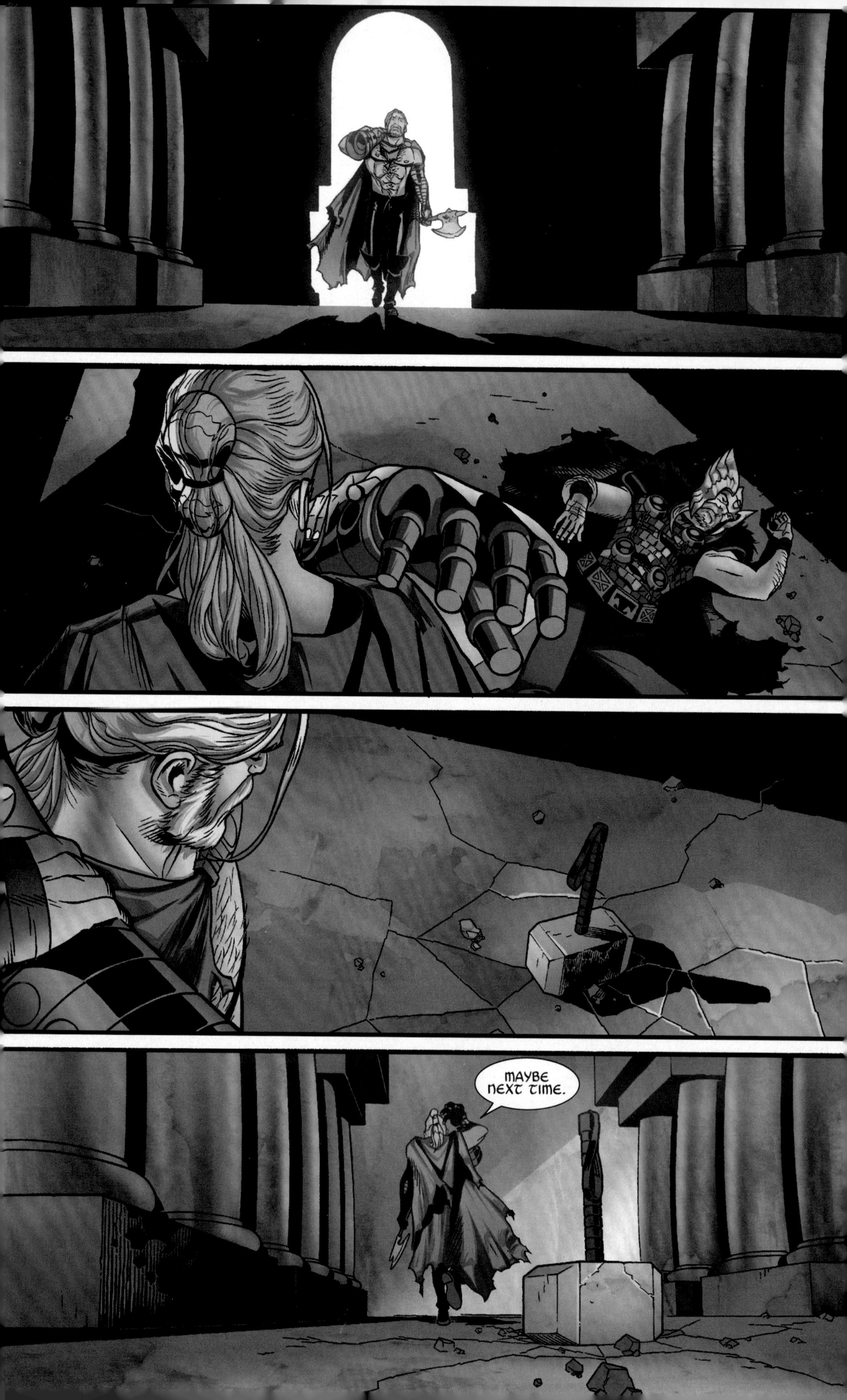
MAYBE NEXT TIME.

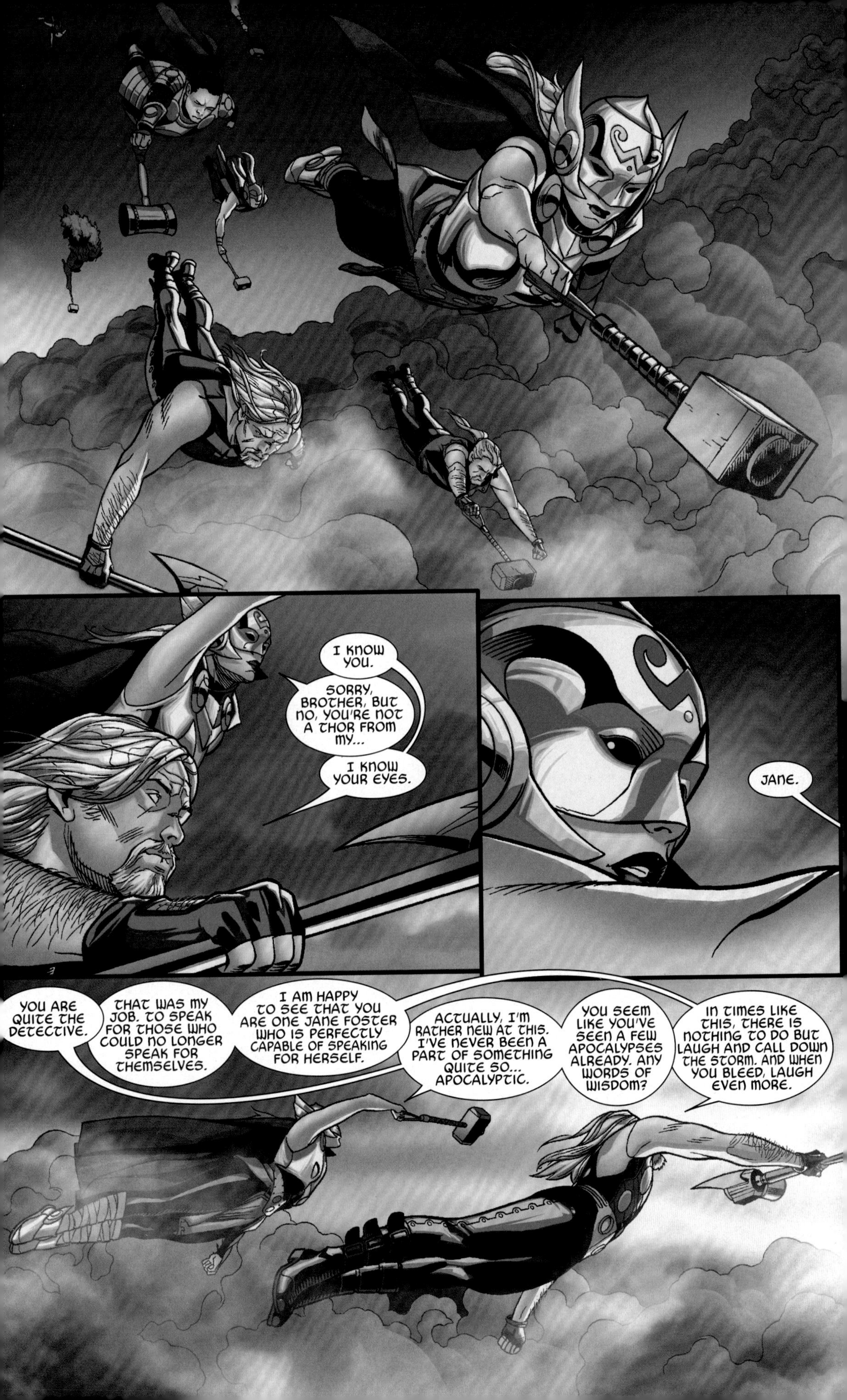
I KNOW YOU.
SORRY, BROTHER, BUT NO, YOU'RE NOT A THOR FROM MY...
I KNOW YOUR EYES.
JANE.
YOU ARE QUITE THE DETECTIVE.
THAT WAS MY JOB. TO SPEAK FOR THOSE WHO COULD NO LONGER SPEAK FOR THEMSELVES.
I AM HAPPY TO SEE THAT YOU ARE ONE JANE FOSTER WHO IS PERFECTLY CAPABLE OF SPEAKING FOR HERSELF.
ACTUALLY, I'M RATHER NEW AT THIS. I'VE NEVER BEEN A PART OF SOMETHING QUITE SO... APOCALYPTIC.
YOU SEEM LIKE YOU'VE SEEN A FEW APOCALYPSES ALREADY. ANY WORDS OF WISDOM?
IN TIMES LIKE THIS, THERE IS NOTHING TO DO BUT LAUGH AND CALL DOWN THE STORM. AND WHEN YOU BLEED, LAUGH EVEN MORE.

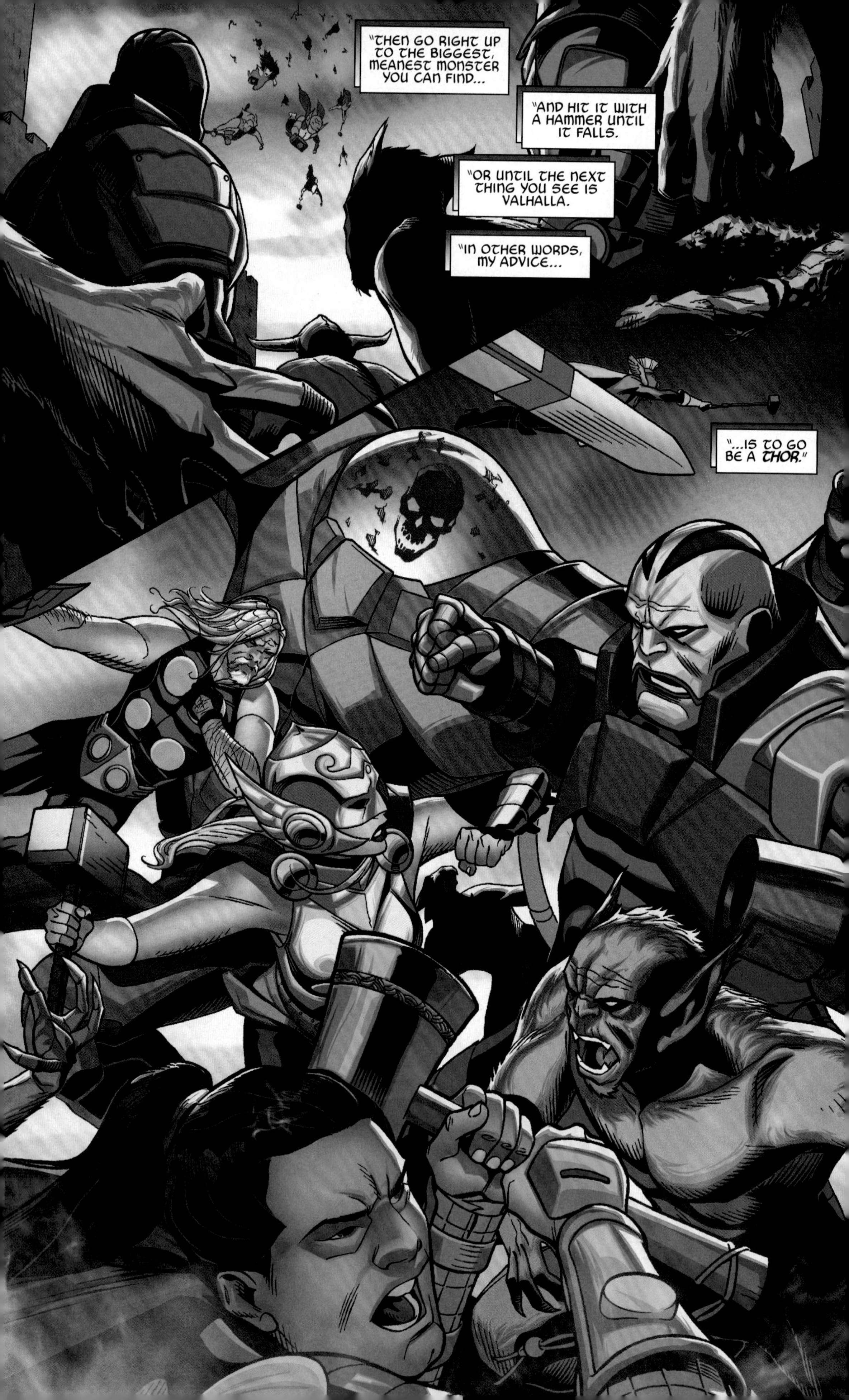
"THEN GO RIGHT UP TO THE BIGGEST, MEANEST MONSTER YOU CAN FIND...
"AND HIT IT WITH A HAMMER UNTIL IT FALLS.
"OR UNTIL THE NEXT THING YOU SEE IS VALHALLA.
"IN OTHER WORDS, MY ADVICE...
"...IS TO GO BE A *THOR*."

FOR THE FIRST TIME IN MY LIFE...I FEEL TRULY WORTHY.

I'M JUST SORRY IT TOOK THE END OF THE WORLD TO MAKE IT HAPPEN.

THOUGH NOTHING MATTERS NOW BUT THE THUNDER RINGING IN MY EARS.

THE FEEL OF MJOLNIR IN MY HAND.

THE TASTE OF BATTLE ON MY LIPS.

MY NAME IS THORLIEF. AND I WAS A THUNDERER. A MURDER POLICE.

THEY CALLED ME THE ULTIMATE THOR.

BUT I WAS JUST YOUR EVERYDAY GOD OF THUNDER. I ONLY DID WHAT WE ALL DO.

I CARRIED A HAMMER. AND WHEN DUTY CALLED, I DID MY BEST TO HURL IT IN THE RIGHT DIRECTION.

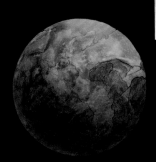

I HURLED IT AS HARD AS I POSSIBLY COULD.

SO HARD I BET IT'LL STILL BE FLYING, LONG AFTER I'M--

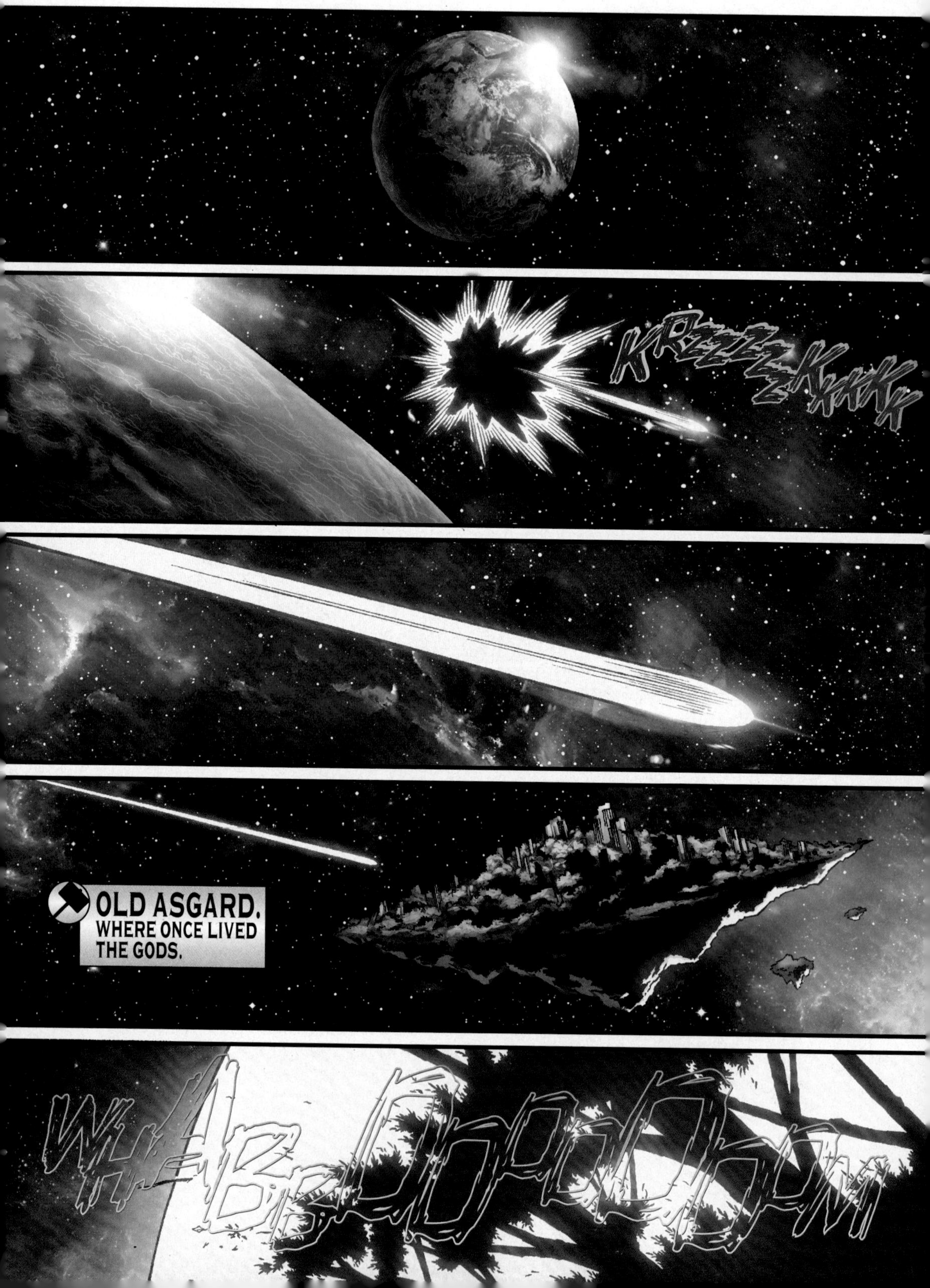
OLD ASGARD.
WHERE ONCE LIVED
THE GODS.

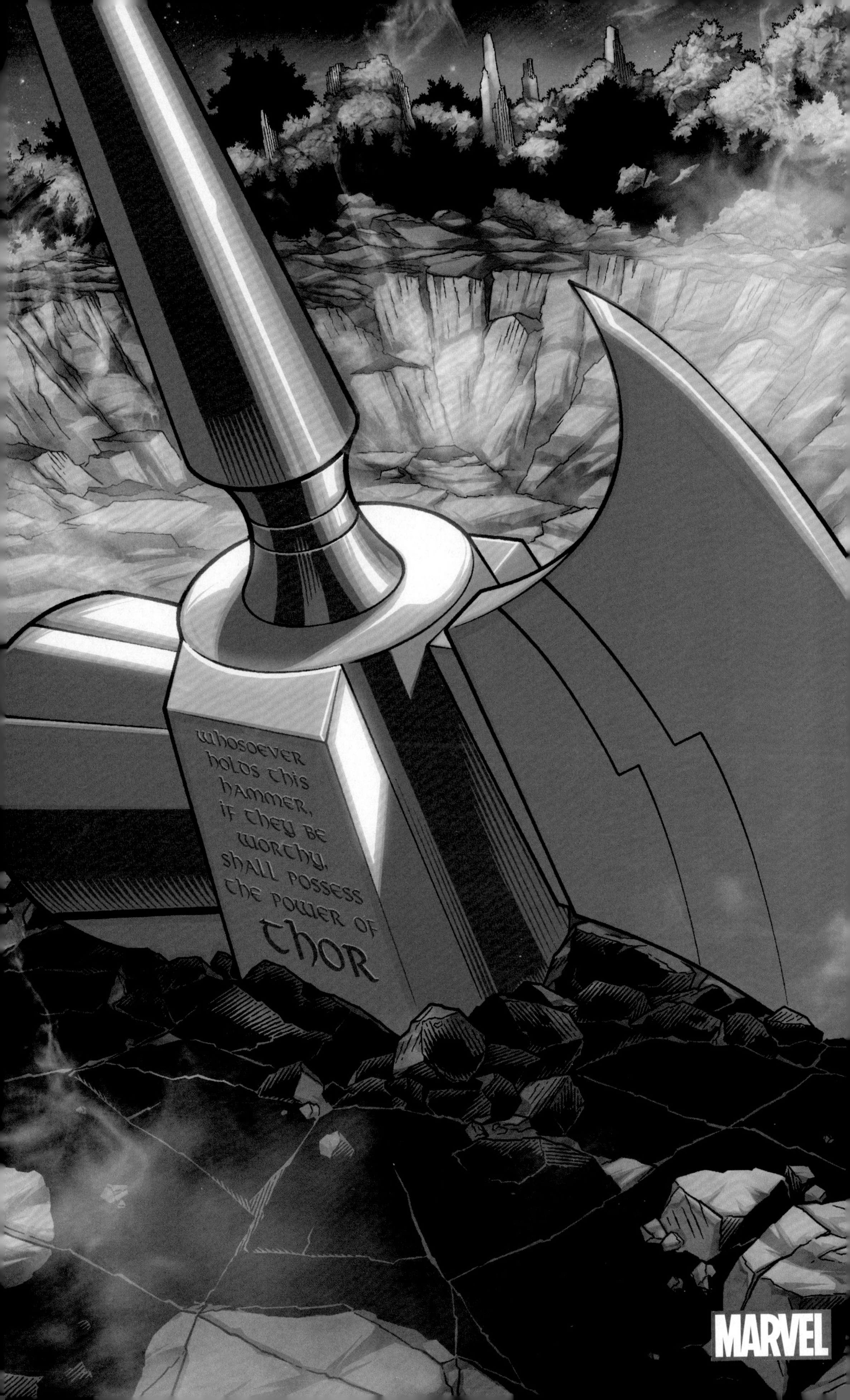
Whosoever
holds this
hammer,
if they be
worthy,
shall possess
the power of
THOR

THOR No. 364

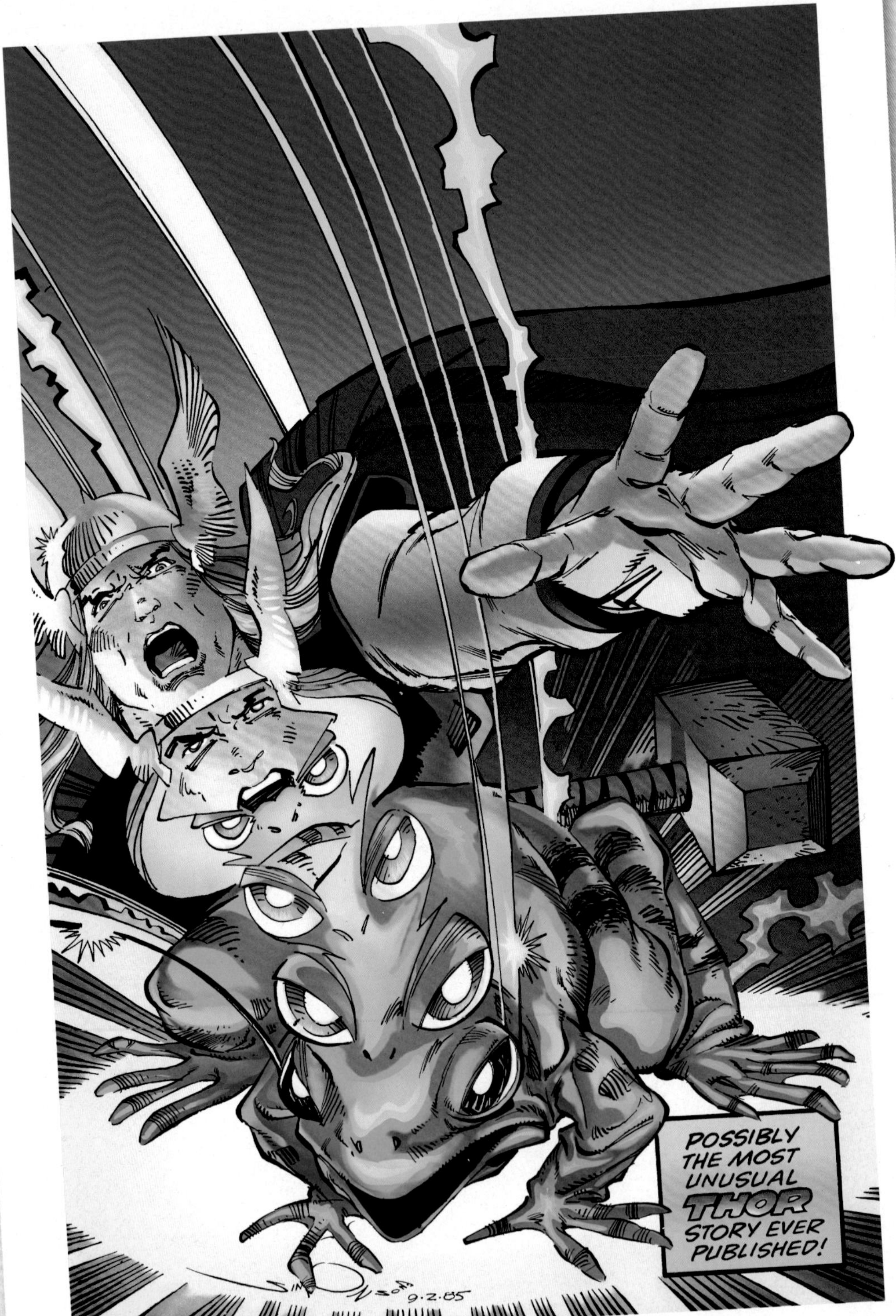
POSSIBLY THE MOST UNUSUAL THOR STORY EVER PUBLISHED!
9.2.85

STAN LEE PRESENTS: the MIGHTY THOR®

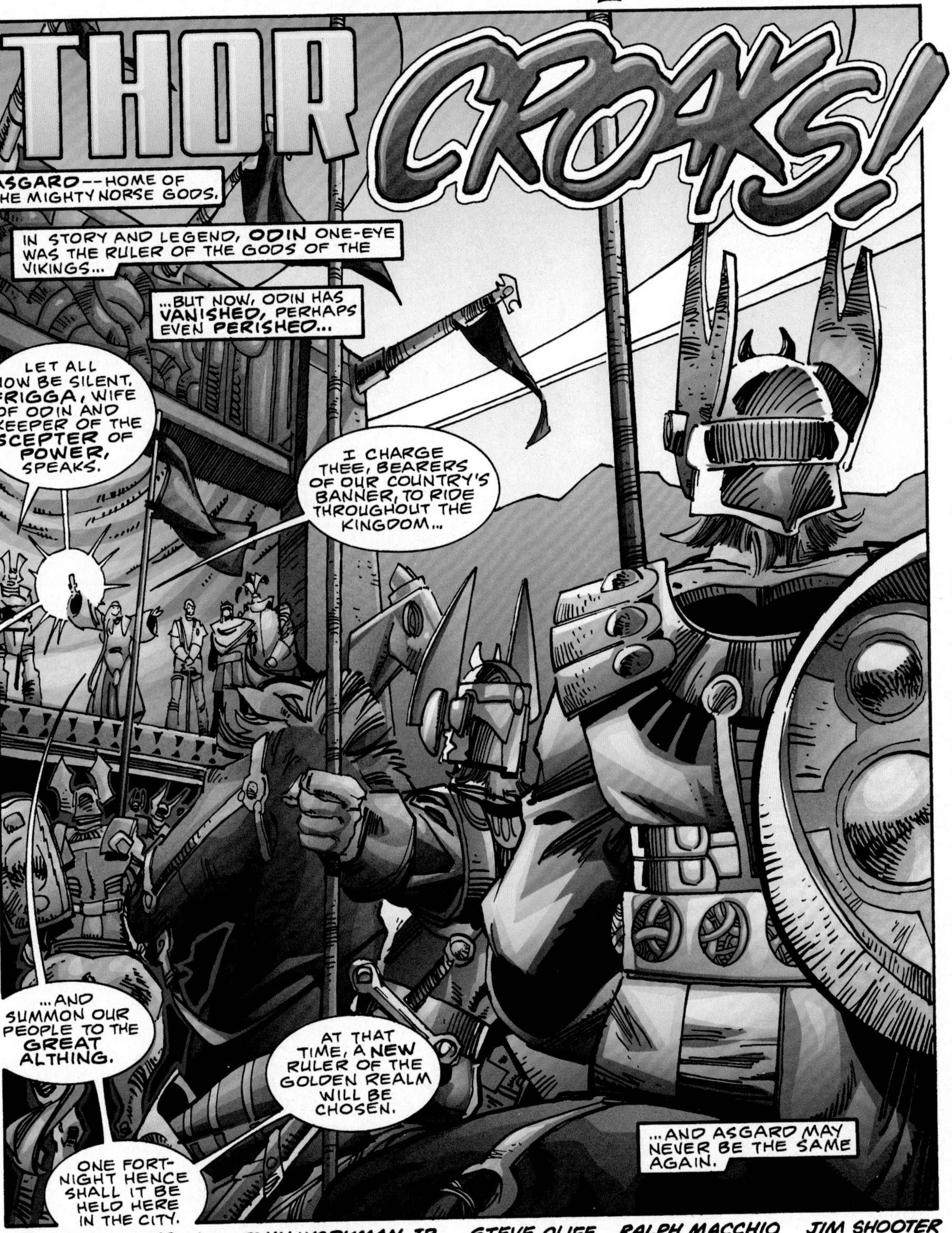
THOR CROAKS!
ASGARD--HOME OF THE MIGHTY NORSE GODS.
IN STORY AND LEGEND, ODIN ONE-EYE WAS THE RULER OF THE GODS OF THE VIKINGS...
...BUT NOW, ODIN HAS VANISHED, PERHAPS EVEN PERISHED...
LET ALL NOW BE SILENT. FRIGGA, WIFE OF ODIN AND KEEPER OF THE SCEPTER OF POWER, SPEAKS.
I CHARGE THEE, BEARERS OF OUR COUNTRY'S BANNER, TO RIDE THROUGHOUT THE KINGDOM...
...AND SUMMON OUR PEOPLE TO THE GREAT ALTHING.
AT THAT TIME, A NEW RULER OF THE GOLDEN REALM WILL BE CHOSEN.
ONE FORT-NIGHT HENCE SHALL IT BE HELD HERE IN THE CITY.
...AND ASGARD MAY NEVER BE THE SAME AGAIN.

WALTER SIMONSON ART & STORY | **JOHN WORKMAN, JR.** LETTERING | **STEVE OLIFF** COLORING | **RALPH MACCHIO** EDITING | **JIM SHOOTER** EDITOR IN CHIEF

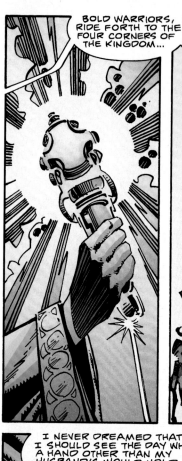

BOLD WARRIORS, RIDE FORTH TO THE FOUR CORNERS OF THE KINGDOM...

...AND MAY THE LIGHT OF ODIN'S SCEPTER SHINE UPON THEE AND KEEP THEE SAFE.

THR-DDBOOM!

I NEVER DREAMED THAT I SHOULD SEE THE DAY WHEN A HAND OTHER THAN MY HUSBAND'S WOULD HOLD HIS RADIANT SCEPTER.

FRIGGA?

I AM ALL RIGHT, HEIMDALL. BUT JUST WHEN YOU THINK YOU HAVE LIVED SO LONG THAT THERE IS NOTHING NEW UNDER THE SUN...

...THE FATES CONSPIRE TO SHOW YOU SOMETHING BEYOND YOUR WILDEST IMAGININGS.

WHO WOULD HAVE BELIEVED I SHOULD DWELL IN MY HOUSE ALONE?

THEN FANDRAL SHALL SEE YOU HOME, LADY.

...THOUGH I THINK ANOTHER SHOULD HAVE HAD THAT HONOR.

WHERE IS THE SON OF ODIN WHO HAS SO OFTEN BEEN PROCLAIMED THE HEIR TO THE THRONE OF ASGARD? WHERE IS MIGHTY THOR?

HE WAS TO HAVE RETURNED TO ASGARD DIRECTLY AFTER DELIVERING THE SOULS OF THE MORTALS RESCUED FROM HEL * TO EARTH.

SURELY, HOGUN, SUCH A TASK WOULD NOT HAVE TAKEN HIM LONG.

MAYHAP THE STORMS BETWEEN ASGARD AND MIDGARD * HAVE GROWN SO STRONG NOW THAT THE RAINBOW BRIDGE HAS BEEN DESTROYED...

...THAT HE IS UNABLE TO CROSS BETWEEN THE REALMS.

*THOR 360-362

*EARTH

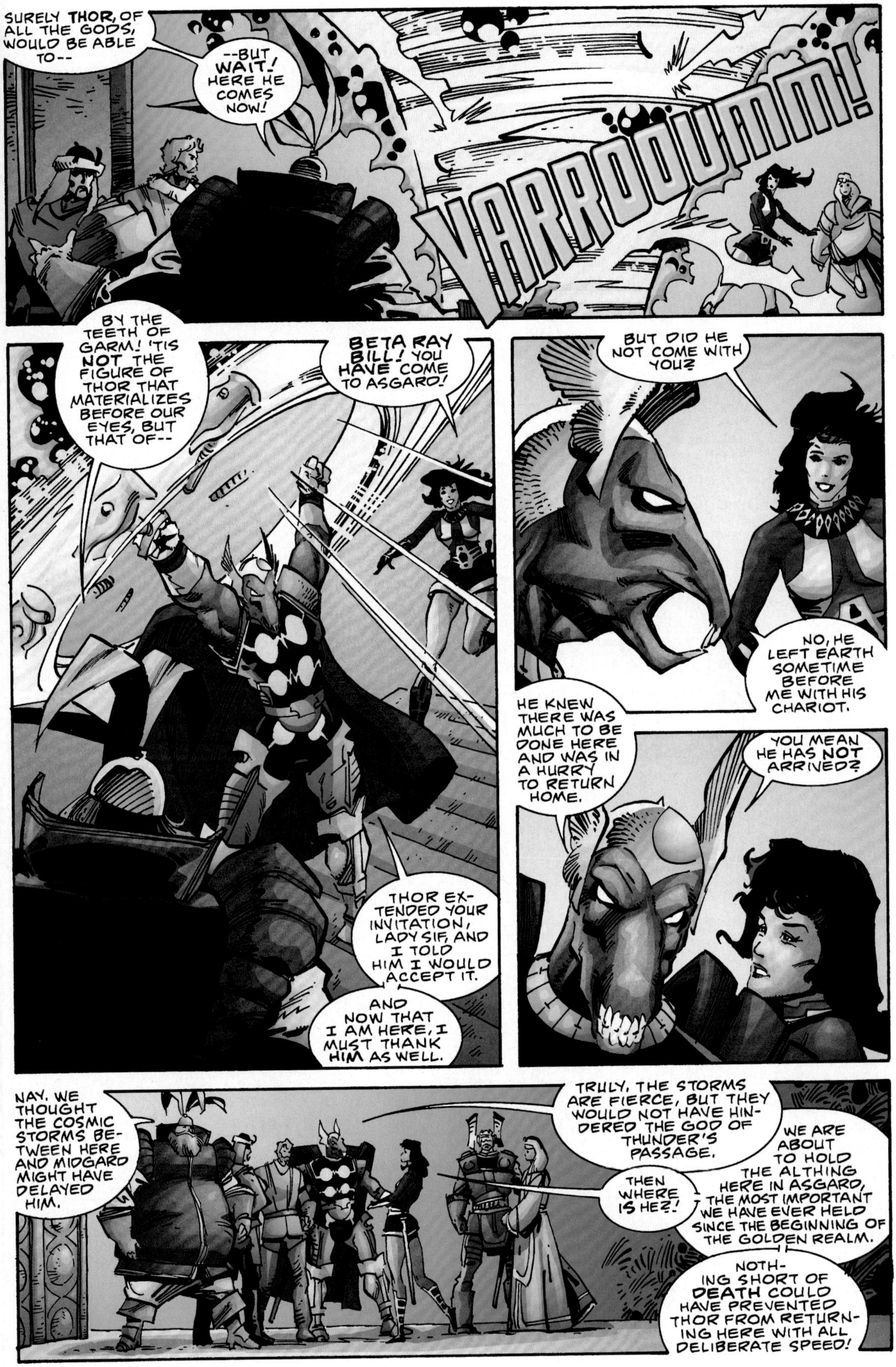
SURELY THOR, OF ALL THE GODS, WOULD BE ABLE TO--
--BUT WAIT! HERE HE COMES NOW!
VARROOUMM!
BY THE TEETH OF GARM! 'TIS NOT THE FIGURE OF THOR THAT MATERIALIZES BEFORE OUR EYES, BUT THAT OF--
BETA RAY BILL! YOU HAVE COME TO ASGARD!
THOR EXTENDED YOUR INVITATION, LADY SIF, AND I TOLD HIM I WOULD ACCEPT IT.
AND NOW THAT I AM HERE, I MUST THANK HIM AS WELL.
BUT DID HE NOT COME WITH YOU?
NO, HE LEFT EARTH SOMETIME BEFORE ME WITH HIS CHARIOT.
HE KNEW THERE WAS MUCH TO BE DONE HERE AND WAS IN A HURRY TO RETURN HOME.
YOU MEAN HE HAS NOT ARRIVED?
NAY. WE THOUGHT THE COSMIC STORMS BETWEEN HERE AND MIDGARD MIGHT HAVE DELAYED HIM.
TRULY, THE STORMS ARE FIERCE, BUT THEY WOULD NOT HAVE HINDERED THE GOD OF THUNDER'S PASSAGE.
THEN WHERE IS HE?!
WE ARE ABOUT TO HOLD THE ALTHING HERE IN ASGARD, THE MOST IMPORTANT WE HAVE EVER HELD SINCE THE BEGINNING OF THE GOLDEN REALM.
NOTHING SHORT OF DEATH COULD HAVE PREVENTED THOR FROM RETURNING HERE WITH ALL DELIBERATE SPEED!

BUT EVEN AS HIS FRIENDS PONDER THE
FATE OF THE MISSING GOD OF THUNDER...

...WE TURN TO LOOK AT THE
REALM OF MORTALS, WHERE
WE FIND THAT THOR IS IN-
DEED STILL IN NEW YORK
CITY...

RIBBIT!!
RIBBIT*!!

*A FROG!
I'VE BECOME
A FROG!**

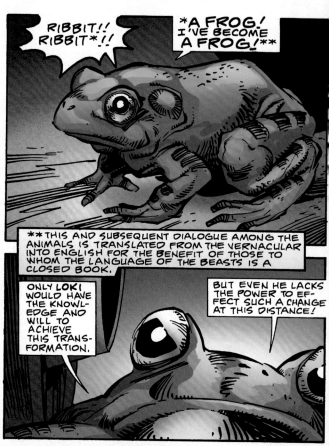

...ALTHOUGH PERHAPS
ANYONE MIGHT BE FOR-
GIVEN IF THEY FAILED
TO RECOGNIZE HIM AT
FIRST GLANCE FOR HE
IS VASTLY CHANGED.

**THIS AND SUBSEQUENT DIALOGUE AMONG THE
ANIMALS IS TRANSLATED FROM THE VERNACULAR
INTO ENGLISH FOR THE BENEFIT OF THOSE TO
WHOM THE LANGUAGE OF THE BEASTS IS A
CLOSED BOOK.

ONLY LOKI
WOULD HAVE
THE KNOWL-
EDGE AND
WILL TO
ACHIEVE
THIS TRANS-
FORMATION.

BUT EVEN HE LACKS
THE POWER TO EF-
FECT SUCH A CHANGE
AT THIS DISTANCE!

NO LONGER IS HE THE MAJESTIC
FIGURE OF LEGEND; INSTEAD, HE
RESEMBLES IN EVERY PARTIC-
ULAR...

EITHER THERE IS SOME
NEW VILLAIN AT WORK...

...OR LOKI HAS
DEVELOPED
POWERS FAR
BEYOND HIS
PREVIOUS
ABILITIES.

AND IT MUST BE
LOKI! WITH THE AL-
THING ABOUT TO
BEGIN, ONLY HE
WOULD HAVE A
VESTED INTEREST
IN PREVENTING MY
RETURN TO ASGARD.

LONG HAS HE LUSTED AFTER MY
FATHER'S THRONE, AND I HAVE
EVER BEEN THE GREATEST OB-
STACLE BETWEEN HIM AND
HIS DESIRES.

IF I DO NOT REACH
ASGARD IN TIME FOR
THE ALTHING, WHO
KNOWS WHAT DASTARD-
LY SCHEMES MY STEP-
BROTHER WILL ATTEMPT?

STILL, THERE
IS NO TIME TO
PONDER THIS
MYSTERY!

I MUST GET HELP
IMMEDIATELY!!

AND THE
AVENGERS'
MANSION
IS THE PLACE
TO GET IT!

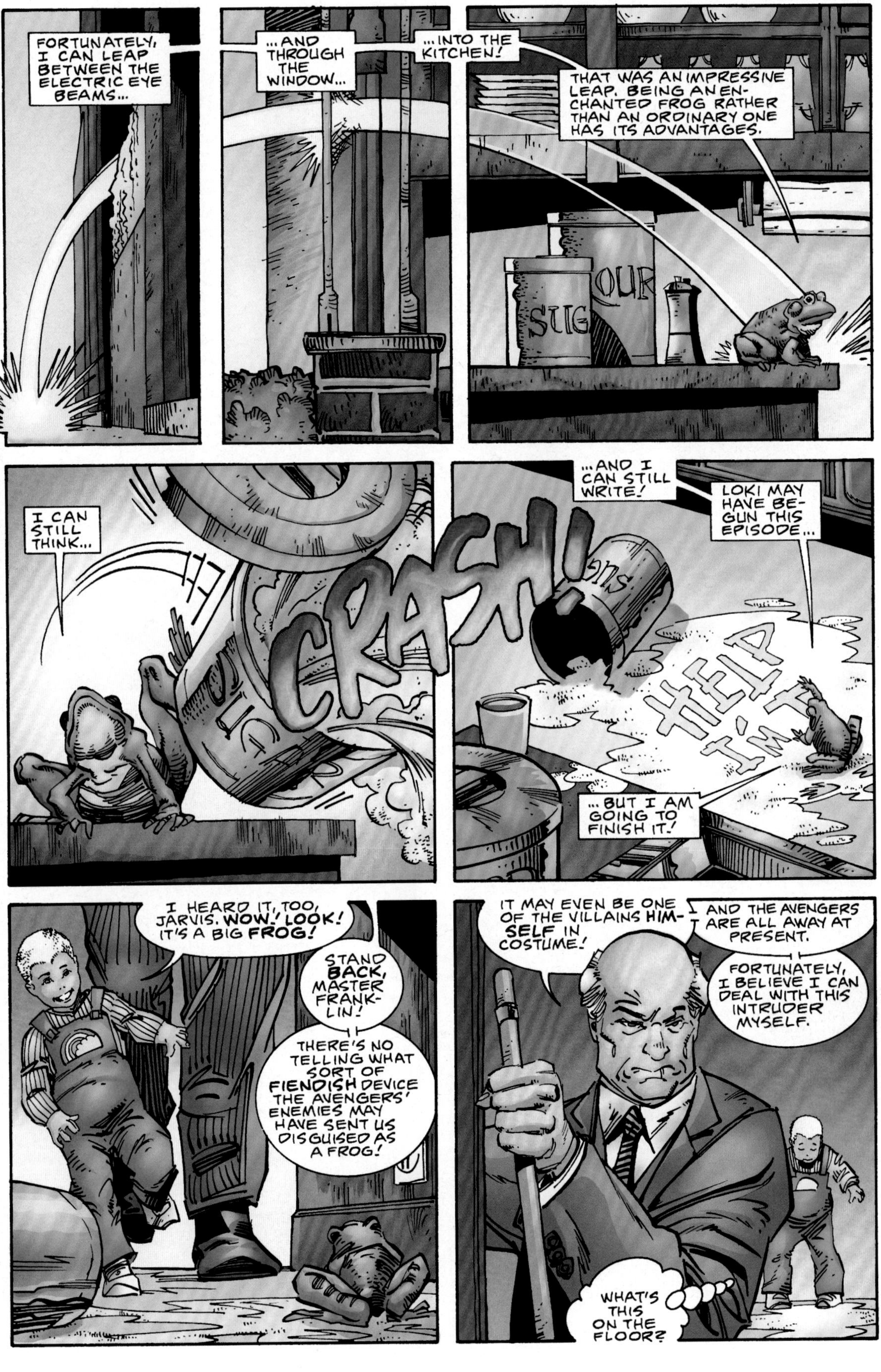
FORTUNATELY, I CAN LEAP BETWEEN THE ELECTRIC EYE BEAMS...
...AND THROUGH THE WINDOW...
...INTO THE KITCHEN!
THAT WAS AN IMPRESSIVE LEAP. BEING AN ENCHANTED FROG RATHER THAN AN ORDINARY ONE HAS ITS ADVANTAGES.
I CAN STILL THINK...
CRASH!
...AND I CAN STILL WRITE!
LOKI MAY HAVE BEGUN THIS EPISODE...
...BUT I AM GOING TO FINISH IT!
I HEARD IT, TOO, JARVIS. WOW! LOOK! IT'S A BIG FROG!
STAND BACK, MASTER FRANKLIN!
THERE'S NO TELLING WHAT SORT OF FIENDISH DEVICE THE AVENGERS' ENEMIES MAY HAVE SENT US DISGUISED AS A FROG!
IT MAY EVEN BE ONE OF THE VILLAINS HIMSELF IN COSTUME!
AND THE AVENGERS ARE ALL AWAY AT PRESENT.
FORTUNATELY, I BELIEVE I CAN DEAL WITH THIS INTRUDER MYSELF.
WHAT'S THIS ON THE FLOOR?

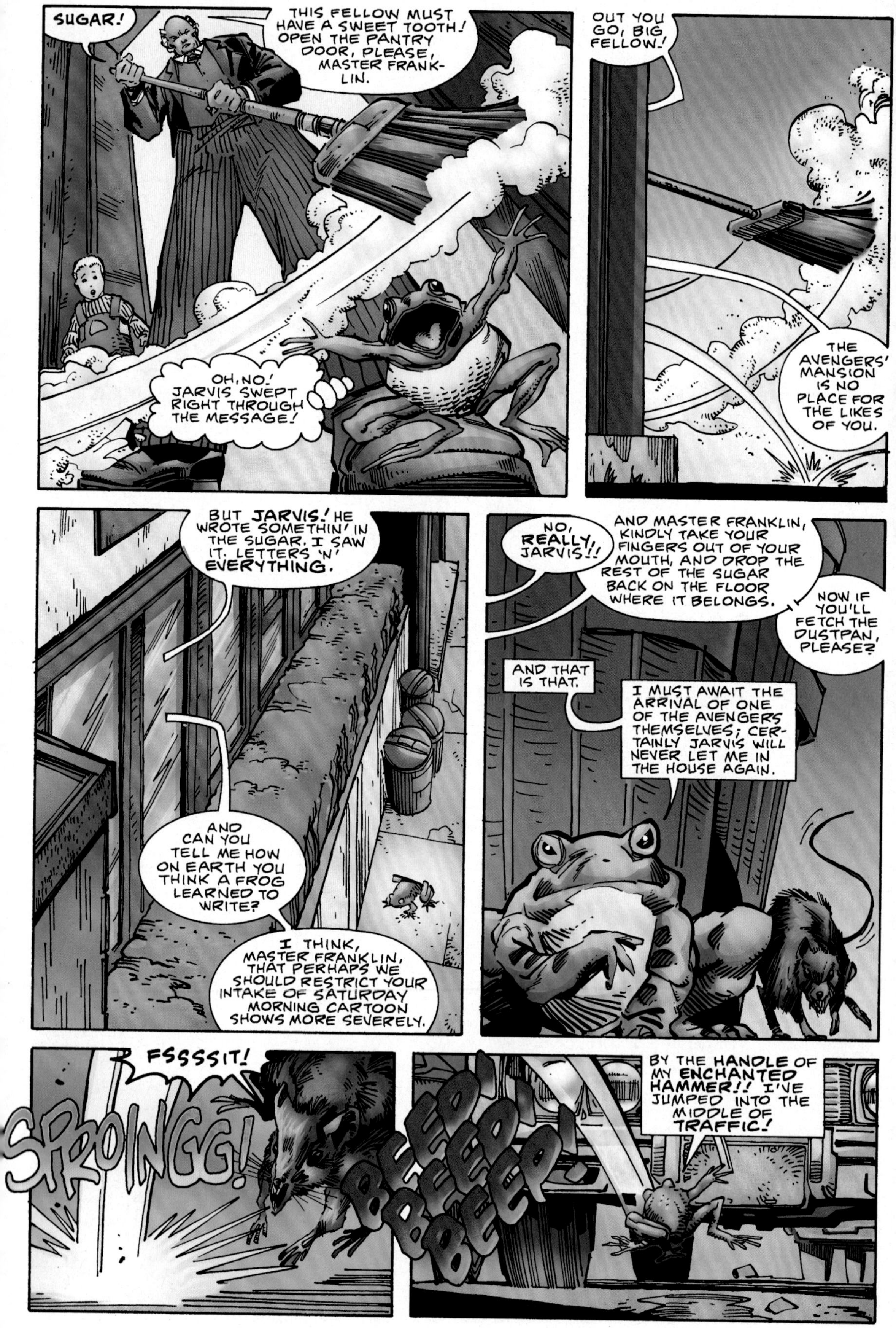
SUGAR!
THIS FELLOW MUST HAVE A SWEET TOOTH! OPEN THE PANTRY DOOR, PLEASE, MASTER FRANK-LIN.
OH, NO! JARVIS SWEPT RIGHT THROUGH THE MESSAGE!
OUT YOU GO, BIG FELLOW!
THE AVENGERS' MANSION IS NO PLACE FOR THE LIKES OF YOU.
BUT JARVIS! HE WROTE SOMETHIN' IN THE SUGAR. I SAW IT. LETTERS 'N' EVERYTHING.
AND CAN YOU TELL ME HOW ON EARTH YOU THINK A FROG LEARNED TO WRITE?
I THINK, MASTER FRANKLIN, THAT PERHAPS WE SHOULD RESTRICT YOUR INTAKE OF SATURDAY MORNING CARTOON SHOWS MORE SEVERELY.
NO, REALLY, JARVIS!!
AND MASTER FRANKLIN, KINDLY TAKE YOUR FINGERS OUT OF YOUR MOUTH, AND DROP THE REST OF THE SUGAR BACK ON THE FLOOR WHERE IT BELONGS.
NOW IF YOU'LL FETCH THE DUSTPAN, PLEASE?
AND THAT IS THAT.
I MUST AWAIT THE ARRIVAL OF ONE OF THE AVENGERS THEMSELVES; CERTAINLY JARVIS WILL NEVER LET ME IN THE HOUSE AGAIN.
FSSSSIT!
SPROINGG!
BEEP! BEEP! BEEEP!
BY THE HANDLE OF MY ENCHANTED HAMMER!! I'VE JUMPED INTO THE MIDDLE OF TRAFFIC!

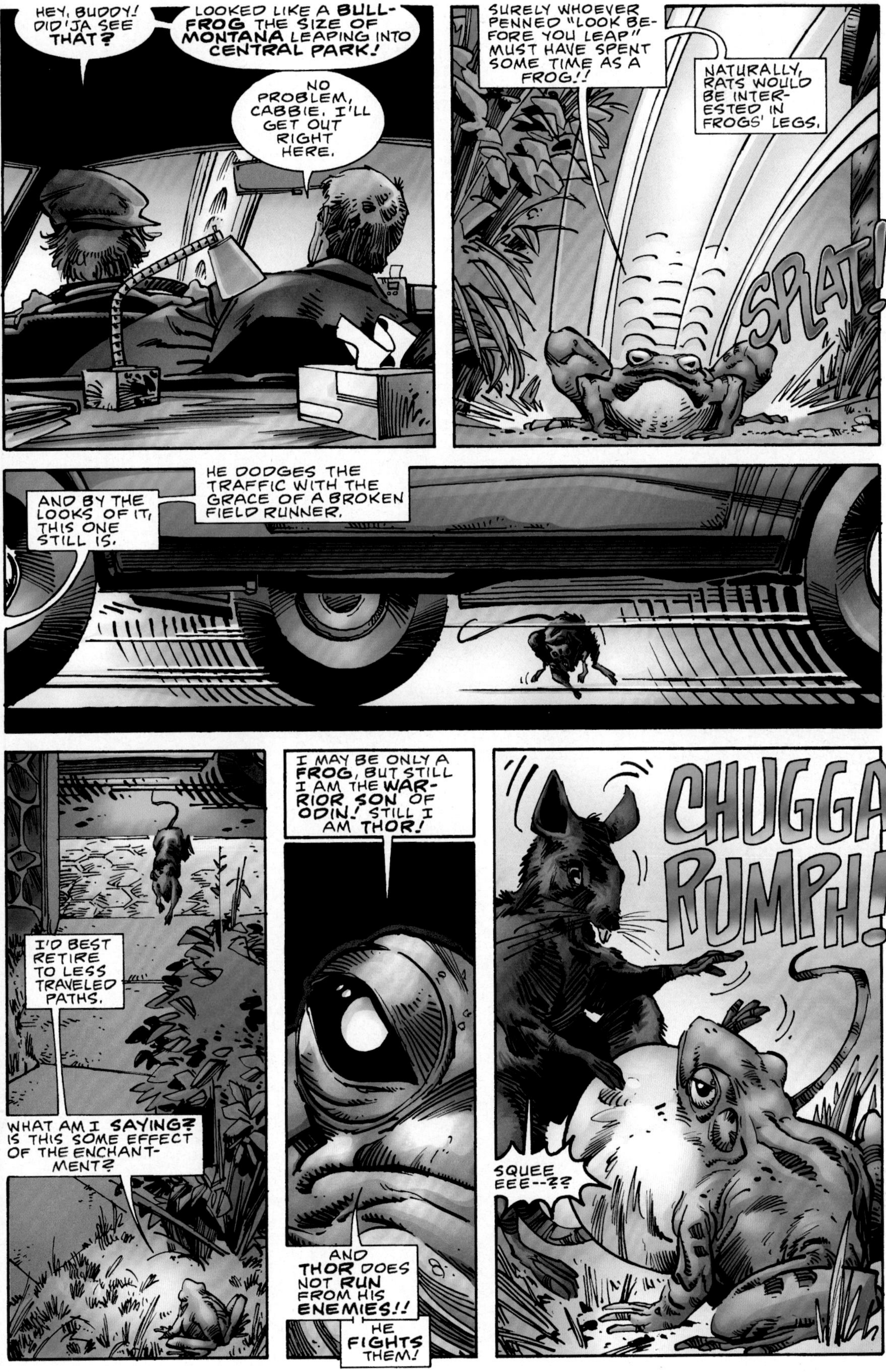
HEY, BUDDY! DID'JA SEE THAT?
LOOKED LIKE A BULL-FROG THE SIZE OF MONTANA LEAPING INTO CENTRAL PARK!
NO PROBLEM, CABBIE. I'LL GET OUT RIGHT HERE.
SURELY WHOEVER PENNED "LOOK BE-FORE YOU LEAP" MUST HAVE SPENT SOME TIME AS A FROG!!
NATURALLY, RATS WOULD BE INTER-ESTED IN FROGS' LEGS.
SPLAT!
HE DODGES THE TRAFFIC WITH THE GRACE OF A BROKEN FIELD RUNNER.
AND BY THE LOOKS OF IT, THIS ONE STILL IS.
I'D BEST RETIRE TO LESS TRAVELED PATHS.
WHAT AM I SAYING? IS THIS SOME EFFECT OF THE ENCHANT-MENT?
I MAY BE ONLY A FROG, BUT STILL I AM THE WAR-RIOR SON OF ODIN! STILL I AM THOR!
AND THOR DOES NOT RUN FROM HIS ENEMIES!!
HE FIGHTS THEM!
CHUGGA RUMPH!
SQUEE EEE--??

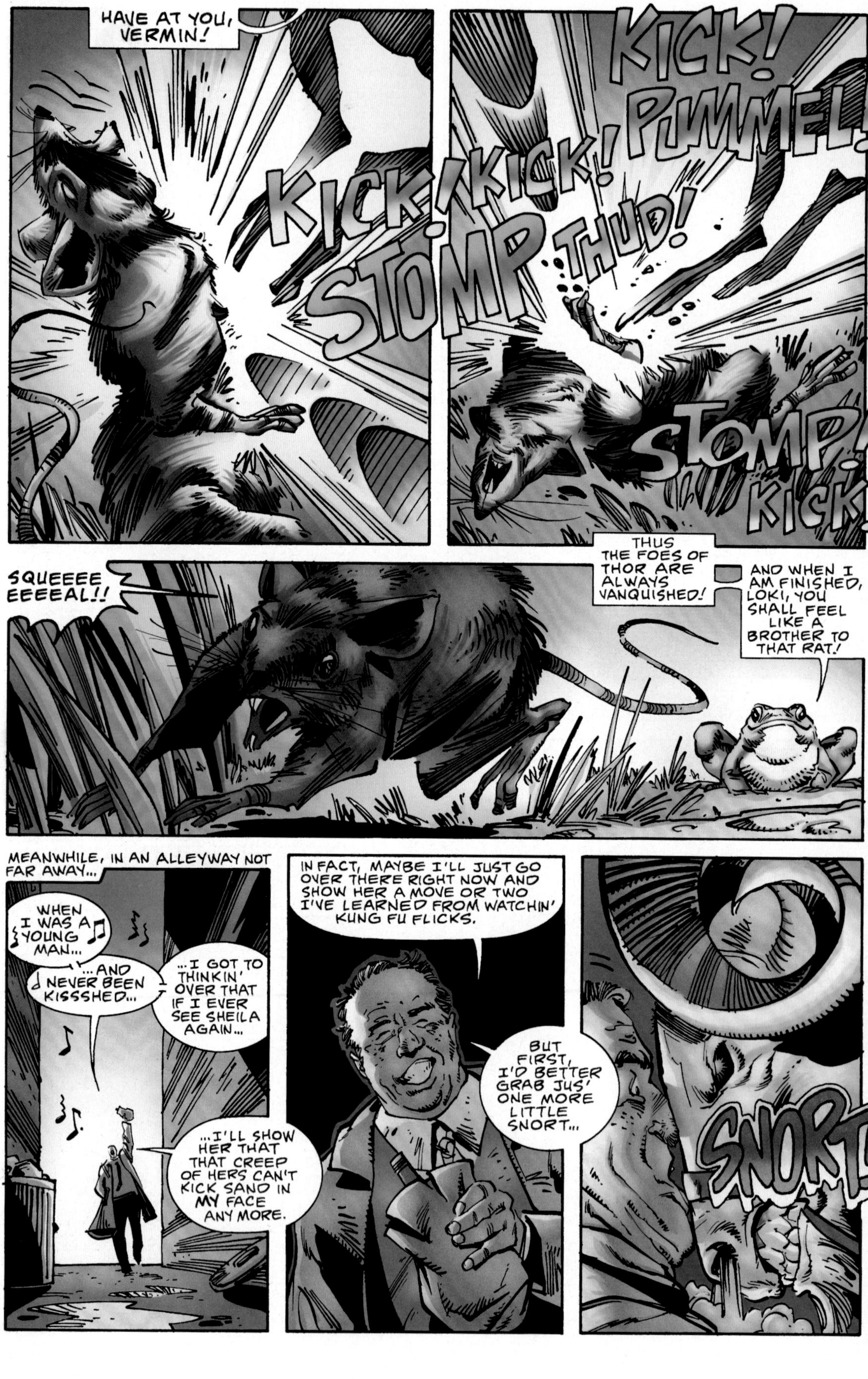
HAVE AT YOU, VERMIN!
KICK! PUMMEL!
KICK! KICK!
STOMP
THUD!
STOMP!
KICK!
SQUEEEE EEEEAL!!
THUS THE FOES OF THOR ARE ALWAYS VANQUISHED!
AND WHEN I AM FINISHED, LOKI, YOU SHALL FEEL LIKE A BROTHER TO THAT RAT!
MEANWHILE, IN AN ALLEYWAY NOT FAR AWAY...
WHEN I WAS A YOUNG MAN...
...AND NEVER BEEN KISSSHED...
...I GOT TO THINKIN' OVER THAT IF I EVER SEE SHEILA AGAIN...
...I'LL SHOW HER THAT THAT CREEP OF HERS CAN'T KICK SAND IN MY FACE ANY MORE.
IN FACT, MAYBE I'LL JUST GO OVER THERE RIGHT NOW AND SHOW HER A MOVE OR TWO I'VE LEARNED FROM WATCHIN' KUNG FU FLICKS.
BUT FIRST, I'D BETTER GRAB JUS' ONE MORE LITTLE SNORT...
SNORT!

THIS ISHN'T REALLY HAPPEN-ING!

I'LL CLOSHE MY EYES AND WHEN I OPEN THEM AGAIN...

SNORT!

THAT'S IT, I'M HISTORY!

SHEILA WAS RIGHT! TOO MUSH OF THISH STUFF DESTROYS THE BRAIN!

IT'S THE WAGON FOR ME!!

AND OVER IN CENTRAL PARK...

NO FROG SHOULD BE ABLE TO DO THAT TO A RAT.

WHEN I WAS TRANSFORMED, I WAS WEARING MY MAGICAL BELT OF STRENGTH.

...STILL I POSSESS POWERS AND ABILITIES FAR BEYOND THAT OF ANY MORTAL FROG.

ALTHOUGH MY POWER HAS BEEN DIMINISHED FAR BELOW THAT OF THE GOD OF THUNDER...

I MUST--

HEY, PAL!

PSSST! OVER HERE!

BETTER GET UNDER COVER FAST. SOUTHSIDE'LL BE COMING BACK WITH SOME BUDDIES ANY MINUTE.

YOUR WORDS ARE WISE, MY FRIEND.

BROTHER, YOU SURE CUT HIM UP. YOU MUST EAT THE RIGHT FLIES FOR BREAKFAST. WHAT'S YOUR NAME?

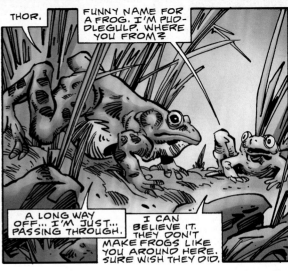

THOR.

FUNNY NAME FOR A FROG. I'M PUDDLEGULP, WHERE YOU FROM?

A LONG WAY OFF... I'M JUST... PASSING THROUGH.

I CAN BELIEVE IT. THEY DON'T MAKE FROGS LIKE YOU AROUND HERE. SURE WISH THEY DID.

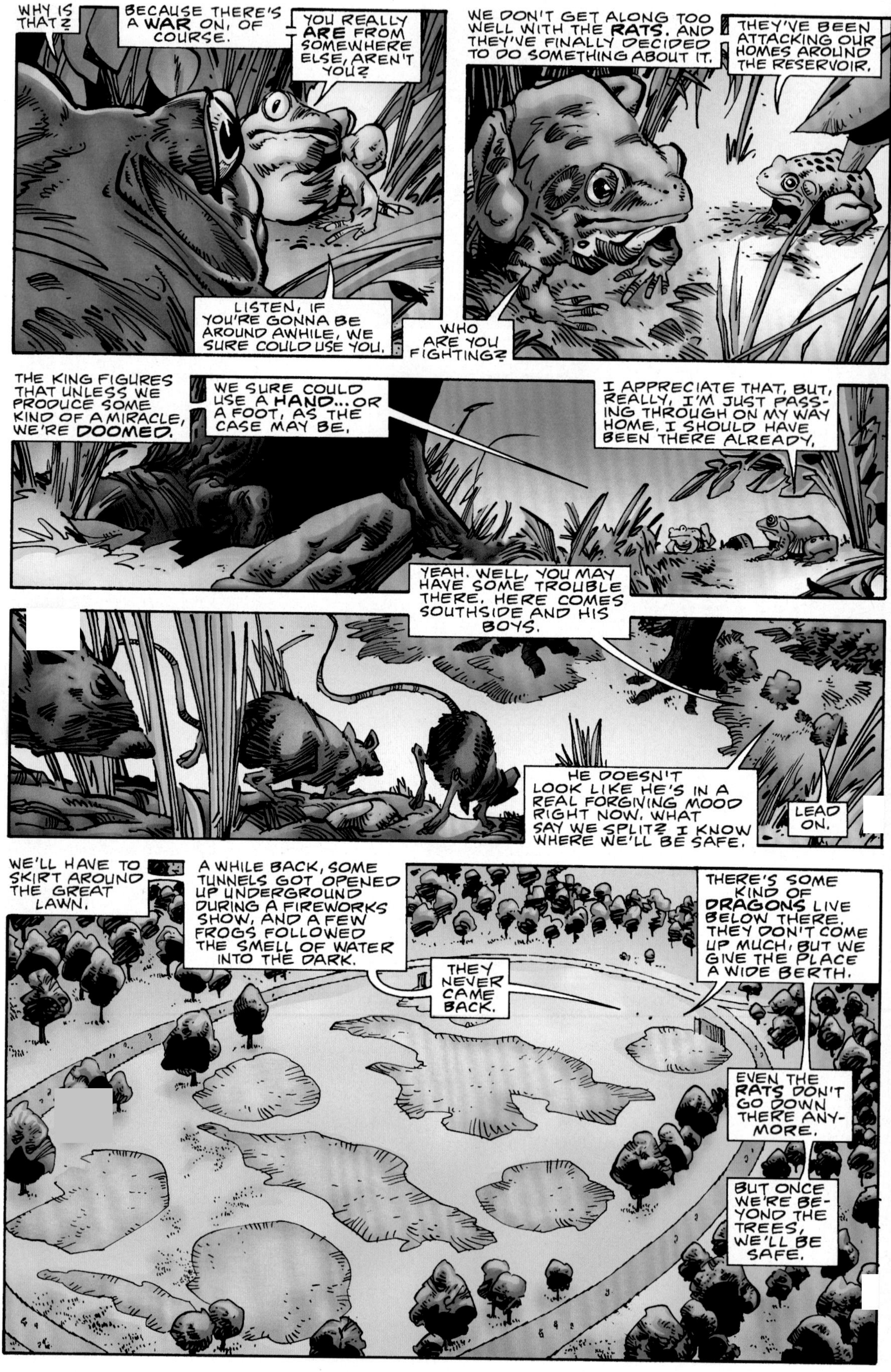
WHY IS THAT?
BECAUSE THERE'S A WAR ON, OF COURSE.
YOU REALLY ARE FROM SOMEWHERE ELSE, AREN'T YOU?
LISTEN, IF YOU'RE GONNA BE AROUND AWHILE, WE SURE COULD USE YOU.
WHO ARE YOU FIGHTING?
WE DON'T GET ALONG TOO WELL WITH THE RATS. AND THEY'VE FINALLY DECIDED TO DO SOMETHING ABOUT IT.
THEY'VE BEEN ATTACKING OUR HOMES AROUND THE RESERVOIR.
THE KING FIGURES THAT UNLESS WE PRODUCE SOME KIND OF A MIRACLE, WE'RE DOOMED.
WE SURE COULD USE A HAND... OR A FOOT, AS THE CASE MAY BE.
I APPRECIATE THAT, BUT, REALLY, I'M JUST PASSING THROUGH ON MY WAY HOME. I SHOULD HAVE BEEN THERE ALREADY.
YEAH. WELL, YOU MAY HAVE SOME TROUBLE THERE. HERE COMES SOUTHSIDE AND HIS BOYS.
HE DOESN'T LOOK LIKE HE'S IN A REAL FORGIVING MOOD RIGHT NOW. WHAT SAY WE SPLIT? I KNOW WHERE WE'LL BE SAFE.
LEAD ON.
WE'LL HAVE TO SKIRT AROUND THE GREAT LAWN.
A WHILE BACK, SOME TUNNELS GOT OPENED UP UNDERGROUND DURING A FIREWORKS SHOW, AND A FEW FROGS FOLLOWED THE SMELL OF WATER INTO THE DARK.
THEY NEVER CAME BACK.
THERE'S SOME KIND OF DRAGONS LIVE BELOW THERE. THEY DON'T COME UP MUCH, BUT WE GIVE THE PLACE A WIDE BERTH.
EVEN THE RATS DON'T GO DOWN THERE ANYMORE.
BUT ONCE WE'RE BEYOND THE TREES, WE'LL BE SAFE.

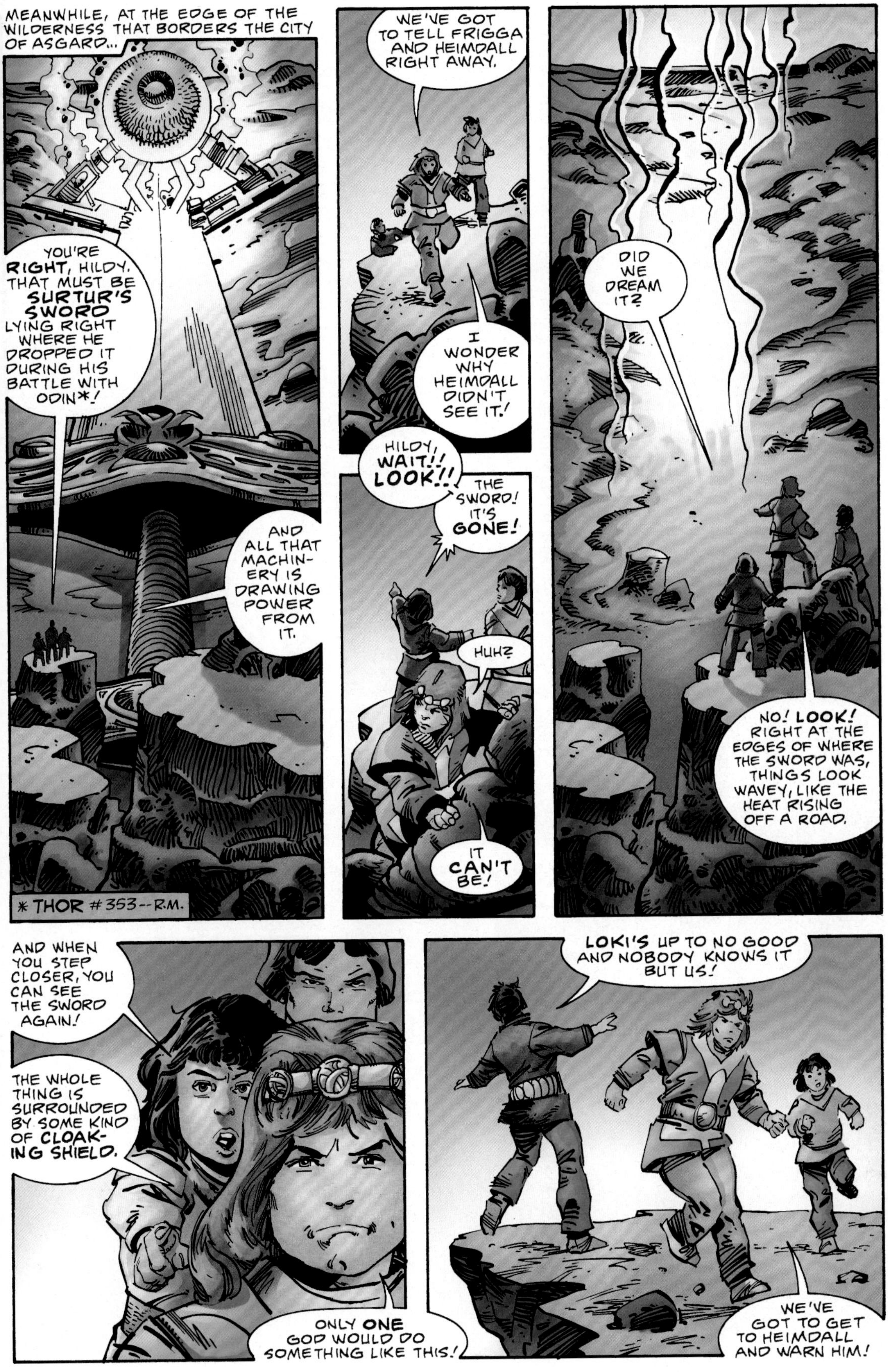
MEANWHILE, AT THE EDGE OF THE WILDERNESS THAT BORDERS THE CITY OF ASGARD...
YOU'RE RIGHT, HILDY. THAT MUST BE SURTUR'S SWORD LYING RIGHT WHERE HE DROPPED IT DURING HIS BATTLE WITH ODIN*!
AND ALL THAT MACHINERY IS DRAWING POWER FROM IT.
* THOR #353--R.M.
WE'VE GOT TO TELL FRIGGA AND HEIMDALL RIGHT AWAY.
I WONDER WHY HEIMDALL DIDN'T SEE IT.
HILDY, WAIT!! LOOK!!
THE SWORD! IT'S GONE!
HUH?
IT CAN'T BE!
DID WE DREAM IT?
NO! LOOK! RIGHT AT THE EDGES OF WHERE THE SWORD WAS, THINGS LOOK WAVEY, LIKE THE HEAT RISING OFF A ROAD.
AND WHEN YOU STEP CLOSER, YOU CAN SEE THE SWORD AGAIN!
THE WHOLE THING IS SURROUNDED BY SOME KIND OF CLOAKING SHIELD.
ONLY ONE GOD WOULD DO SOMETHING LIKE THIS!
LOKI'S UP TO NO GOOD AND NOBODY KNOWS IT BUT US!
WE'VE GOT TO GET TO HEIMDALL AND WARN HIM!

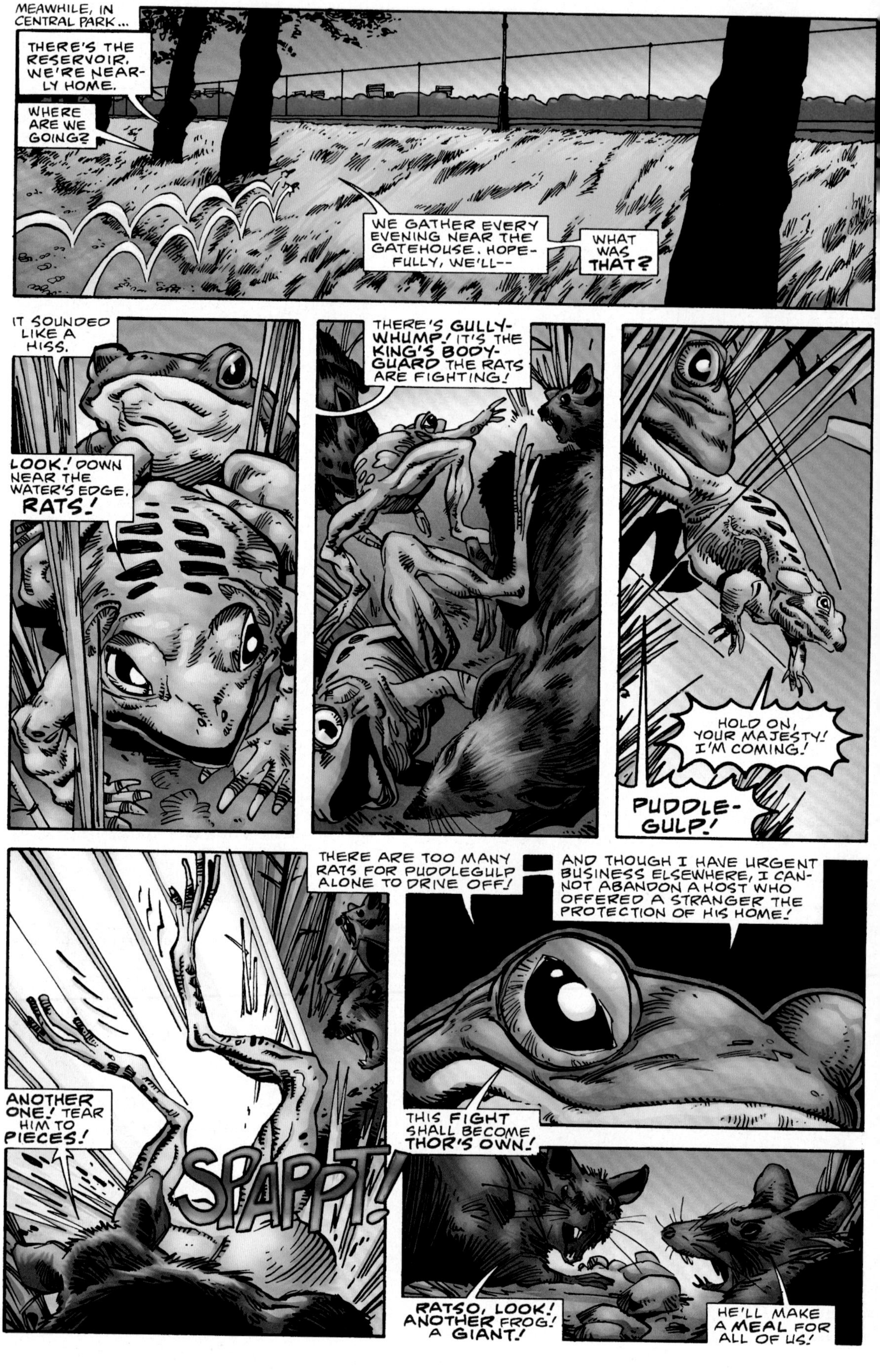
MEAWHILE, IN CENTRAL PARK...
THERE'S THE RESERVOIR. WE'RE NEARLY HOME.
WHERE ARE WE GOING?
WE GATHER EVERY EVENING NEAR THE GATEHOUSE. HOPEFULLY, WE'LL--
WHAT WAS THAT?
IT SOUNDED LIKE A HISS.
LOOK! DOWN NEAR THE WATER'S EDGE. RATS!
THERE'S GULLY-WHUMP! IT'S THE KING'S BODYGUARD THE RATS ARE FIGHTING!
HOLD ON, YOUR MAJESTY! I'M COMING!
PUDDLE-GULP!
THERE ARE TOO MANY RATS FOR PUDDLEGULP ALONE TO DRIVE OFF!
AND THOUGH I HAVE URGENT BUSINESS ELSEWHERE, I CANNOT ABANDON A HOST WHO OFFERED A STRANGER THE PROTECTION OF HIS HOME!
THIS FIGHT SHALL BECOME THOR'S OWN!
ANOTHER ONE! TEAR HIM TO PIECES!
SPAPPT!
RATSO, LOOK! ANOTHER FROG! A GIANT!
HE'LL MAKE A MEAL FOR ALL OF US!

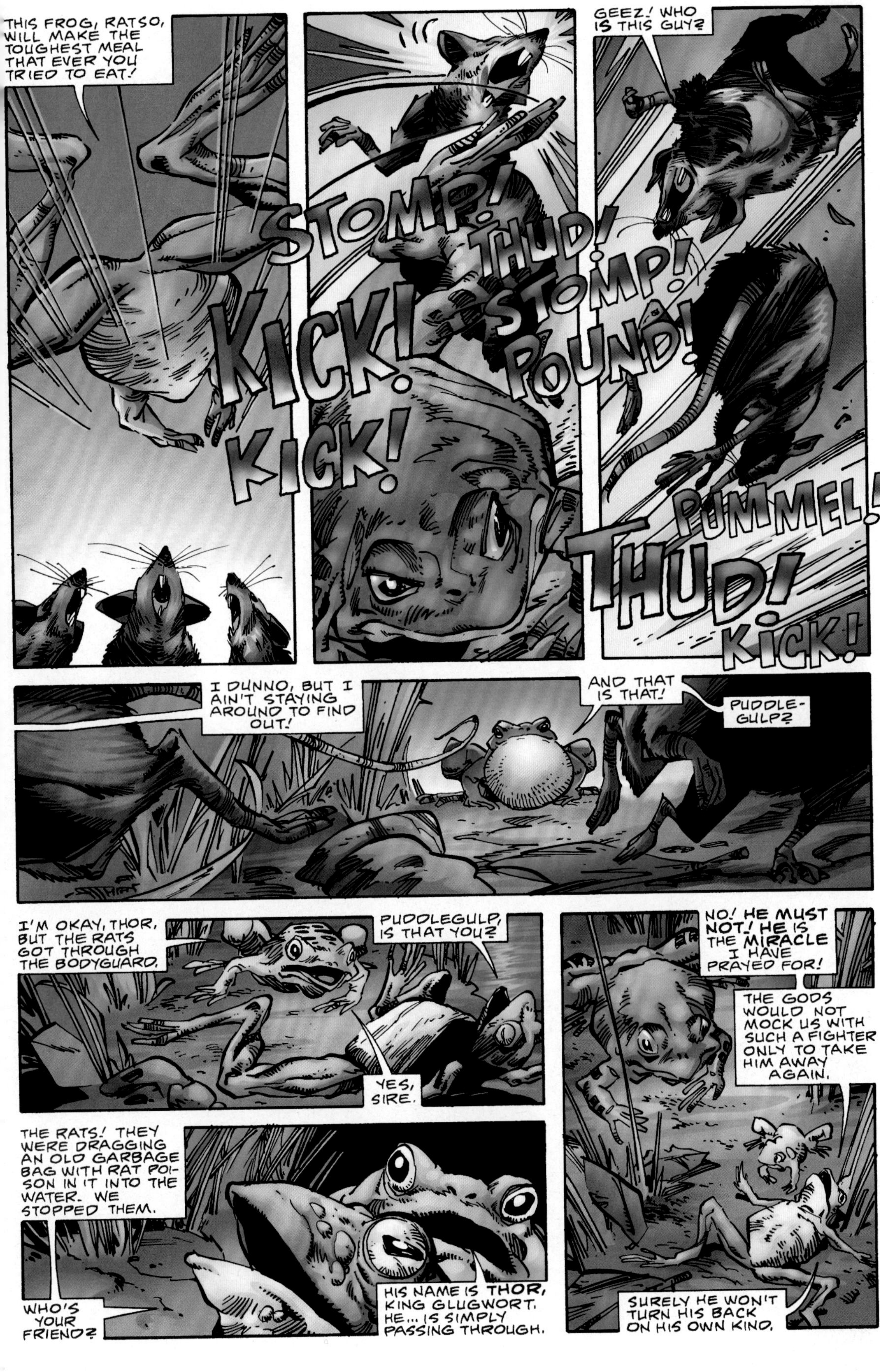
THIS FROG, RATSO, WILL MAKE THE TOUGHEST MEAL THAT EVER YOU TRIED TO EAT!
STOMP! KICK! KICK!
THUD! STOMP! POUND!
GEEZ! WHO IS THIS GUY?
PUMMEL! THUD! KICK!
I DUNNO, BUT I AIN'T STAYING AROUND TO FIND OUT!
AND THAT IS THAT!
PUDDLE-GULP?
I'M OKAY, THOR, BUT THE RATS GOT THROUGH THE BODYGUARD.
PUDDLEGULP, IS THAT YOU?
YES, SIRE.
NO! HE MUST NOT! HE IS THE MIRACLE I HAVE PRAYED FOR!
THE GODS WOULD NOT MOCK US WITH SUCH A FIGHTER ONLY TO TAKE HIM AWAY AGAIN.
THE RATS! THEY WERE DRAGGING AN OLD GARBAGE BAG WITH RAT POISON IN IT INTO THE WATER. WE STOPPED THEM.
WHO'S YOUR FRIEND?
HIS NAME IS THOR, KING GLUGWORT. HE... IS SIMPLY PASSING THROUGH.
SURELY HE WON'T TURN HIS BACK ON HIS OWN KIND.

THOR! MY KINGDOM! MY **DAUGHTER!** TAKE WHATEVER YOU WANT, BUT **SAVE** OUR PEOPLE!

PROMISE... PROMISE... PROMISE...

MAY YOU SWIM TO SAFE HAVEN, KING GLUGWORT. GOODBYE.

FOLLOW ME, THOR. THE RATS'LL BE BACK WITH REINFORCEMENTS ANY MINUTE!

PLOOSH! PLOOSH!

HERE UNDER THE GATE-HOUSE, WE CAN GATHER IN SAFETY.

LOOK! PUDDLE-GULP'S **BACK!**

HAVE YOU SEEN MY FATHER?

PRINCESS, THE KING IS DEAD, HE WAS SLAIN BY OUR ENEMIES.

I AM SORRY, GREENSONG.

MY FATHER? **DEAD?**

AND YOU'RE **STILL ALIVE,** PUDDLEGULP? I WOULD HAVE GIVEN MY **LIFE** TO SAVE MY LORD.

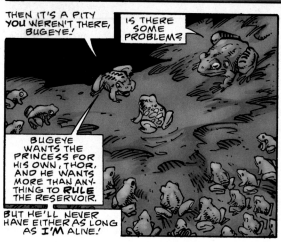

THEN IT'S A PITY YOU WEREN'T THERE, BUGEYE!

IS THERE SOME PROBLEM?

BUGEYE WANTS THE PRINCESS FOR HIS OWN, THOR, AND HE WANTS MORE THAN ANY-THING TO **RULE** THE RESERVOIR.

BUT HE'LL NEVER HAVE EITHER AS LONG AS I'M ALIVE!

MY FELLOW BULLFROGS, MEET THOR!

HE FOUGHT FEROCIOUSLY TO SAVE OUR KING, BUT HE AND I WERE TOO LATE.

WITH HIS DYING BREATH, GLUGWORT CHARGED THAT WE DO EVERY-THING WE COULD TO PERSUADE THOR TO STAY AND HELP US.

EVEN IF WE HAD TO GIVE UP THE **KINGDOM...** OR THE **PRINCESS!**

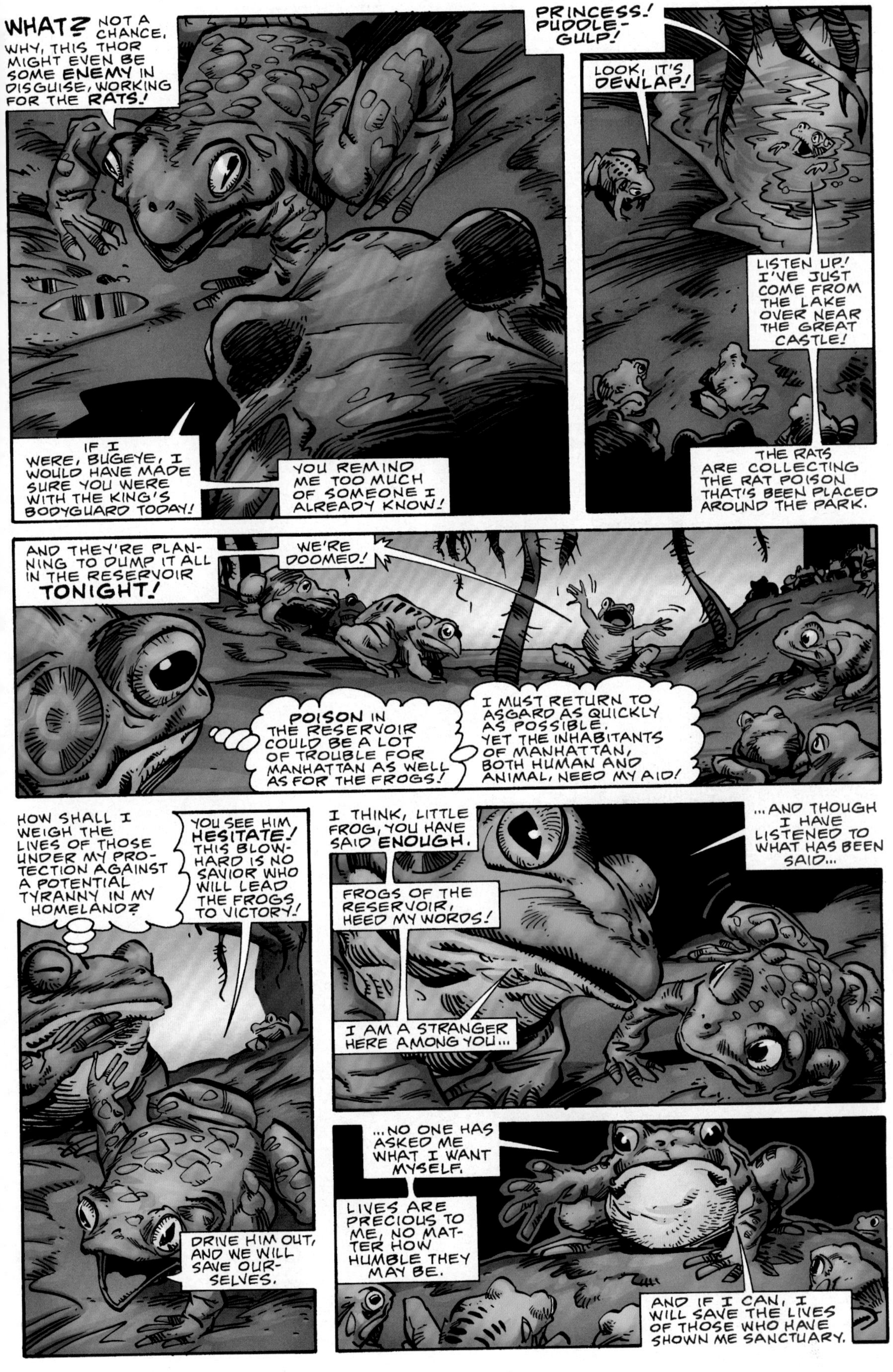
WHAT? NOT A CHANCE. WHY, THIS THOR MIGHT EVEN BE SOME ENEMY IN DISGUISE, WORKING FOR THE RATS!
IF I WERE, BUGEYE, I WOULD HAVE MADE SURE YOU WERE WITH THE KING'S BODYGUARD TODAY!
YOU REMIND ME TOO MUCH OF SOMEONE I ALREADY KNOW!
PRINCESS! PUDDLE-GULP!
LOOK, IT'S DEWLAP!
LISTEN UP! I'VE JUST COME FROM THE LAKE OVER NEAR THE GREAT CASTLE!
THE RATS ARE COLLECTING THE RAT POISON THAT'S BEEN PLACED AROUND THE PARK.
AND THEY'RE PLANNING TO DUMP IT ALL IN THE RESERVOIR TONIGHT!
WE'RE DOOMED!
POISON IN THE RESERVOIR COULD BE A LOT OF TROUBLE FOR MANHATTAN AS WELL AS FOR THE FROGS!
I MUST RETURN TO ASGARD AS QUICKLY AS POSSIBLE. YET THE INHABITANTS OF MANHATTAN, BOTH HUMAN AND ANIMAL, NEED MY AID!
HOW SHALL I WEIGH THE LIVES OF THOSE UNDER MY PROTECTION AGAINST A POTENTIAL TYRANNY IN MY HOMELAND?
YOU SEE HIM HESITATE! THIS BLOWHARD IS NO SAVIOR WHO WILL LEAD THE FROGS TO VICTORY!
DRIVE HIM OUT, AND WE WILL SAVE OURSELVES.
I THINK, LITTLE FROG, YOU HAVE SAID ENOUGH.
FROGS OF THE RESERVOIR, HEED MY WORDS!
I AM A STRANGER HERE AMONG YOU...
...AND THOUGH I HAVE LISTENED TO WHAT HAS BEEN SAID...
...NO ONE HAS ASKED ME WHAT I WANT MYSELF.
LIVES ARE PRECIOUS TO ME, NO MATTER HOW HUMBLE THEY MAY BE.
AND IF I CAN, I WILL SAVE THE LIVES OF THOSE WHO HAVE SHOWN ME SANCTUARY.

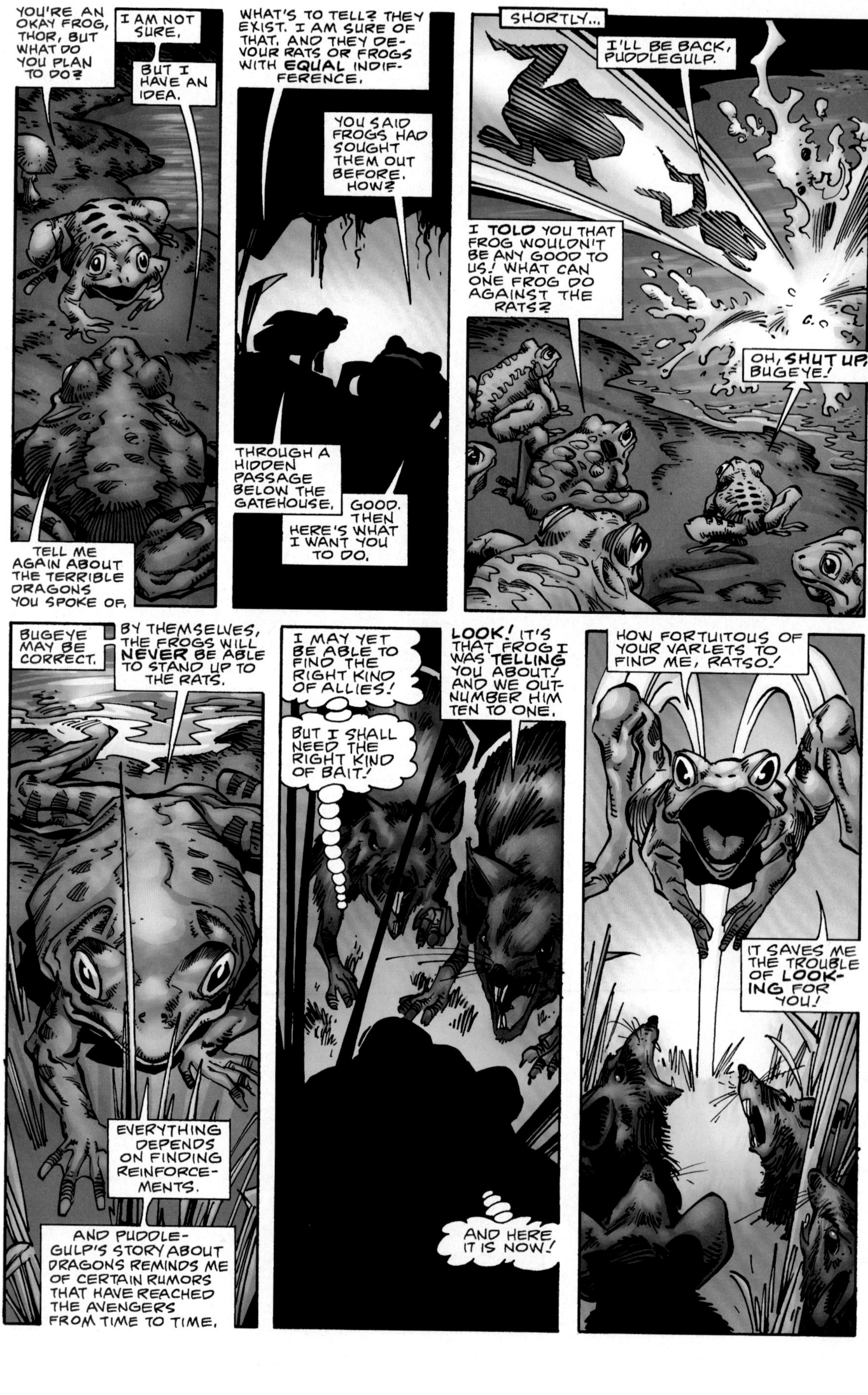

YOU'RE AN OKAY FROG, THOR, BUT WHAT DO YOU PLAN TO DO?
I AM NOT SURE.
BUT I HAVE AN IDEA.
TELL ME AGAIN ABOUT THE TERRIBLE DRAGONS YOU SPOKE OF.
WHAT'S TO TELL? THEY EXIST. I AM SURE OF THAT. AND THEY DE-VOUR RATS OR FROGS WITH EQUAL INDIF-FERENCE.
YOU SAID FROGS HAD SOUGHT THEM OUT BEFORE. HOW?
THROUGH A HIDDEN PASSAGE BELOW THE GATEHOUSE.
GOOD. THEN HERE'S WHAT I WANT YOU TO DO.
SHORTLY...
I'LL BE BACK, PUDDLEGULP.
I TOLD YOU THAT FROG WOULDN'T BE ANY GOOD TO US! WHAT CAN ONE FROG DO AGAINST THE RATS?
OH, SHUT UP, BUGEYE!
BUGEYE MAY BE CORRECT.
BY THEMSELVES, THE FROGS WILL NEVER BE ABLE TO STAND UP TO THE RATS.
EVERYTHING DEPENDS ON FINDING REINFORCE-MENTS.
AND PUDDLE-GULP'S STORY ABOUT DRAGONS REMINDS ME OF CERTAIN RUMORS THAT HAVE REACHED THE AVENGERS FROM TIME TO TIME.
I MAY YET BE ABLE TO FIND THE RIGHT KIND OF ALLIES!
BUT I SHALL NEED THE RIGHT KIND OF BAIT!
LOOK! IT'S THAT FROG I WAS TELLING YOU ABOUT! AND WE OUT-NUMBER HIM TEN TO ONE.
AND HERE IT IS NOW!
HOW FORTUITOUS OF YOUR VARLETS TO FIND ME, RATSO!
IT SAVES ME THE TROUBLE OF LOOK-ING FOR YOU!

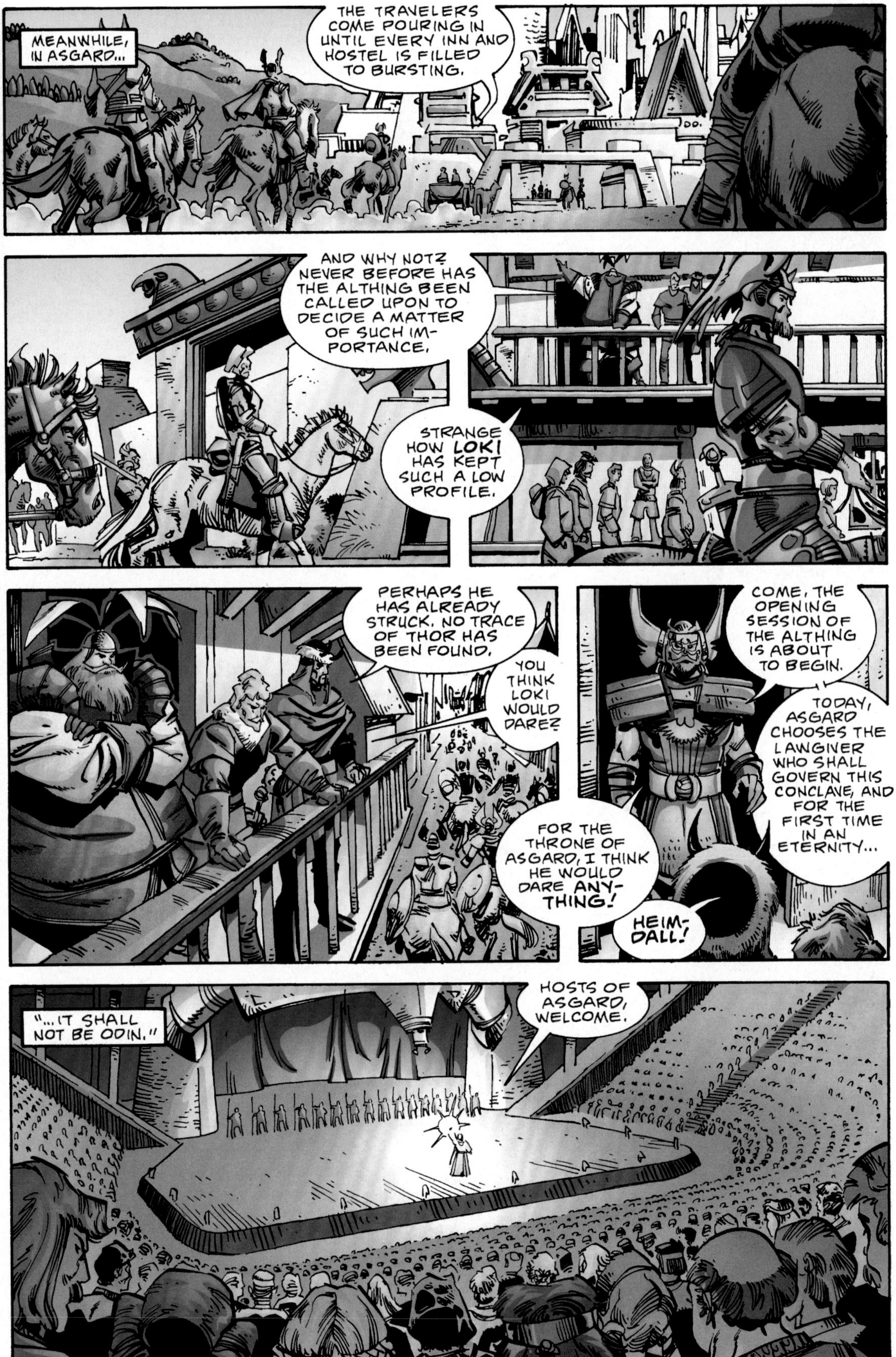
MEANWHILE, IN ASGARD...
THE TRAVELERS COME POURING IN UNTIL EVERY INN AND HOSTEL IS FILLED TO BURSTING.
AND WHY NOT? NEVER BEFORE HAS THE ALTHING BEEN CALLED UPON TO DECIDE A MATTER OF SUCH IMPORTANCE.
STRANGE HOW LOKI HAS KEPT SUCH A LOW PROFILE.
PERHAPS HE HAS ALREADY STRUCK. NO TRACE OF THOR HAS BEEN FOUND.
YOU THINK LOKI WOULD DARE?
FOR THE THRONE OF ASGARD, I THINK HE WOULD DARE ANYTHING!
COME. THE OPENING SESSION OF THE ALTHING IS ABOUT TO BEGIN.
TODAY, ASGARD CHOOSES THE LAWGIVER WHO SHALL GOVERN THIS CONCLAVE, AND FOR THE FIRST TIME IN AN ETERNITY...
HEIMDALL!
"...IT SHALL NOT BE ODIN."
HOSTS OF ASGARD, WELCOME.

I HOLD ABOVE ME THE GREAT **SCEPTER** OF **POWER.**

BY ITS LIGHT, WE SHALL SOLEMNIZE OUR DECISIONS HERE.

CLICK!

I, **FRIGGA,** WIFE OF ODIN, AND MOTHER OF THE GODS, DECLARE THE GREAT ALTHING OF ASGARD OPEN.

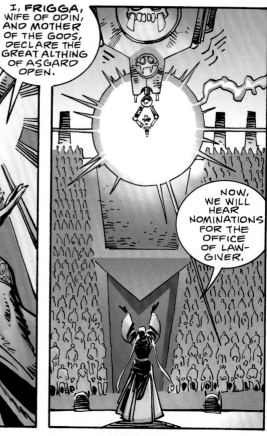

NOW, WE WILL HEAR NOMINATIONS FOR THE OFFICE OF LAW-GIVER.

LET ALL MEN AND WOMEN SEARCH THEIR HEARTS, AND FIND THE COURAGE THEREIN TO SPEAK ONLY **TRUTH** WITHIN THIS AMPHITHEATER.

MY FRIENDS, LOKI CLAIMS THE RIGHT AS ODIN'S STEPSON TO STAND BEFORE YOU NOW.

CAN THERE BE ANY DOUBT AS TO WHO WOULD BEST SERVE ASGARD IN HER HOUR OF NEED AS THE LAWGIVER OF THE ALTHING?

SURELY, ONLY ODIN'S TRUSTED ADVISOR AND CONFIDANT, THE **GRAND VIZIER,** SHOULD STAND IN THIS ASSEMBLY AS LAWGIVER.

WHO ELSE WOULD HONOR THAT SACRED TRUST OR FULFILL THAT OFFICE SO WELL?

SPEAK, ASGARDIANS, AND TELL ME YOU AGREE THAT NO OTHER COULD SO FAITHFULLY EXECUTE THOSE DUTIES IN THIS SOLEMN HOUR!

AND THE CHEERS GO UP FROM THE MULTITUDES AS THE GRAND VIZIER STEPS FORWARD TO RECEIVE THE OFFICE OF LAW-GIVER.

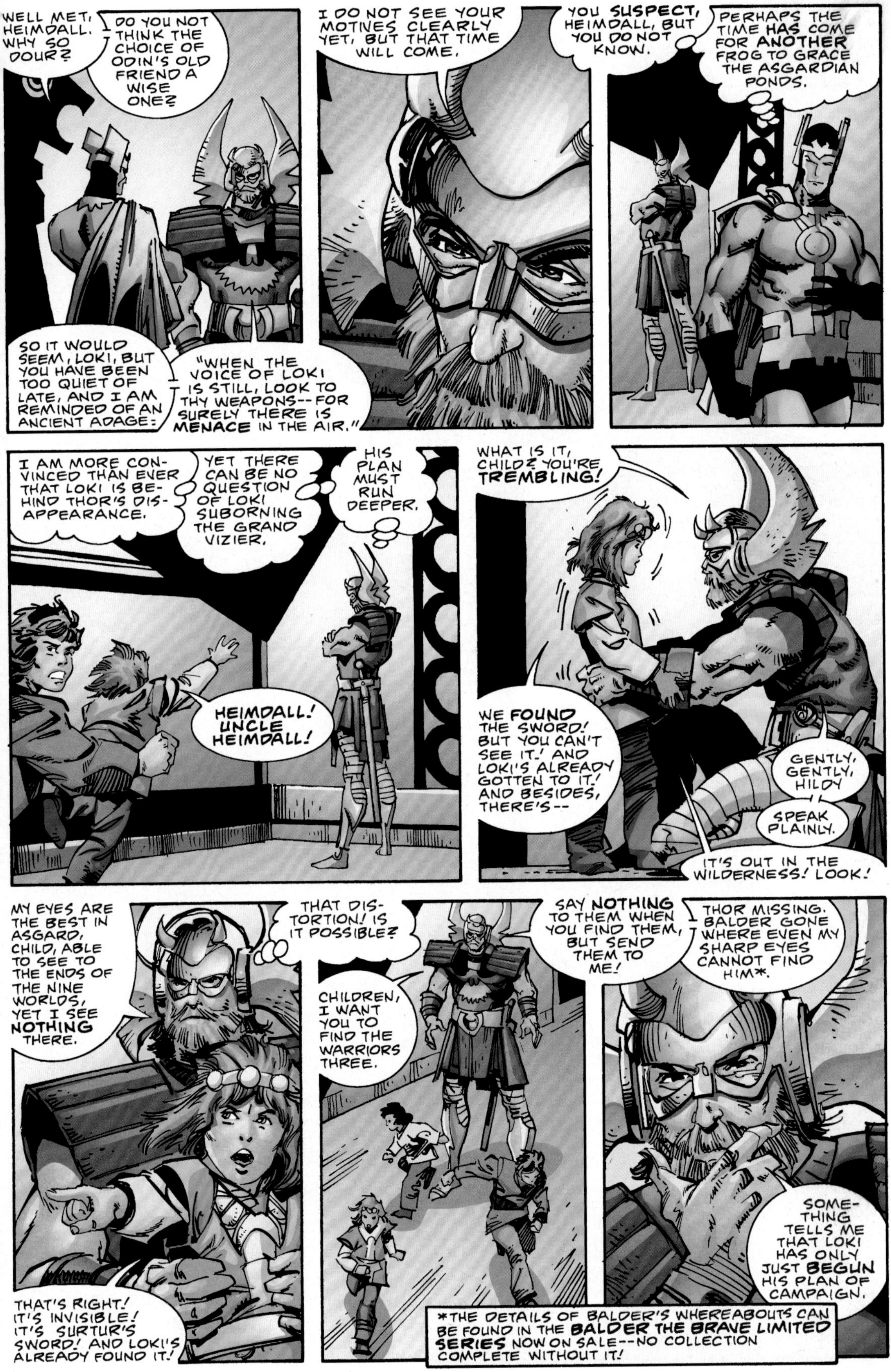
WELL MET, HEIMDALL. WHY SO DOUR?
DO YOU NOT THINK THE CHOICE OF ODIN'S OLD FRIEND A WISE ONE?
SO IT WOULD SEEM, LOKI, BUT YOU HAVE BEEN TOO QUIET OF LATE, AND I AM REMINDED OF AN ANCIENT ADAGE:
"WHEN THE VOICE OF LOKI IS STILL, LOOK TO THY WEAPONS--FOR SURELY THERE IS MENACE IN THE AIR."
I DO NOT SEE YOUR MOTIVES CLEARLY YET, BUT THAT TIME WILL COME.
YOU SUSPECT, HEIMDALL, BUT YOU DO NOT KNOW.
PERHAPS THE TIME HAS COME FOR ANOTHER FROG TO GRACE THE ASGARDIAN PONDS.
I AM MORE CONVINCED THAN EVER THAT LOKI IS BEHIND THOR'S DISAPPEARANCE.
YET THERE CAN BE NO QUESTION OF LOKI SUBORNING THE GRAND VIZIER.
HIS PLAN MUST RUN DEEPER.
HEIMDALL! UNCLE HEIMDALL!
WHAT IS IT, CHILD? YOU'RE TREMBLING!
WE FOUND THE SWORD! BUT YOU CAN'T SEE IT! AND LOKI'S ALREADY GOTTEN TO IT! AND BESIDES, THERE'S--
GENTLY, GENTLY, HILDY
SPEAK PLAINLY.
IT'S OUT IN THE WILDERNESS! LOOK!
MY EYES ARE THE BEST IN ASGARD, CHILD, ABLE TO SEE TO THE ENDS OF THE NINE WORLDS, YET I SEE NOTHING THERE.
THAT DISTORTION! IS IT POSSIBLE?
THAT'S RIGHT! IT'S INVISIBLE! IT'S SURTUR'S SWORD! AND LOKI'S ALREADY FOUND IT!
CHILDREN, I WANT YOU TO FIND THE WARRIORS THREE.
SAY NOTHING TO THEM WHEN YOU FIND THEM, BUT SEND THEM TO ME!
THOR MISSING. BALDER GONE WHERE EVEN MY SHARP EYES CANNOT FIND HIM*.
SOMETHING TELLS ME THAT LOKI HAS ONLY JUST BEGUN HIS PLAN OF CAMPAIGN.
*THE DETAILS OF BALDER'S WHEREABOUTS CAN BE FOUND IN THE BALDER THE BRAVE LIMITED SERIES NOW ON SALE--NO COLLECTION COMPLETE WITHOUT IT!

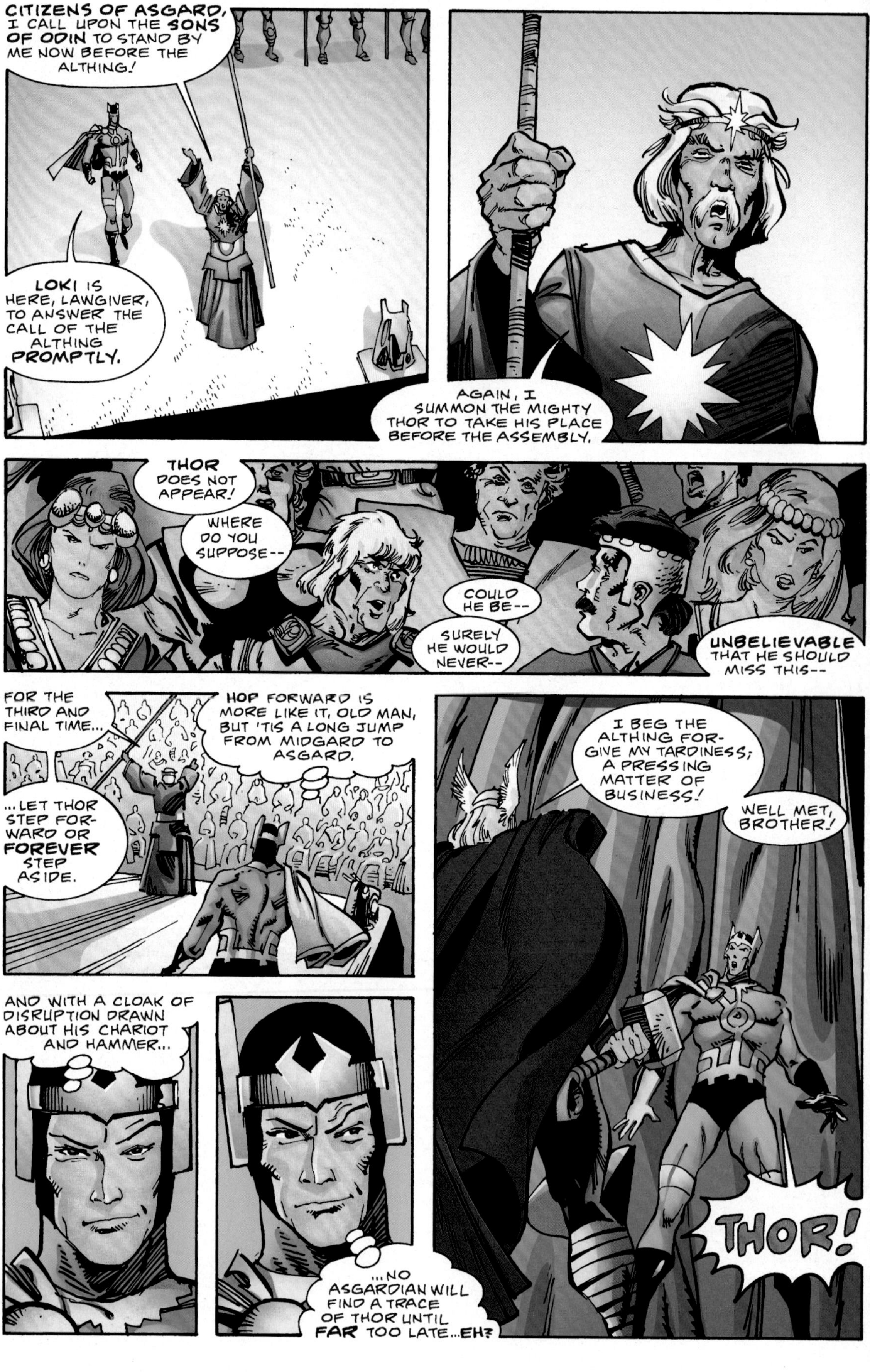
CITIZENS OF ASGARD, I CALL UPON THE SONS OF ODIN TO STAND BY ME NOW BEFORE THE ALTHING!
LOKI IS HERE, LAWGIVER, TO ANSWER THE CALL OF THE ALTHING PROMPTLY.
AGAIN, I SUMMON THE MIGHTY THOR TO TAKE HIS PLACE BEFORE THE ASSEMBLY.
THOR DOES NOT APPEAR!
WHERE DO YOU SUPPOSE--
COULD HE BE--
SURELY HE WOULD NEVER--
UNBELIEVABLE THAT HE SHOULD MISS THIS--
FOR THE THIRD AND FINAL TIME...
HOP FORWARD IS MORE LIKE IT, OLD MAN, BUT 'TIS A LONG JUMP FROM MIDGARD TO ASGARD.
...LET THOR STEP FORWARD OR FOREVER STEP ASIDE.
AND WITH A CLOAK OF DISRUPTION DRAWN ABOUT HIS CHARIOT AND HAMMER...
...NO ASGARDIAN WILL FIND A TRACE OF THOR UNTIL FAR TOO LATE...EH?
I BEG THE ALTHING FORGIVE MY TARDINESS; A PRESSING MATTER OF BUSINESS!
WELL MET, BROTHER!
THOR!

BUT LET US TURN FROM THIS ASTONISHING APPEARANCE IN THE FABLED REALM OF AS-GARD AND PEER FAR BENEATH THE SURFACE OF CENTRAL PARK IN NEW YORK CITY...

...WHERE WE FIND...

IT APPEARS THAT THE RUMORS WERE CORRECT.

THE OPENING IN THE GATEHOUSE HAS LED ME TO A SERIES OF INTERCONNECTED TUNNELS THAT ANGLE EVER DEEPER INTO THE DARK.

AND PUDDLE-GULP'S TALE OF THE DRAGONS BE-GINS TO MAKE SENSE.

NOW 'TIS TIME TO LEAVE **ANOTHER** RAT IN THE TRAIL ALONG MY PATH FROM THE PARK.

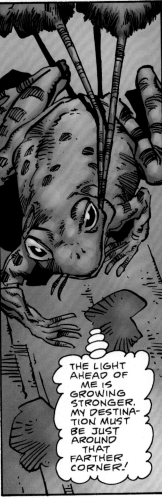

THE LIGHT AHEAD OF ME IS GROWING STRONGER. MY DESTINA-TION MUST BE JUST AROUND THAT FARTHER CORNER.!

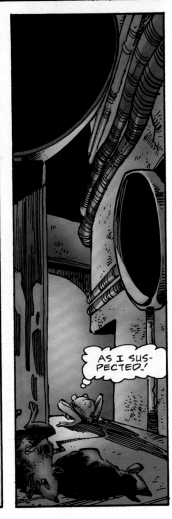

AS I SUS-PECTED.!

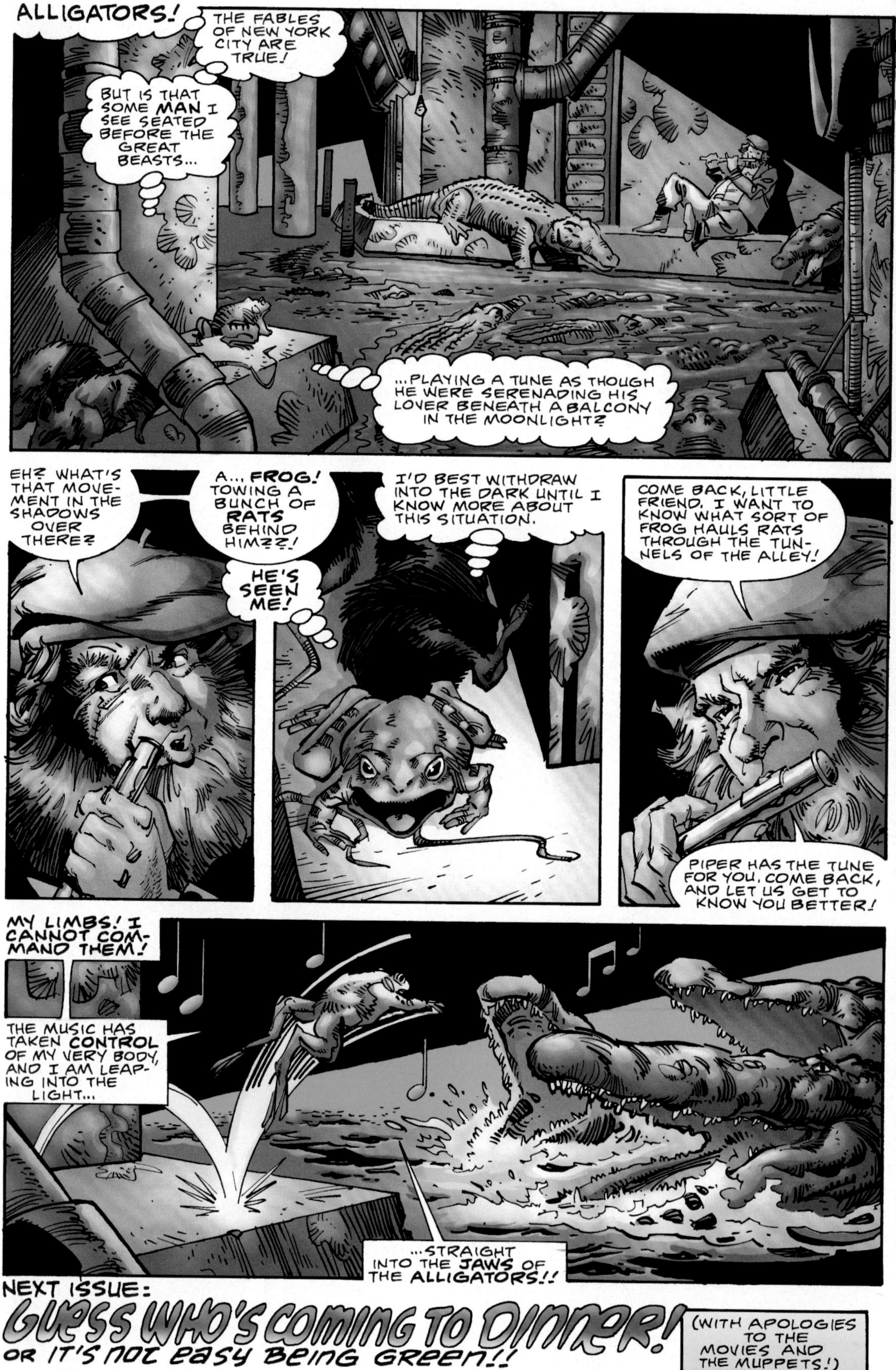
ALLIGATORS!
THE FABLES OF NEW YORK CITY ARE TRUE!
BUT IS THAT SOME MAN I SEE SEATED BEFORE THE GREAT BEASTS...
...PLAYING A TUNE AS THOUGH HE WERE SERENADING HIS LOVER BENEATH A BALCONY IN THE MOONLIGHT?
EH? WHAT'S THAT MOVEMENT IN THE SHADOWS OVER THERE?
A... FROG! TOWING A BUNCH OF RATS BEHIND HIM??!
HE'S SEEN ME!
I'D BEST WITHDRAW INTO THE DARK UNTIL I KNOW MORE ABOUT THIS SITUATION.
COME BACK, LITTLE FRIEND. I WANT TO KNOW WHAT SORT OF FROG HAULS RATS THROUGH THE TUNNELS OF THE ALLEY!
PIPER HAS THE TUNE FOR YOU. COME BACK, AND LET US GET TO KNOW YOU BETTER!
MY LIMBS! I CANNOT COMMAND THEM!
THE MUSIC HAS TAKEN CONTROL OF MY VERY BODY, AND I AM LEAPING INTO THE LIGHT...
...STRAIGHT INTO THE JAWS OF THE ALLIGATORS!!

NEXT ISSUE:

GUESS WHO'S COMING TO DINNER! (WITH APOLOGIES TO THE MOVIES AND THE MUPPETS!)

OR IT'S NOT EASY BEING GREEN!!

THIS ISSUE IS FOR CATAPULT, CARL BARKS AND ALL THE OTHER HEROES AND VILLAINS OF DUCKBURG.

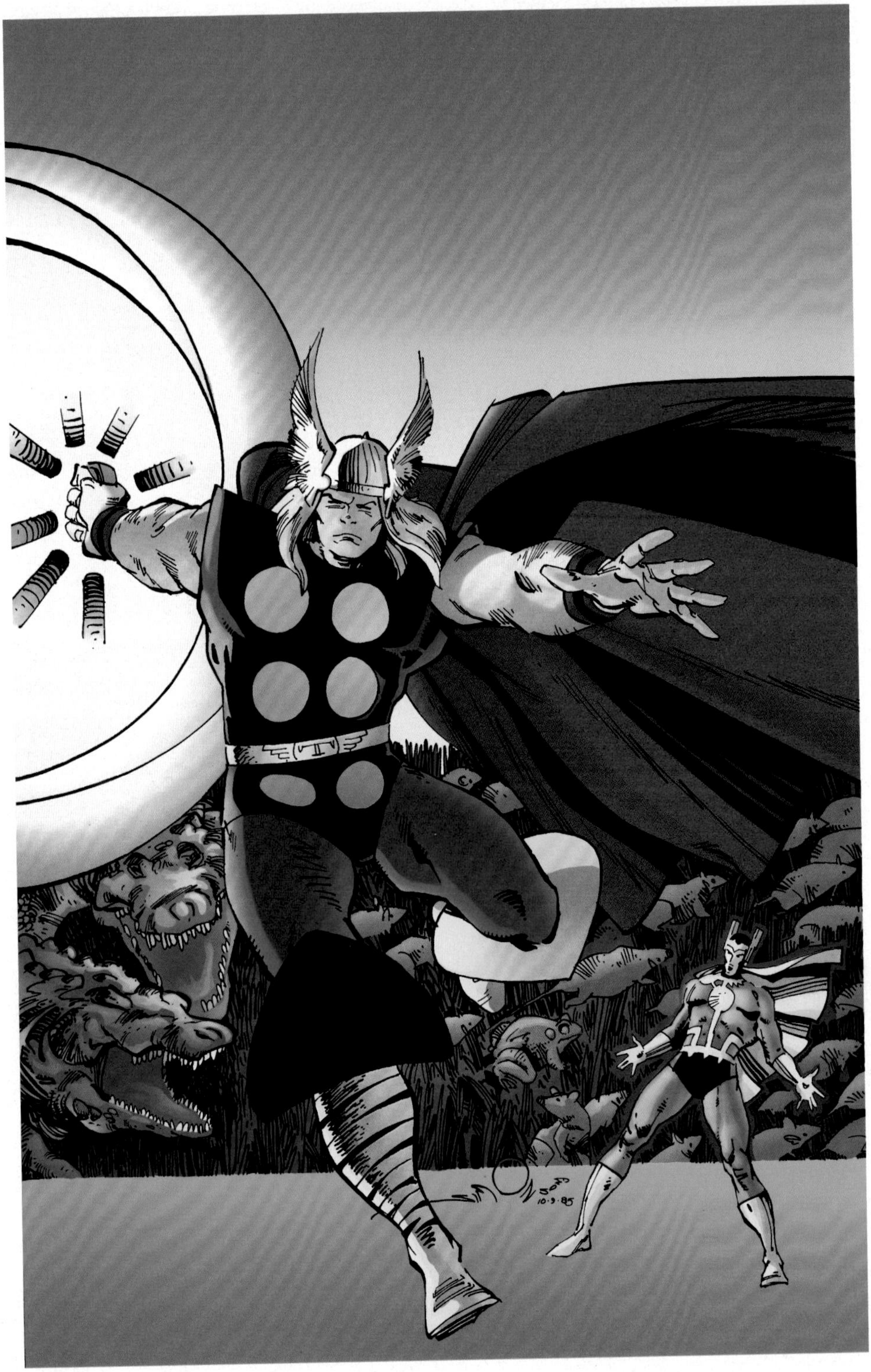

THOR No. 365

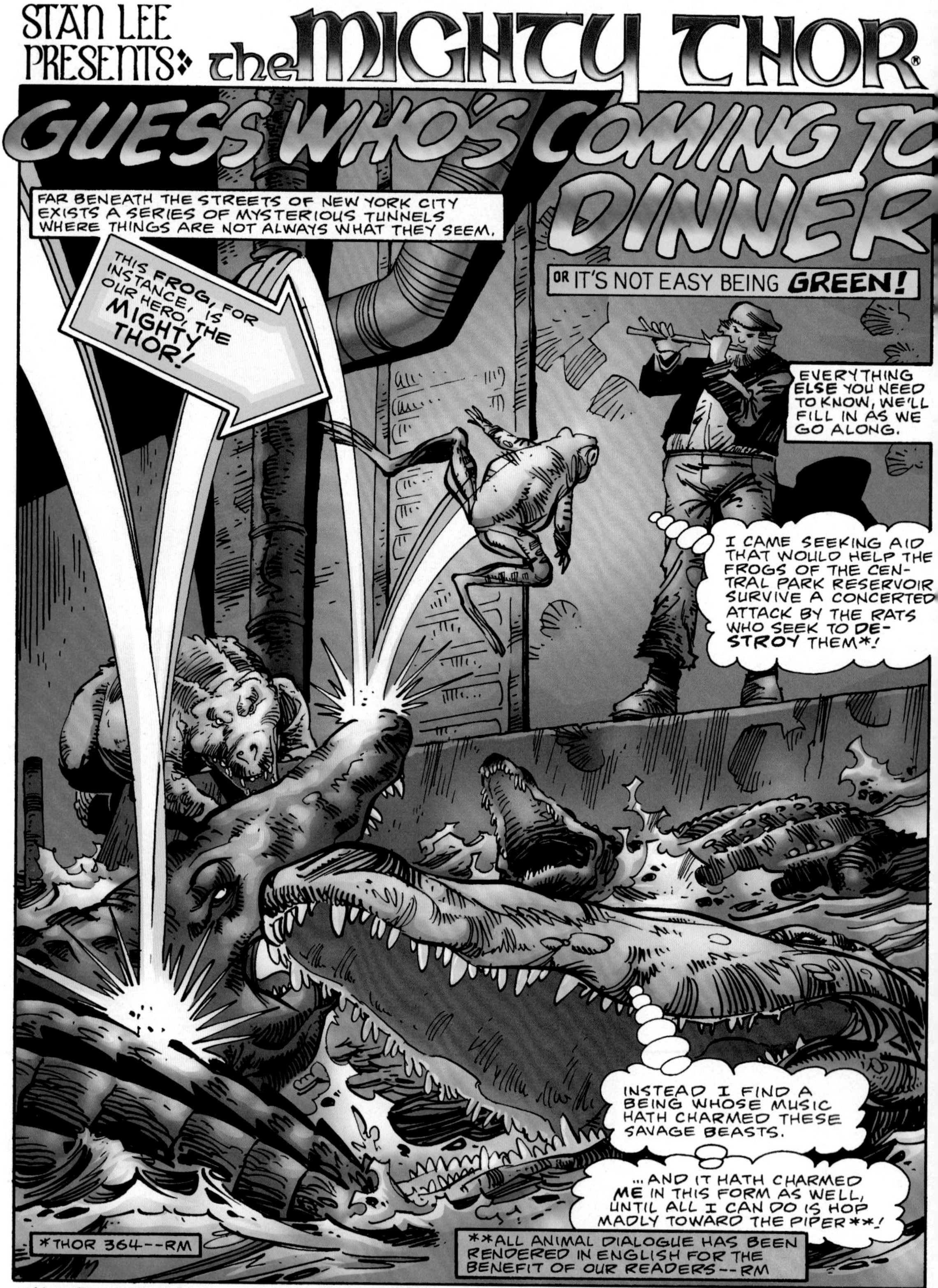
STAN LEE PRESENTS: the MIGHTY THOR®
GUESS WHO'S COMING TO DINNER
FAR BENEATH THE STREETS OF NEW YORK CITY EXISTS A SERIES OF MYSTERIOUS TUNNELS WHERE THINGS ARE NOT ALWAYS WHAT THEY SEEM.
THIS FROG, FOR INSTANCE, IS OUR HERO, THE MIGHTY THOR!
OR IT'S NOT EASY BEING GREEN!
EVERYTHING ELSE YOU NEED TO KNOW, WE'LL FILL IN AS WE GO ALONG.
I CAME SEEKING AID THAT WOULD HELP THE FROGS OF THE CENTRAL PARK RESERVOIR SURVIVE A CONCERTED ATTACK BY THE RATS WHO SEEK TO DESTROY THEM*!
INSTEAD I FIND A BEING WHOSE MUSIC HATH CHARMED THESE SAVAGE BEASTS.
...AND IT HATH CHARMED ME IN THIS FORM AS WELL, UNTIL ALL I CAN DO IS HOP MADLY TOWARD THE PIPER**!
*THOR 364--RM
**ALL ANIMAL DIALOGUE HAS BEEN RENDERED IN ENGLISH FOR THE BENEFIT OF OUR READERS--RM

WALTER SIMONSON ART & STORY | JOHN WORKMAN LETTERING | STEVE OLIFF COLORING | RALPH MACCHIO EDITING | JIM SHOOTER EDITOR IN CHIEF

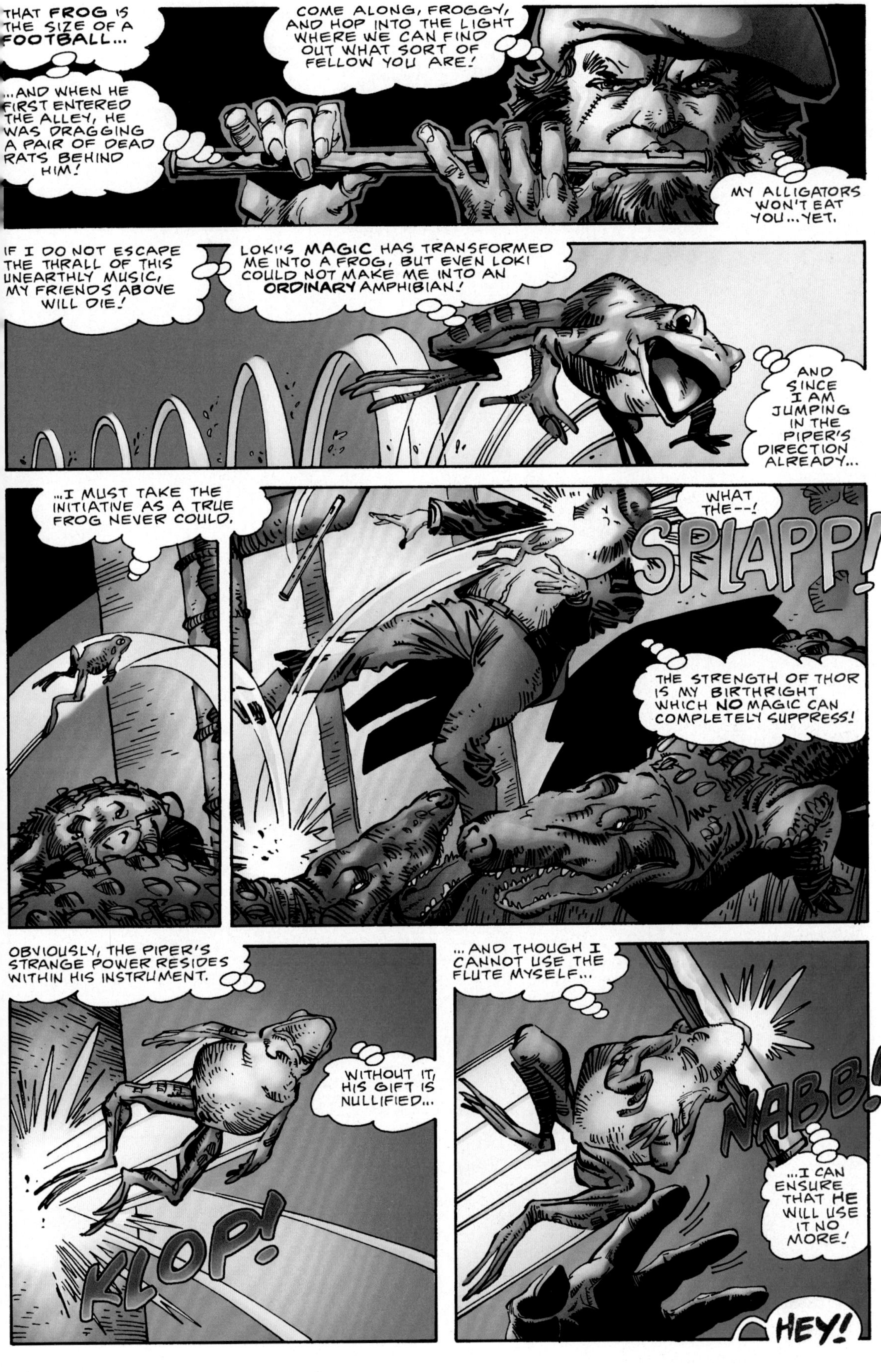
THAT FROG IS THE SIZE OF A FOOTBALL...
...AND WHEN HE FIRST ENTERED THE ALLEY, HE WAS DRAGGING A PAIR OF DEAD RATS BEHIND HIM!
COME ALONG, FROGGY, AND HOP INTO THE LIGHT WHERE WE CAN FIND OUT WHAT SORT OF FELLOW YOU ARE!
MY ALLIGATORS WON'T EAT YOU...YET.
IF I DO NOT ESCAPE THE THRALL OF THIS UNEARTHLY MUSIC, MY FRIENDS ABOVE WILL DIE!
LOKI'S MAGIC HAS TRANSFORMED ME INTO A FROG, BUT EVEN LOKI COULD NOT MAKE ME INTO AN ORDINARY AMPHIBIAN!
AND SINCE I AM JUMPING IN THE PIPER'S DIRECTION ALREADY...
...I MUST TAKE THE INITIATIVE AS A TRUE FROG NEVER COULD.
WHAT THE--!
SPLAPP!
THE STRENGTH OF THOR IS MY BIRTHRIGHT WHICH NO MAGIC CAN COMPLETELY SUPPRESS!
OBVIOUSLY, THE PIPER'S STRANGE POWER RESIDES WITHIN HIS INSTRUMENT.
WITHOUT IT, HIS GIFT IS NULLIFIED...
KLOP!
...AND THOUGH I CANNOT USE THE FLUTE MYSELF...
NABB!
...I CAN ENSURE THAT HE WILL USE IT NO MORE!
HEY!

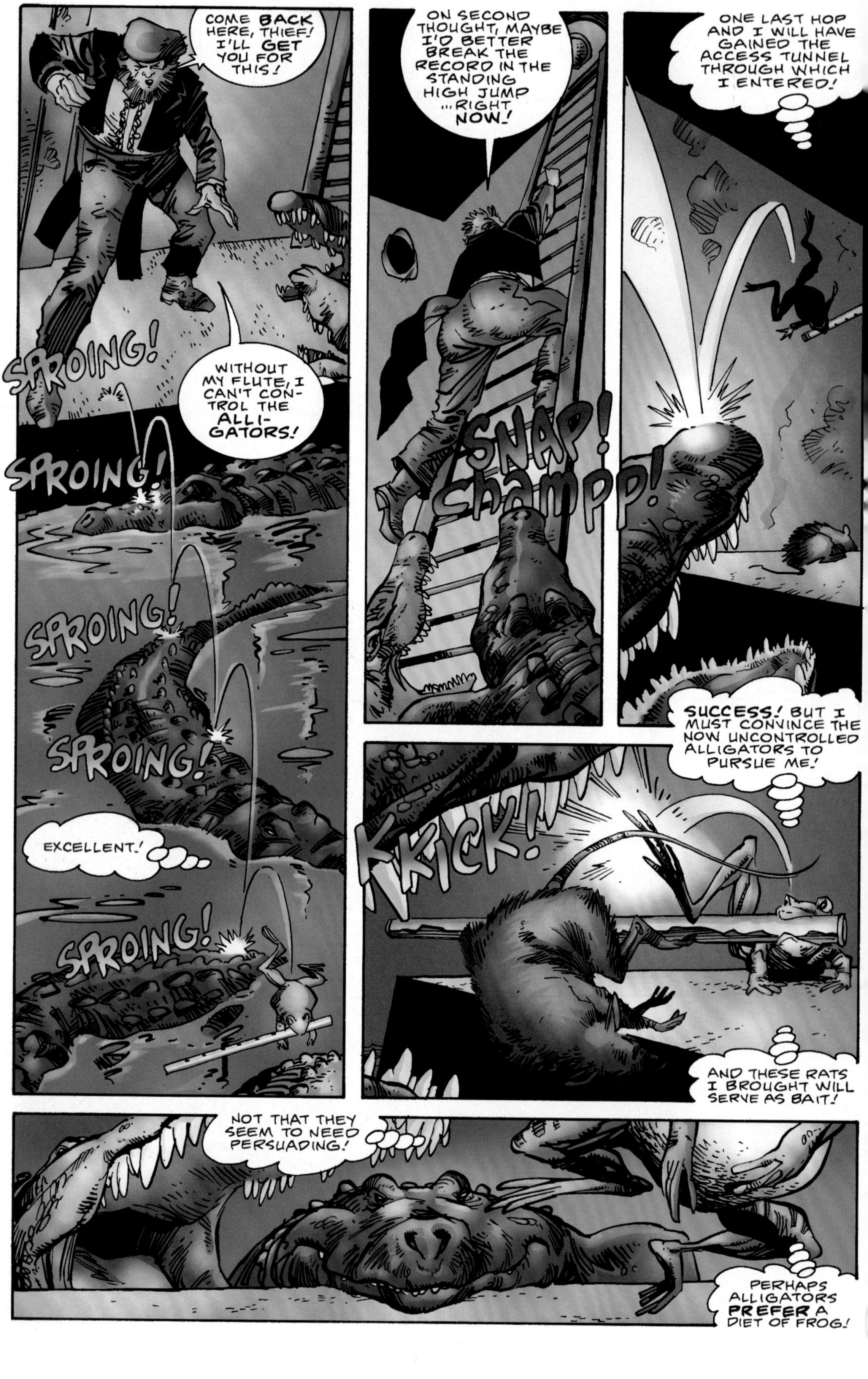
COME BACK HERE, THIEF! I'LL GET YOU FOR THIS!
SPROING!
WITHOUT MY FLUTE, I CAN'T CONTROL THE ALLIGATORS!
SPROING!
SPROING!
SPROING!
EXCELLENT!
SPROING!
ON SECOND THOUGHT, MAYBE I'D BETTER BREAK THE RECORD IN THE STANDING HIGH JUMP ...RIGHT NOW!
SNAP!
CHAMPP!
ONE LAST HOP AND I WILL HAVE GAINED THE ACCESS TUNNEL THROUGH WHICH I ENTERED!
SUCCESS! BUT I MUST CONVINCE THE NOW UNCONTROLLED ALLIGATORS TO PURSUE ME!
KKICK!
AND THESE RATS I BROUGHT WILL SERVE AS BAIT!
NOT THAT THEY SEEM TO NEED PERSUADING!
PERHAPS ALLIGATORS PREFER A DIET OF FROG!

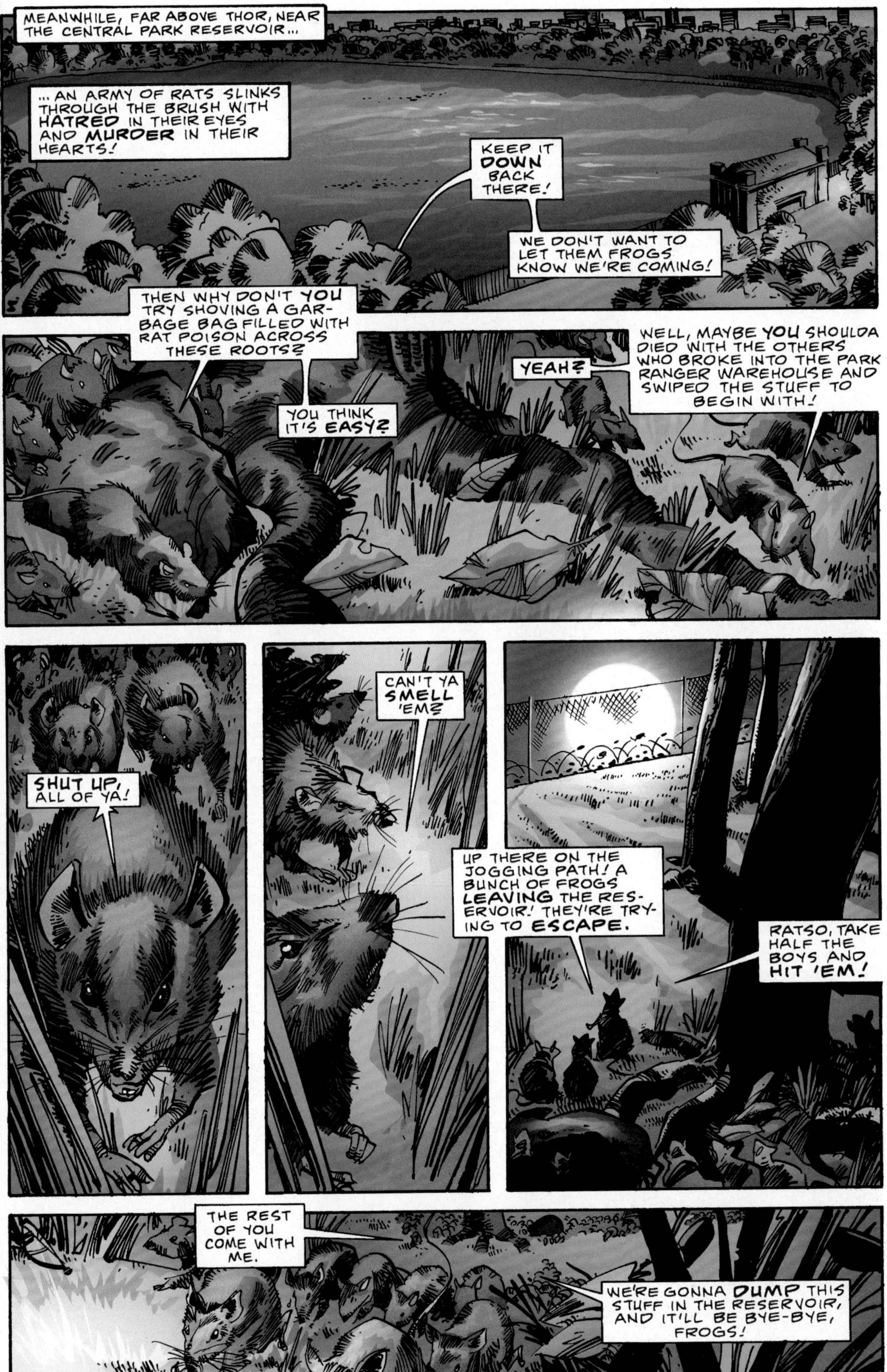

MEANWHILE, FAR ABOVE THOR, NEAR THE CENTRAL PARK RESERVOIR...
...AN ARMY OF RATS SLINKS THROUGH THE BRUSH WITH HATRED IN THEIR EYES AND MURDER IN THEIR HEARTS!
KEEP IT DOWN BACK THERE!
WE DON'T WANT TO LET THEM FROGS KNOW WE'RE COMING!
THEN WHY DON'T YOU TRY SHOVING A GARBAGE BAG FILLED WITH RAT POISON ACROSS THESE ROOTS?
YOU THINK IT'S EASY?
YEAH?
WELL, MAYBE YOU SHOULDA DIED WITH THE OTHERS WHO BROKE INTO THE PARK RANGER WAREHOUSE AND SWIPED THE STUFF TO BEGIN WITH!
SHUT UP, ALL OF YA!
CAN'T YA SMELL 'EM?
UP THERE ON THE JOGGING PATH! A BUNCH OF FROGS LEAVING THE RESERVOIR! THEY'RE TRYING TO ESCAPE.
RATSO, TAKE HALF THE BOYS AND HIT 'EM!
THE REST OF YOU COME WITH ME.
WE'RE GONNA DUMP THIS STUFF IN THE RESERVOIR, AND IT'LL BE BYE-BYE, FROGS!

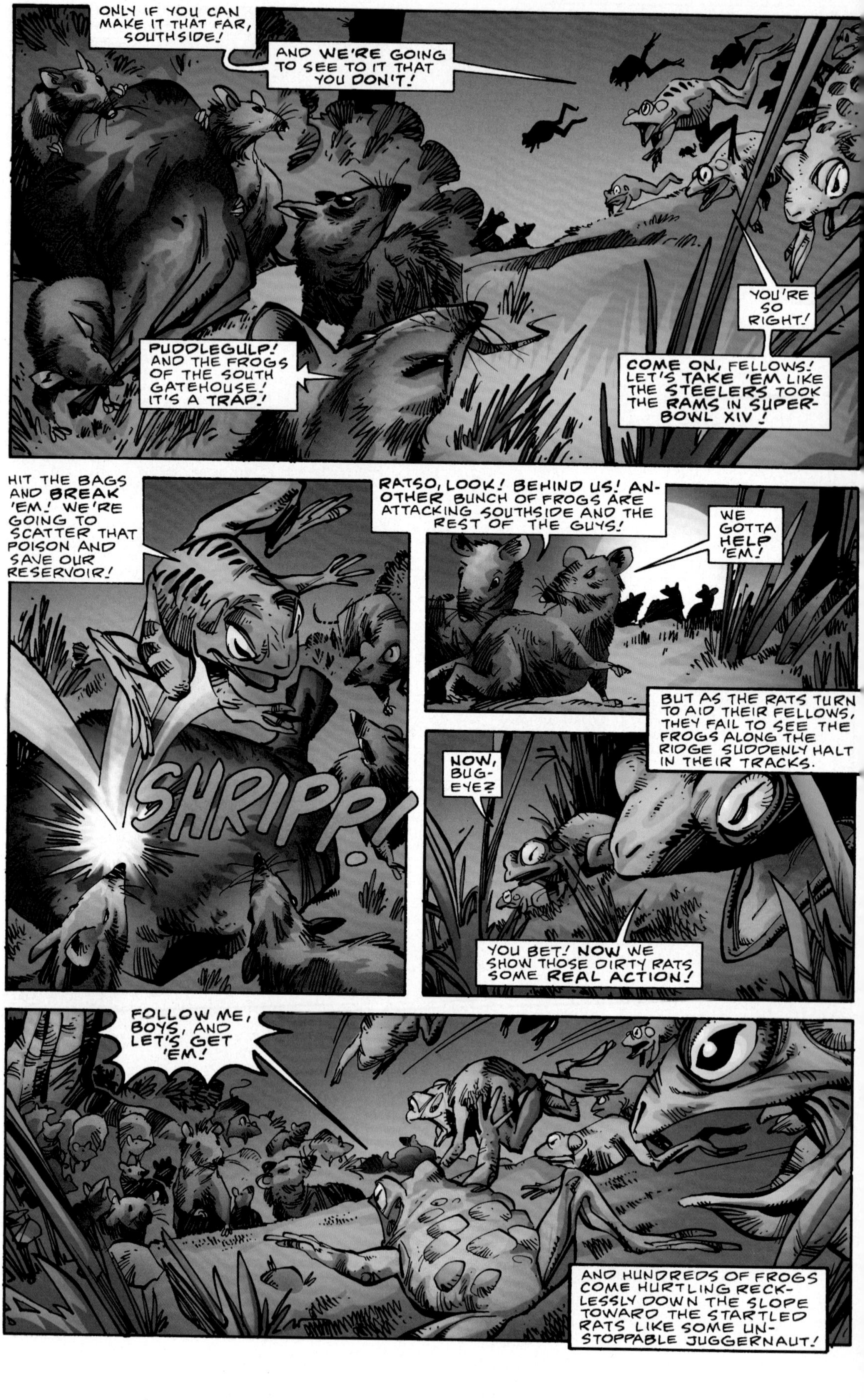
ONLY IF YOU CAN MAKE IT THAT FAR, SOUTHSIDE!
AND WE'RE GOING TO SEE TO IT THAT YOU DON'T!
PUDDLEGULP! AND THE FROGS OF THE SOUTH GATEHOUSE! IT'S A TRAP!
YOU'RE SO RIGHT!
COME ON, FELLOWS! LET'S TAKE 'EM LIKE THE STEELERS TOOK THE RAMS IN SUPER-BOWL XIV!
HIT THE BAGS AND BREAK 'EM! WE'RE GOING TO SCATTER THAT POISON AND SAVE OUR RESERVOIR!
SHRIPP!
RATSO, LOOK! BEHIND US! AN-OTHER BUNCH OF FROGS ARE ATTACKING SOUTHSIDE AND THE REST OF THE GUYS!
WE GOTTA HELP 'EM!
BUT AS THE RATS TURN TO AID THEIR FELLOWS, THEY FAIL TO SEE THE FROGS ALONG THE RIDGE SUDDENLY HALT IN THEIR TRACKS.
NOW, BUG-EYEZ?
YOU BET! NOW WE SHOW THOSE DIRTY RATS SOME REAL ACTION!
FOLLOW ME, BOYS, AND LET'S GET 'EM!
AND HUNDREDS OF FROGS COME HURTLING RECK-LESSLY DOWN THE SLOPE TOWARD THE STARTLED RATS LIKE SOME UN-STOPPABLE JUGGERNAUT!

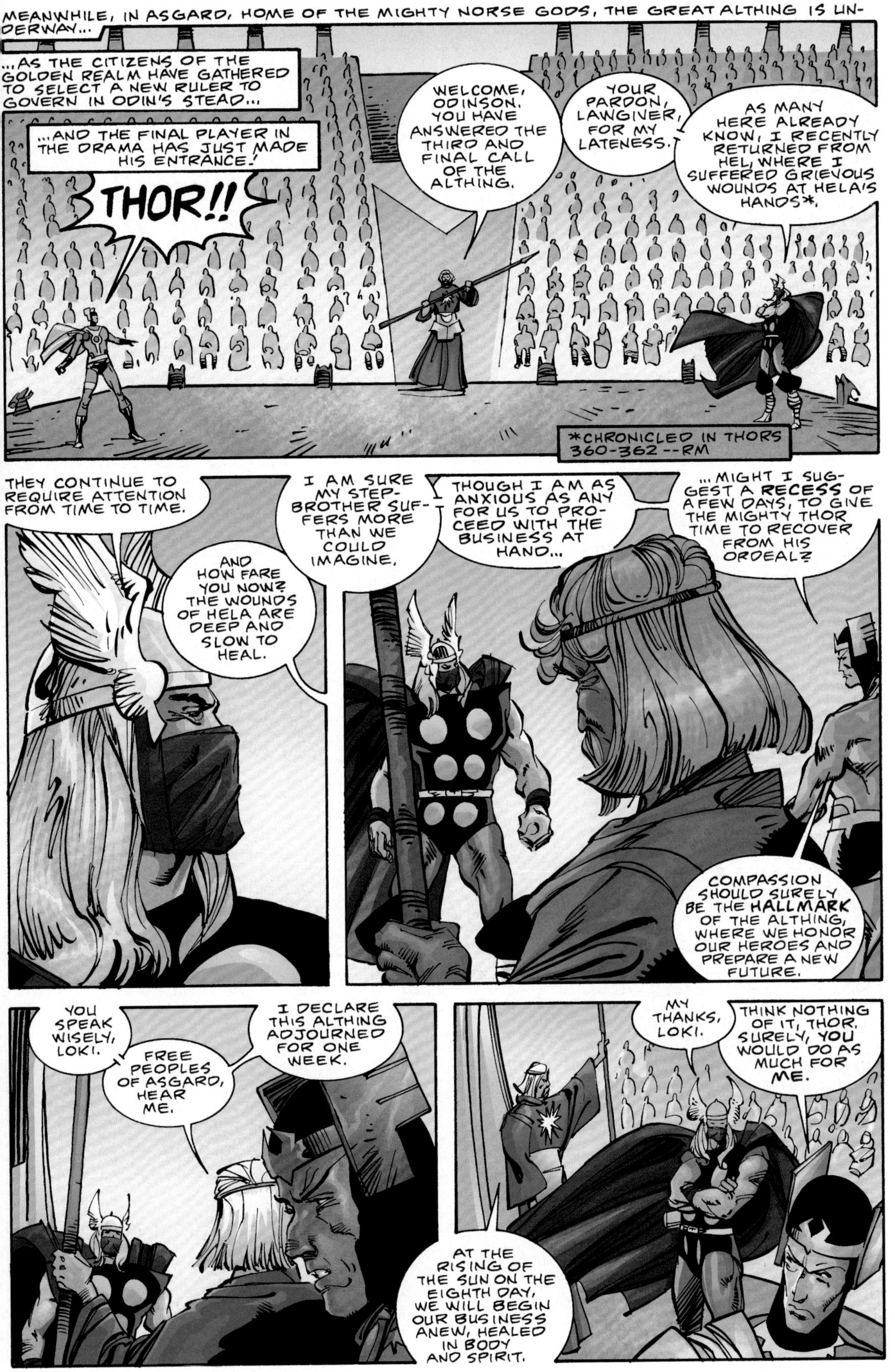
MEANWHILE, IN ASGARD, HOME OF THE MIGHTY NORSE GODS, THE GREAT ALTHING IS UNDERWAY...
...AS THE CITIZENS OF THE GOLDEN REALM HAVE GATHERED TO SELECT A NEW RULER TO GOVERN IN ODIN'S STEAD...
...AND THE FINAL PLAYER IN THE DRAMA HAS JUST MADE HIS ENTRANCE!
THOR!!
WELCOME, ODINSON. YOU HAVE ANSWERED THE THIRD AND FINAL CALL OF THE ALTHING.
YOUR PARDON, LAWGIVER, FOR MY LATENESS.
AS MANY HERE ALREADY KNOW, I RECENTLY RETURNED FROM HEL, WHERE I SUFFERED GRIEVOUS WOUNDS AT HELA'S HANDS*.
*CHRONICLED IN THORS 360-362 --RM
THEY CONTINUE TO REQUIRE ATTENTION FROM TIME TO TIME.
AND HOW FARE YOU NOW? THE WOUNDS OF HELA ARE DEEP AND SLOW TO HEAL.
I AM SURE MY STEP-BROTHER SUFFERS MORE THAN WE COULD IMAGINE.
THOUGH I AM AS ANXIOUS AS ANY FOR US TO PROCEED WITH THE BUSINESS AT HAND...
...MIGHT I SUGGEST A FEW DAYS' RECESS, TO GIVE THE MIGHTY THOR TIME TO RECOVER FROM HIS ORDEAL?
COMPASSION SHOULD SURELY BE THE HALLMARK OF THE ALTHING, WHERE WE HONOR OUR HEROES AND PREPARE A NEW FUTURE.
YOU SPEAK WISELY, LOKI.
FREE PEOPLES OF ASGARD, HEAR ME.
I DECLARE THIS ALTHING ADJOURNED FOR ONE WEEK.
AT THE RISING OF THE SUN ON THE EIGHTH DAY, WE WILL BEGIN OUR BUSINESS ANEW, HEALED IN BODY AND SPIRIT.
MY THANKS, LOKI.
THINK NOTHING OF IT, THOR. SURELY, YOU WOULD DO AS MUCH FOR ME.

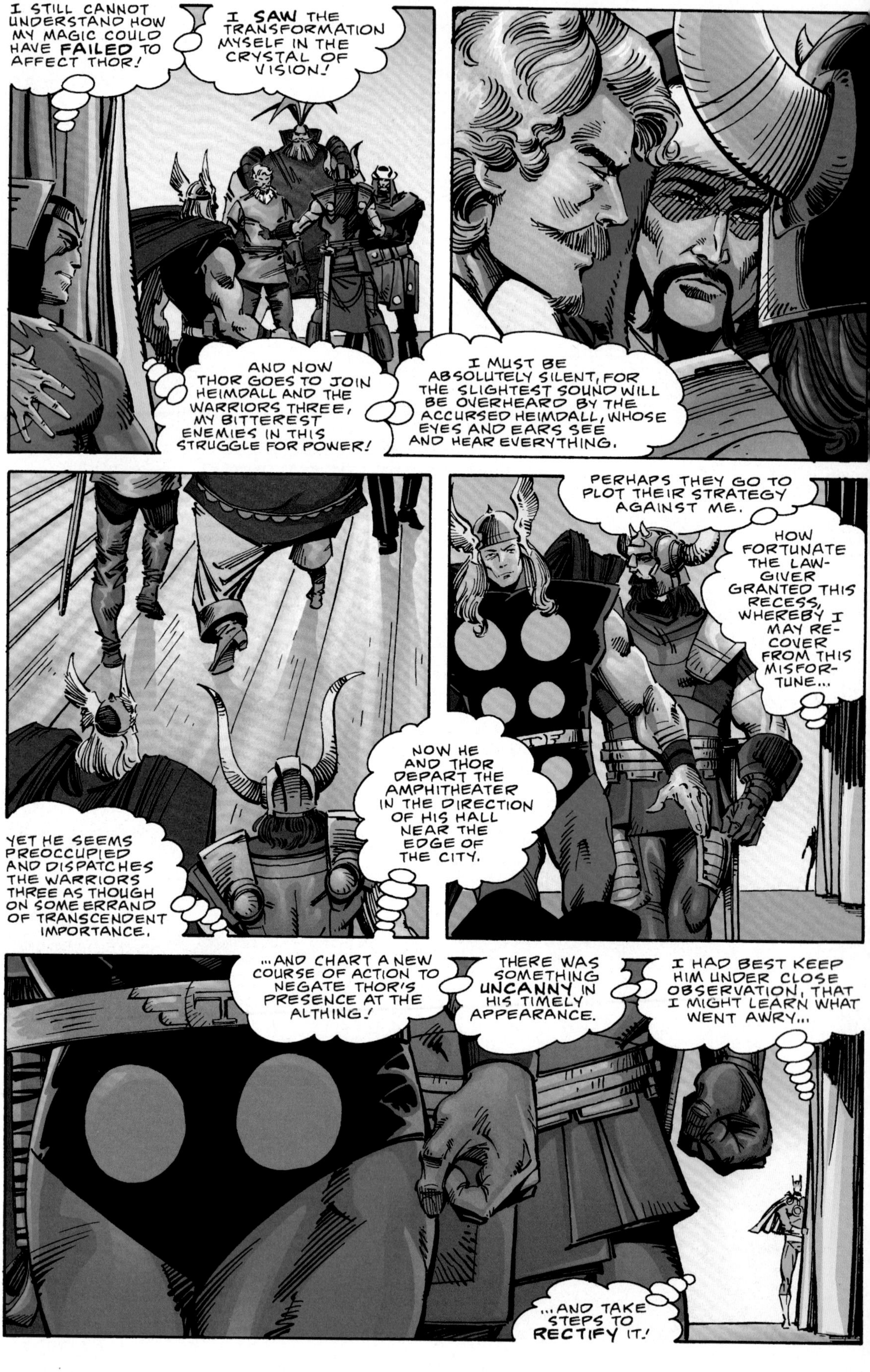
I STILL CANNOT UNDERSTAND HOW MY MAGIC COULD HAVE FAILED TO AFFECT THOR!
I SAW THE TRANSFORMATION MYSELF IN THE CRYSTAL OF VISION!
AND NOW THOR GOES TO JOIN HEIMDALL AND THE WARRIORS THREE, MY BITTEREST ENEMIES IN THIS STRUGGLE FOR POWER!
I MUST BE ABSOLUTELY SILENT, FOR THE SLIGHTEST SOUND WILL BE OVERHEARD BY THE ACCURSED HEIMDALL, WHOSE EYES AND EARS SEE AND HEAR EVERYTHING.
YET HE SEEMS PREOCCUPIED AND DISPATCHES THE WARRIORS THREE AS THOUGH ON SOME ERRAND OF TRANSCENDENT IMPORTANCE.
NOW HE AND THOR DEPART THE AMPHITHEATER IN THE DIRECTION OF HIS HALL NEAR THE EDGE OF THE CITY.
PERHAPS THEY GO TO PLOT THEIR STRATEGY AGAINST ME.
HOW FORTUNATE THE LAW-GIVER GRANTED THIS RECESS, WHEREBY I MAY RECOVER FROM THIS MISFORTUNE...
...AND CHART A NEW COURSE OF ACTION TO NEGATE THOR'S PRESENCE AT THE ALTHING!
THERE WAS SOMETHING UNCANNY IN HIS TIMELY APPEARANCE.
I HAD BEST KEEP HIM UNDER CLOSE OBSERVATION, THAT I MIGHT LEARN WHAT WENT AWRY...
...AND TAKE STEPS TO RECTIFY IT!

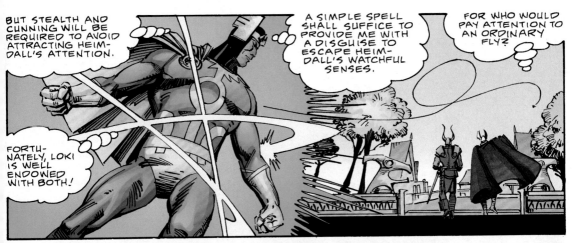

BUT STEALTH AND CUNNING WILL BE REQUIRED TO AVOID ATTRACTING HEIMDALL'S ATTENTION.

A SIMPLE SPELL SHALL SUFFICE TO PROVIDE ME WITH A DISGUISE TO ESCAPE HEIMDALL'S WATCHFUL SENSES.

FOR WHO WOULD PAY ATTENTION TO AN ORDINARY FLY?

FORTUNATELY, LOKI IS WELL ENDOWED WITH BOTH!

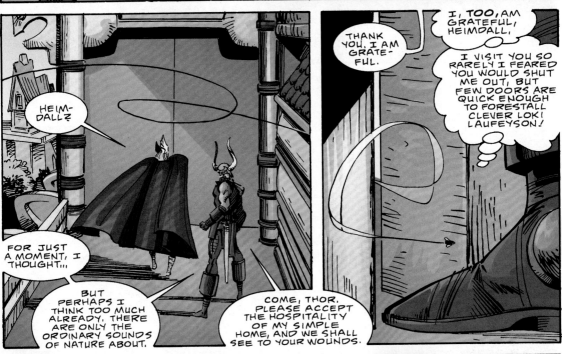

HEIMDALL?

FOR JUST A MOMENT, I THOUGHT...

BUT PERHAPS I THINK TOO MUCH ALREADY. THERE ARE ONLY THE ORDINARY SOUNDS OF NATURE ABOUT.

THANK YOU, I AM GRATEFUL.

COME, THOR, PLEASE ACCEPT THE HOSPITALITY OF MY SIMPLE HOME, AND WE SHALL SEE TO YOUR WOUNDS.

I, TOO, AM GRATEFUL, HEIMDALL.

I VISIT YOU SO RARELY I FEARED YOU WOULD SHUT ME OUT, BUT FEW DOORS ARE QUICK ENOUGH TO FORESTALL CLEVER LOKI LAUFEYSON!

LET US RETIRE TO MY PRIVATE CHAMBERS, THOR, AND THERE WE SHALL DISCUSS ALL THAT IS NEEDFUL.

BUT I THINK THAT WE HAD BEST TAKE PRECAUTIONS AGAINST BEING OVERHEARD, MY LORD.

I WILL SEAL THE DOORWAY WITH MY URU SWORD.

SHOULD ANY CREATURE, GREAT OR SMALL, ATTEMPT TO PASS THIS BARRIER...

...THE BLADE WILL HUM AND I SHALL KNOW THAT THERE ARE SPIES ABOUT.

CURSES!

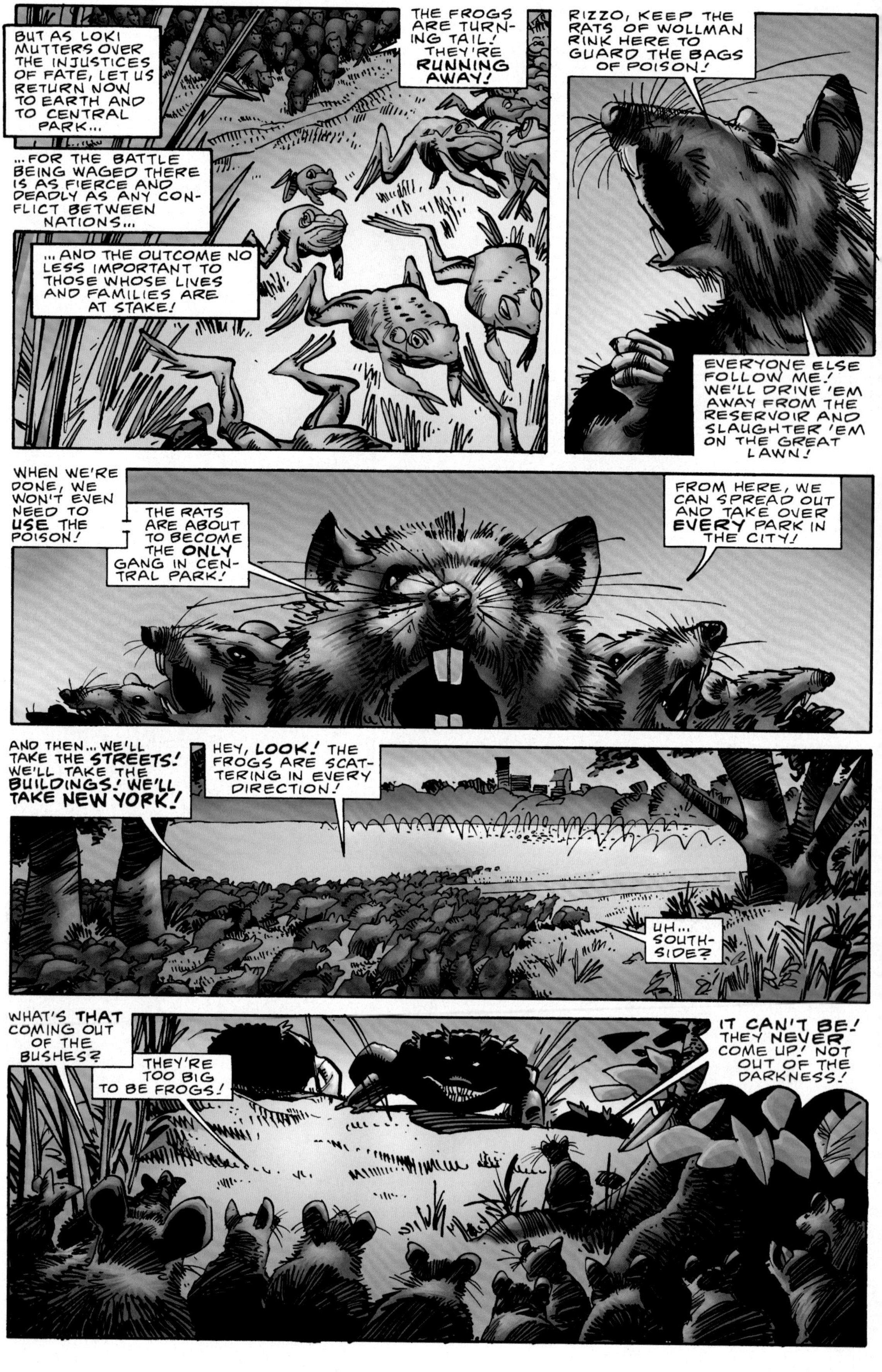

BUT AS LOKI MUTTERS OVER THE INJUSTICES OF FATE, LET US RETURN NOW TO EARTH AND TO CENTRAL PARK...
...FOR THE BATTLE BEING WAGED THERE IS AS FIERCE AND DEADLY AS ANY CONFLICT BETWEEN NATIONS...
...AND THE OUTCOME NO LESS IMPORTANT TO THOSE WHOSE LIVES AND FAMILIES ARE AT STAKE!
THE FROGS ARE TURNING TAIL! THEY'RE RUNNING AWAY!
RIZZO, KEEP THE RATS OF WOLLMAN RINK HERE TO GUARD THE BAGS OF POISON!
EVERYONE ELSE FOLLOW ME! WE'LL DRIVE 'EM AWAY FROM THE RESERVOIR AND SLAUGHTER 'EM ON THE GREAT LAWN!
WHEN WE'RE DONE, WE WON'T EVEN NEED TO USE THE POISON!
THE RATS ARE ABOUT TO BECOME THE ONLY GANG IN CENTRAL PARK!
FROM HERE, WE CAN SPREAD OUT AND TAKE OVER EVERY PARK IN THE CITY!
AND THEN... WE'LL TAKE THE STREETS! WE'LL TAKE THE BUILDINGS! WE'LL TAKE NEW YORK!
HEY, LOOK! THE FROGS ARE SCATTERING IN EVERY DIRECTION!
UH... SOUTHSIDE?
WHAT'S THAT COMING OUT OF THE BUSHES?
THEY'RE TOO BIG TO BE FROGS!
IT CAN'T BE! THEY NEVER COME UP! NOT OUT OF THE DARKNESS!

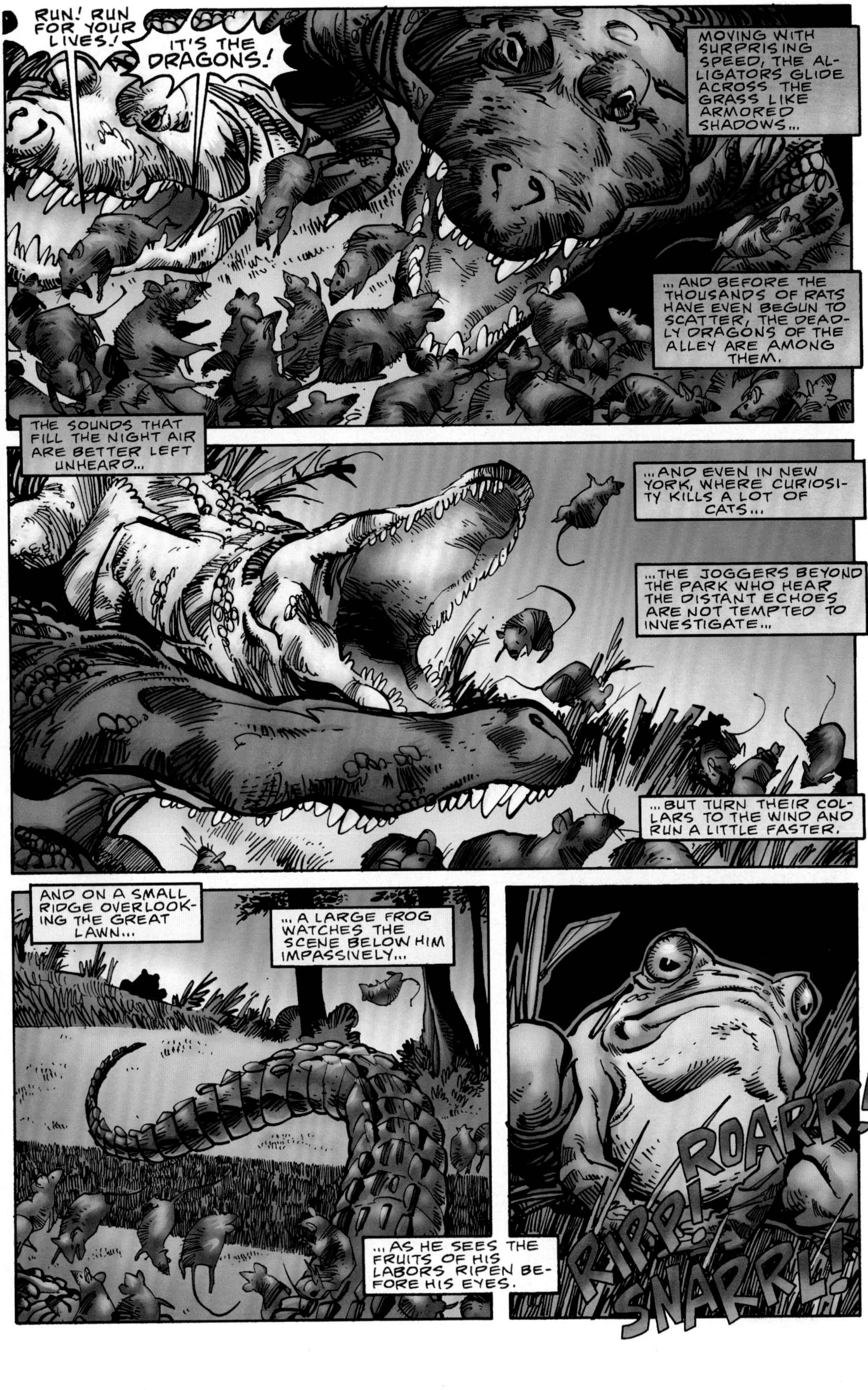
RUN! RUN FOR YOUR LIVES!
IT'S THE DRAGONS!
MOVING WITH SURPRISING SPEED, THE ALLIGATORS GLIDE ACROSS THE GRASS LIKE ARMORED SHADOWS...
...AND BEFORE THE THOUSANDS OF RATS HAVE EVEN BEGUN TO SCATTER, THE DEADLY DRAGONS OF THE ALLEY ARE AMONG THEM.
THE SOUNDS THAT FILL THE NIGHT AIR ARE BETTER LEFT UNHEARD...
...AND EVEN IN NEW YORK, WHERE CURIOSITY KILLS A LOT OF CATS...
...THE JOGGERS BEYOND THE PARK WHO HEAR THE DISTANT ECHOES ARE NOT TEMPTED TO INVESTIGATE...
...BUT TURN THEIR COLLARS TO THE WIND AND RUN A LITTLE FASTER.
AND ON A SMALL RIDGE OVERLOOKING THE GREAT LAWN...
...A LARGE FROG WATCHES THE SCENE BELOW HIM IMPASSIVELY...
...AS HE SEES THE FRUITS OF HIS LABORS RIPEN BEFORE HIS EYES.
ROARR!
RIPP!
SNARRL!

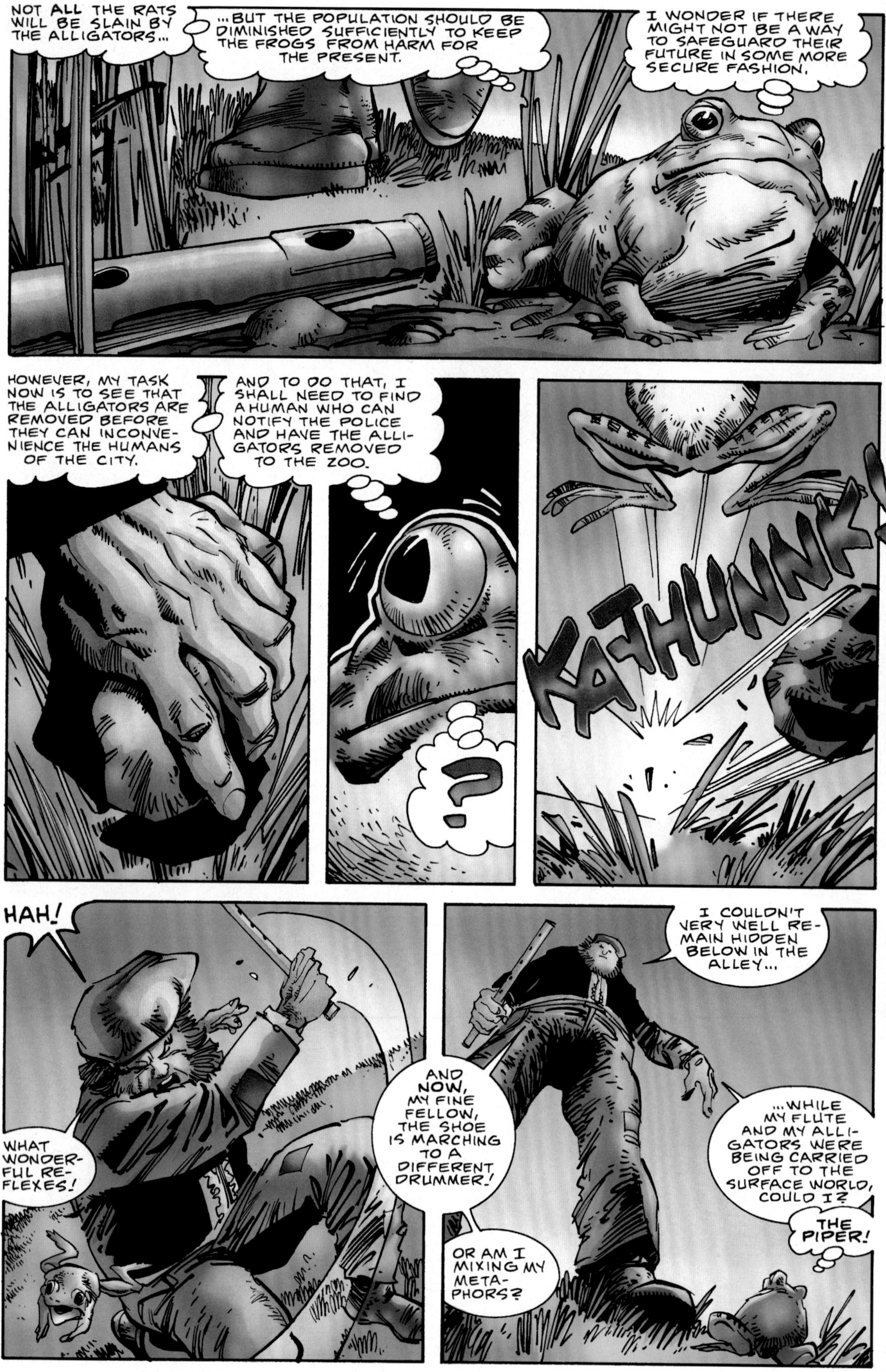
NOT ALL THE RATS WILL BE SLAIN BY THE ALLIGATORS...
...BUT THE POPULATION SHOULD BE DIMINISHED SUFFICIENTLY TO KEEP THE FROGS FROM HARM FOR THE PRESENT.
I WONDER IF THERE MIGHT NOT BE A WAY TO SAFEGUARD THEIR FUTURE IN SOME MORE SECURE FASHION.
HOWEVER, MY TASK NOW IS TO SEE THAT THE ALLIGATORS ARE REMOVED BEFORE THEY CAN INCONVENIENCE THE HUMANS OF THE CITY.
AND TO DO THAT, I SHALL NEED TO FIND A HUMAN WHO CAN NOTIFY THE POLICE AND HAVE THE ALLIGATORS REMOVED TO THE ZOO.
?
KATHUNNK!
HAH!
WHAT WONDERFUL REFLEXES!
AND NOW, MY FINE FELLOW, THE SHOE IS MARCHING TO A DIFFERENT DRUMMER!
OR AM I MIXING MY METAPHORS?
I COULDN'T VERY WELL REMAIN HIDDEN BELOW IN THE ALLEY...
...WHILE MY FLUTE AND MY ALLIGATORS WERE BEING CARRIED OFF TO THE SURFACE WORLD, COULD I?
THE PIPER!

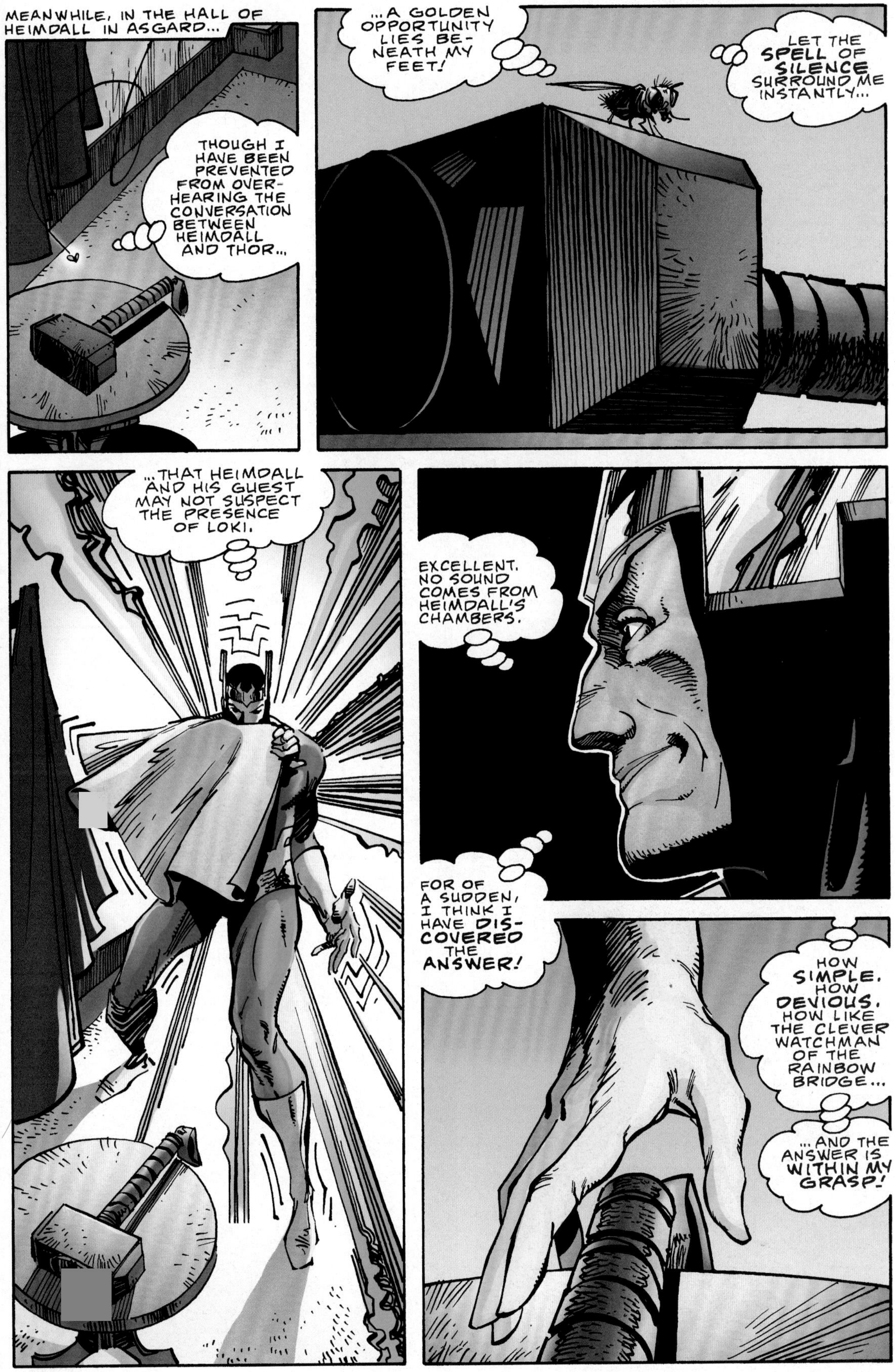
MEANWHILE, IN THE HALL OF HEIMDALL IN ASGARD...
THOUGH I HAVE BEEN PREVENTED FROM OVER-HEARING THE CONVERSATION BETWEEN HEIMDALL AND THOR...
...A GOLDEN OPPORTUNITY LIES BE-NEATH MY FEET!
LET THE SPELL OF SILENCE SURROUND ME INSTANTLY...
...THAT HEIMDALL AND HIS GUEST MAY NOT SUSPECT THE PRESENCE OF LOKI.
EXCELLENT. NO SOUND COMES FROM HEIMDALL'S CHAMBERS.
FOR OF A SUDDEN, I THINK I HAVE DIS-COVERED THE ANSWER!
HOW SIMPLE. HOW DEVIOUS. HOW LIKE THE CLEVER WATCHMAN OF THE RAINBOW BRIDGE...
...AND THE ANSWER IS WITHIN MY GRASP!

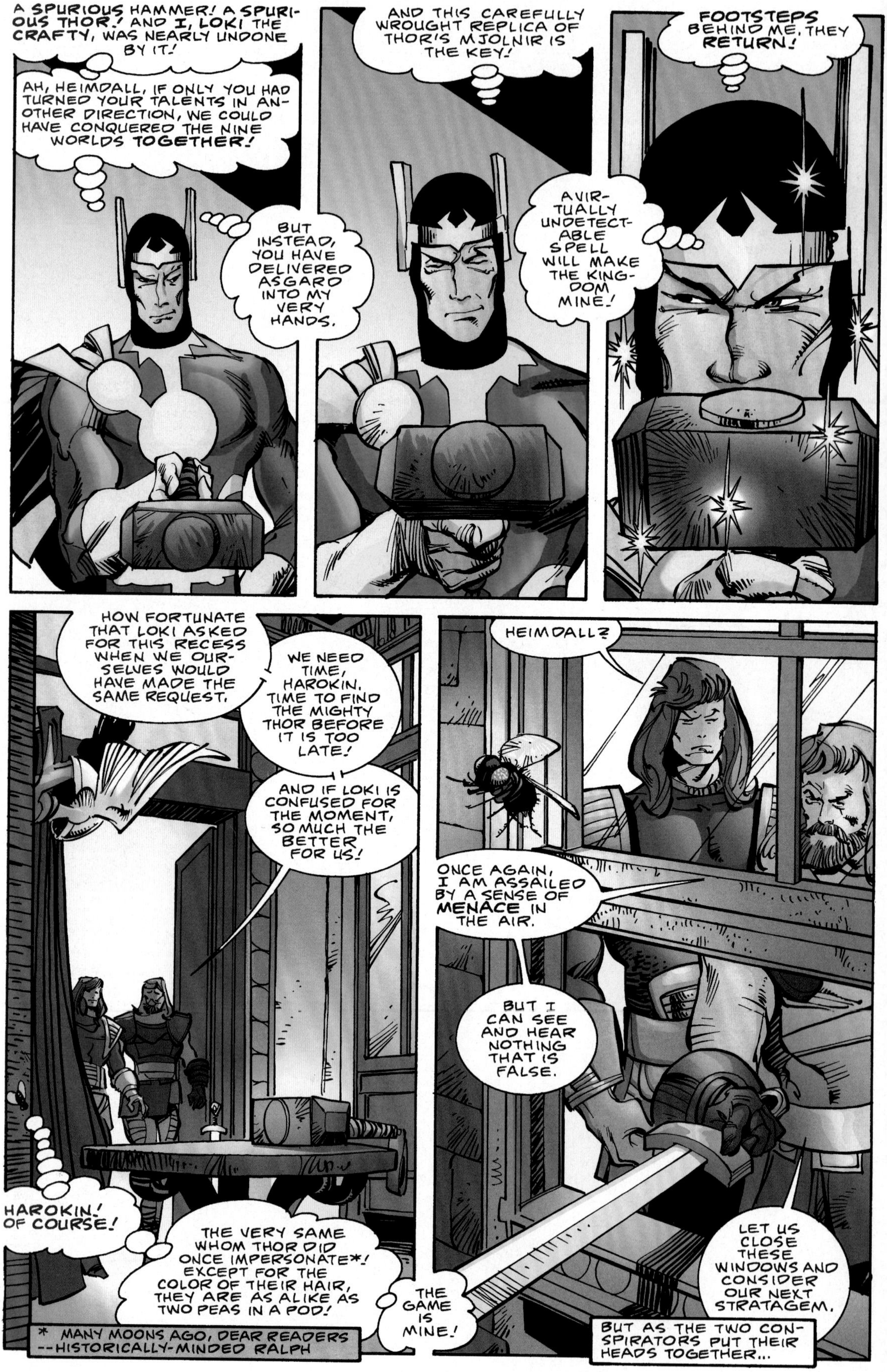
A SPURIOUS HAMMER! A SPURIOUS THOR! AND I, LOKI THE CRAFTY, WAS NEARLY UNDONE BY IT!
AH, HEIMDALL, IF ONLY YOU HAD TURNED YOUR TALENTS IN ANOTHER DIRECTION, WE COULD HAVE CONQUERED THE NINE WORLDS TOGETHER!
BUT INSTEAD, YOU HAVE DELIVERED ASGARD INTO MY VERY HANDS.
AND THIS CAREFULLY WROUGHT REPLICA OF THOR'S MJOLNIR IS THE KEY!
A VIRTUALLY UNDETECTABLE SPELL WILL MAKE THE KINGDOM MINE!
FOOTSTEPS BEHIND ME, THEY RETURN!
HOW FORTUNATE THAT LOKI ASKED FOR THIS RECESS WHEN WE OURSELVES WOULD HAVE MADE THE SAME REQUEST.
WE NEED TIME, HAROKIN. TIME TO FIND THE MIGHTY THOR BEFORE IT IS TOO LATE!
AND IF LOKI IS CONFUSED FOR THE MOMENT, SO MUCH THE BETTER FOR US!
HAROKIN! OF COURSE!
THE VERY SAME WHOM THOR DID ONCE IMPERSONATE*! EXCEPT FOR THE COLOR OF THEIR HAIR, THEY ARE AS ALIKE AS TWO PEAS IN A POD!
* MANY MOONS AGO, DEAR READERS --HISTORICALLY-MINDED RALPH
THE GAME IS MINE!
HEIMDALL?
ONCE AGAIN, I AM ASSAILED BY A SENSE OF MENACE IN THE AIR.
BUT I CAN SEE AND HEAR NOTHING THAT IS FALSE.
LET US CLOSE THESE WINDOWS AND CONSIDER OUR NEXT STRATAGEM.
BUT AS THE TWO CONSPIRATORS PUT THEIR HEADS TOGETHER...

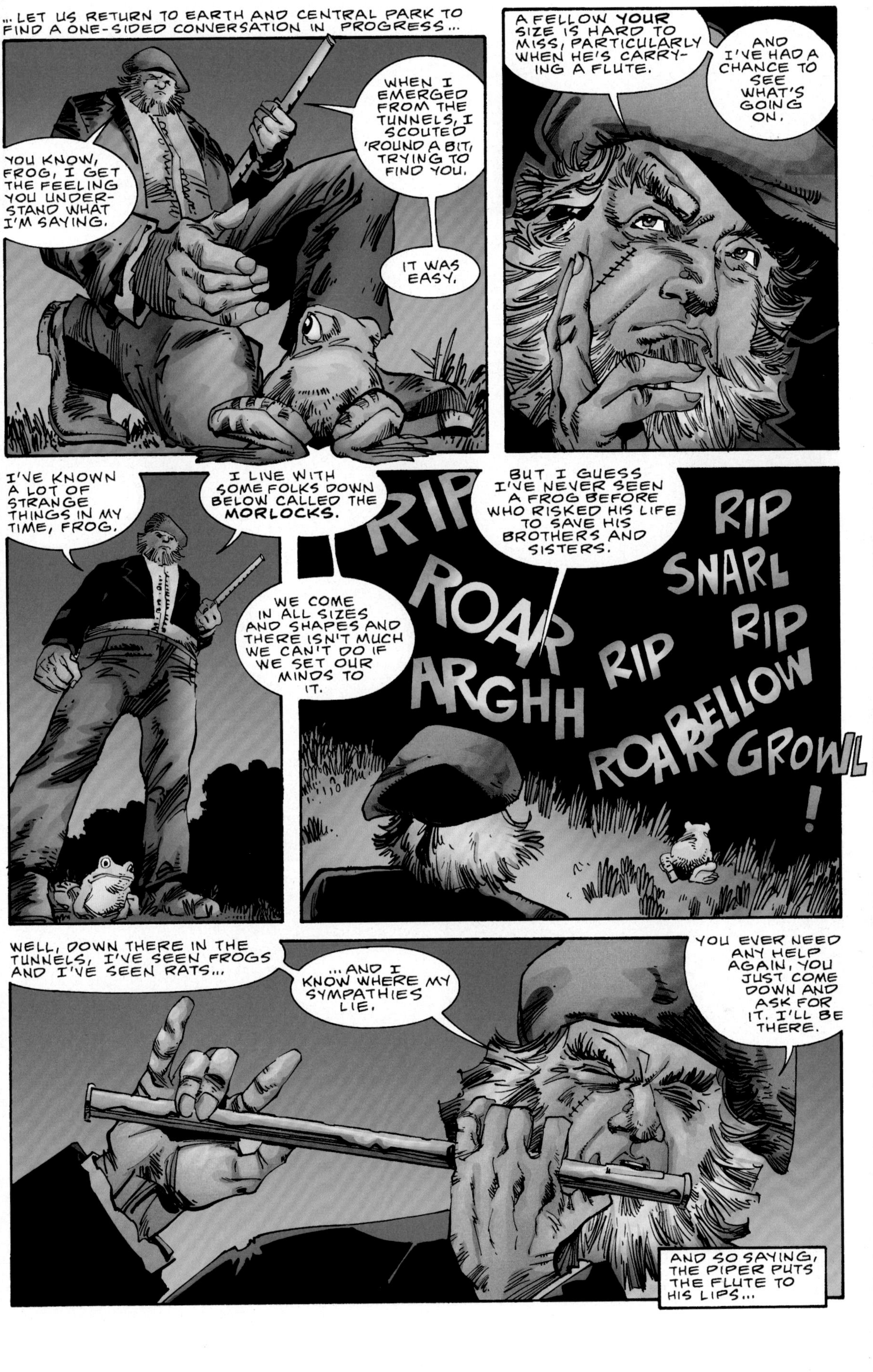
...LET US RETURN TO EARTH AND CENTRAL PARK TO FIND A ONE-SIDED CONVERSATION IN PROGRESS...
YOU KNOW, FROG, I GET THE FEELING YOU UNDERSTAND WHAT I'M SAYING.
WHEN I EMERGED FROM THE TUNNELS, I SCOUTED 'ROUND A BIT, TRYING TO FIND YOU.
IT WAS EASY.
A FELLOW YOUR SIZE IS HARD TO MISS, PARTICULARLY WHEN HE'S CARRYING A FLUTE.
AND I'VE HAD A CHANCE TO SEE WHAT'S GOING ON.
I'VE KNOWN A LOT OF STRANGE THINGS IN MY TIME, FROG.
I LIVE WITH SOME FOLKS DOWN BELOW CALLED THE MORLOCKS.
WE COME IN ALL SIZES AND SHAPES AND THERE ISN'T MUCH WE CAN'T DO IF WE SET OUR MINDS TO IT.
BUT I GUESS I'VE NEVER SEEN A FROG BEFORE WHO RISKED HIS LIFE TO SAVE HIS BROTHERS AND SISTERS.
RIP RIP SNARL ROAR RIP RIP ARGHH ROAR BELLOW GROWL !
WELL, DOWN THERE IN THE TUNNELS, I'VE SEEN FROGS AND I'VE SEEN RATS...
...AND I KNOW WHERE MY SYMPATHIES LIE.
YOU EVER NEED ANY HELP AGAIN, YOU JUST COME DOWN AND ASK FOR IT. I'LL BE THERE.
AND SO SAYING, THE PIPER PUTS THE FLUTE TO HIS LIPS...

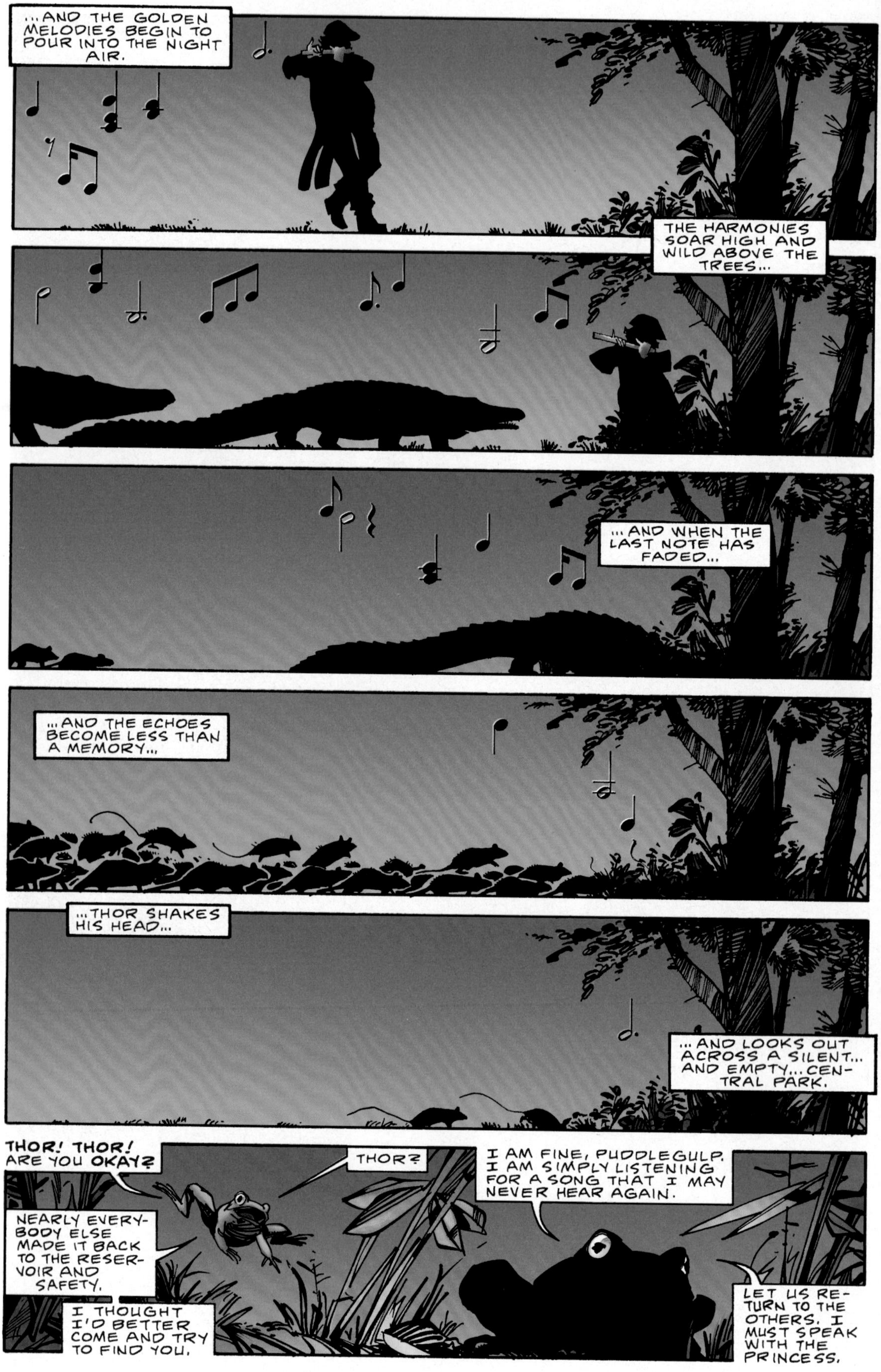

...AND THE GOLDEN MELODIES BEGIN TO POUR INTO THE NIGHT AIR.
THE HARMONIES SOAR HIGH AND WILD ABOVE THE TREES...
...AND WHEN THE LAST NOTE HAS FADED...
...AND THE ECHOES BECOME LESS THAN A MEMORY...
...THOR SHAKES HIS HEAD...
...AND LOOKS OUT ACROSS A SILENT... AND EMPTY... CENTRAL PARK.
THOR! THOR! ARE YOU OKAY?
NEARLY EVERYBODY ELSE MADE IT BACK TO THE RESERVOIR AND SAFETY.
I THOUGHT I'D BETTER COME AND TRY TO FIND YOU.
THOR?
I AM FINE, PUDDLEGULP. I AM SIMPLY LISTENING FOR A SONG THAT I MAY NEVER HEAR AGAIN.
LET US RETURN TO THE OTHERS. I MUST SPEAK WITH THE PRINCESS.

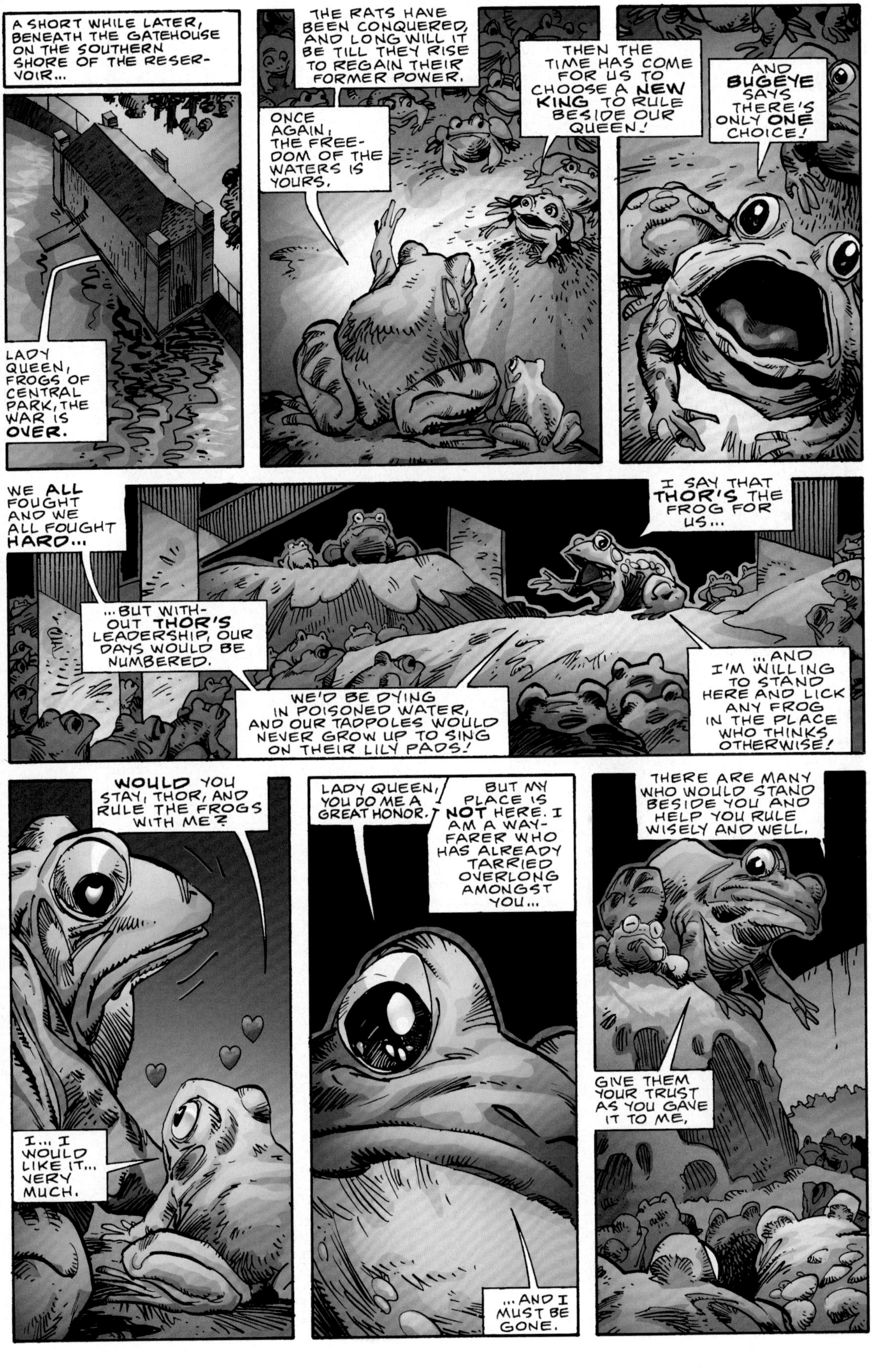

A SHORT WHILE LATER, BENEATH THE GATEHOUSE ON THE SOUTHERN SHORE OF THE RESERVOIR...
LADY QUEEN, FROGS OF CENTRAL PARK, THE WAR IS **OVER.**
THE RATS HAVE BEEN CONQUERED, AND LONG WILL IT BE TILL THEY RISE TO REGAIN THEIR FORMER POWER.
ONCE AGAIN, THE FREEDOM OF THE WATERS IS YOURS.
THEN THE TIME HAS COME FOR US TO CHOOSE A **NEW KING** TO RULE BESIDE OUR QUEEN!
AND **BUGEYE** SAYS THERE'S ONLY **ONE** CHOICE!
WE **ALL** FOUGHT AND WE ALL FOUGHT **HARD...**
...BUT WITHOUT **THOR'S** LEADERSHIP, OUR DAYS WOULD BE NUMBERED.
WE'D BE DYING IN POISONED WATER, AND OUR TADPOLES WOULD NEVER GROW UP TO SING ON THEIR LILY PADS!
I SAY THAT **THOR'S** THE FROG FOR US...
...AND I'M WILLING TO STAND HERE AND LICK ANY FROG IN THE PLACE WHO THINKS OTHERWISE!
WOULD YOU STAY, THOR, AND RULE THE FROGS WITH ME?
I... I WOULD LIKE IT... VERY MUCH.
LADY QUEEN, YOU DO ME A GREAT HONOR.
BUT MY PLACE IS **NOT** HERE. I AM A WAYFARER WHO HAS ALREADY TARRIED OVERLONG AMONGST YOU...
...AND I MUST BE GONE.
THERE ARE MANY WHO WOULD STAND BESIDE YOU AND HELP YOU RULE WISELY AND WELL.
GIVE THEM YOUR TRUST AS YOU GAVE IT TO ME.

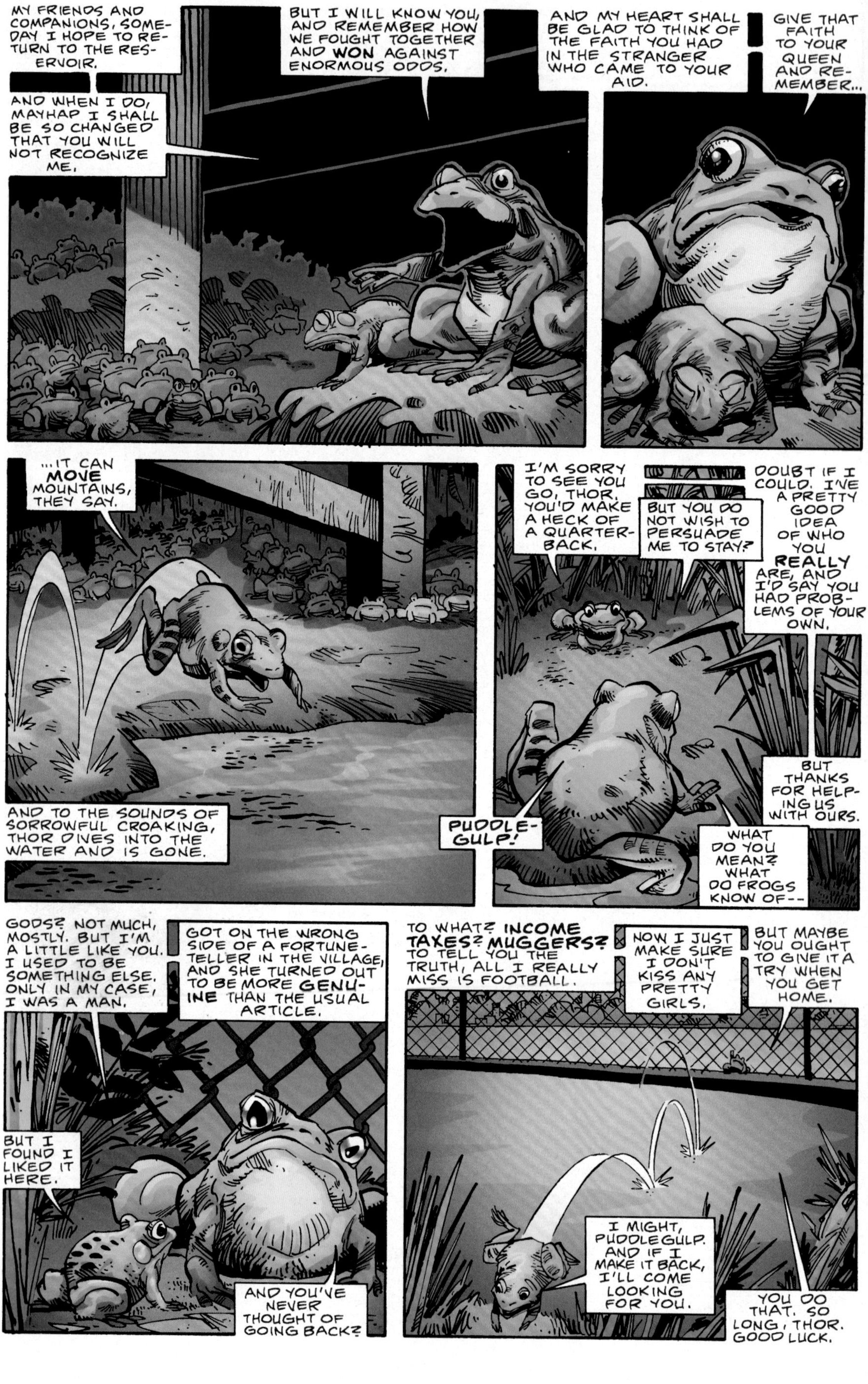
MY FRIENDS AND COMPANIONS, SOME-DAY I HOPE TO RE-TURN TO THE RES-ERVOIR.
AND WHEN I DO, MAYHAP I SHALL BE SO CHANGED THAT YOU WILL NOT RECOGNIZE ME.
BUT I WILL KNOW YOU, AND REMEMBER HOW WE FOUGHT TOGETHER AND WON AGAINST ENORMOUS ODDS.
AND MY HEART SHALL BE GLAD TO THINK OF THE FAITH YOU HAD IN THE STRANGER WHO CAME TO YOUR AID.
GIVE THAT FAITH TO YOUR QUEEN AND RE-MEMBER...
...IT CAN MOVE MOUNTAINS, THEY SAY.
AND TO THE SOUNDS OF SORROWFUL CROAKING, THOR DIVES INTO THE WATER AND IS GONE.
I'M SORRY TO SEE YOU GO, THOR. YOU'D MAKE A HECK OF A QUARTER-BACK.
BUT YOU DO NOT WISH TO PERSUADE ME TO STAY?
DOUBT IF I COULD. I'VE A PRETTY GOOD IDEA OF WHO YOU REALLY ARE, AND I'D SAY YOU HAD PROB-LEMS OF YOUR OWN.
BUT THANKS FOR HELP-ING US WITH OURS.
PUDDLE-GULP!
WHAT DO YOU MEAN? WHAT DO FROGS KNOW OF--
GODS? NOT MUCH, MOSTLY. BUT I'M A LITTLE LIKE YOU. I USED TO BE SOMETHING ELSE. ONLY IN MY CASE, I WAS A MAN.
GOT ON THE WRONG SIDE OF A FORTUNE-TELLER IN THE VILLAGE, AND SHE TURNED OUT TO BE MORE GENU-INE THAN THE USUAL ARTICLE.
BUT I FOUND I LIKED IT HERE.
AND YOU'VE NEVER THOUGHT OF GOING BACK?
TO WHAT? INCOME TAXES? MUGGERS? TO TELL YOU THE TRUTH, ALL I REALLY MISS IS FOOTBALL.
NOW I JUST MAKE SURE I DON'T KISS ANY PRETTY GIRLS.
BUT MAYBE YOU OUGHT TO GIVE IT A TRY WHEN YOU GET HOME.
I MIGHT, PUDDLEGULP. AND IF I MAKE IT BACK, I'LL COME LOOKING FOR YOU.
YOU DO THAT. SO LONG, THOR. GOOD LUCK.

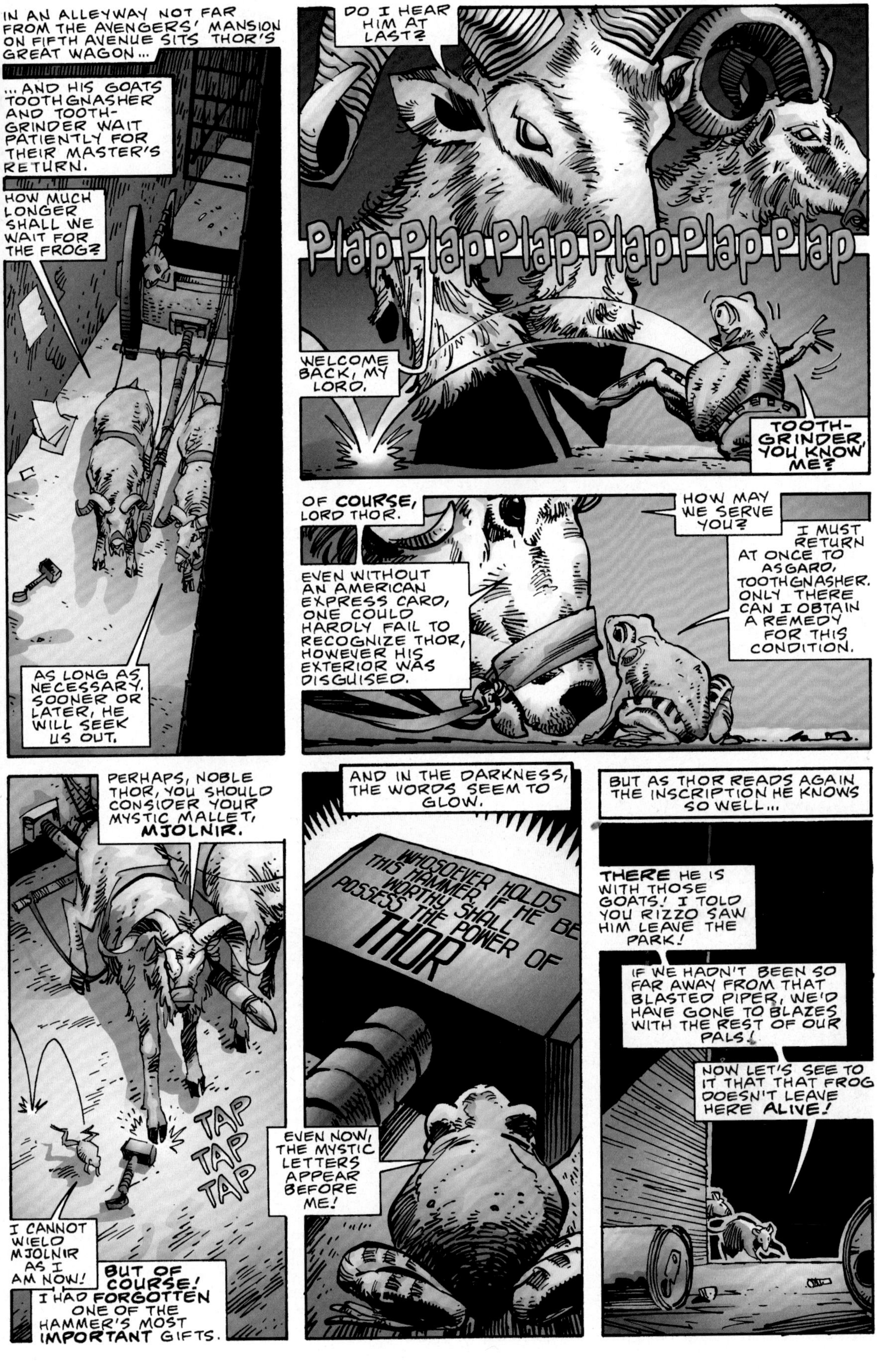
IN AN ALLEYWAY NOT FAR FROM THE AVENGERS' MANSION ON FIFTH AVENUE SITS THOR'S GREAT WAGON...
...AND HIS GOATS TOOTHGNASHER AND TOOTH-GRINDER WAIT PATIENTLY FOR THEIR MASTER'S RETURN.
HOW MUCH LONGER SHALL WE WAIT FOR THE FROG?
AS LONG AS NECESSARY. SOONER OR LATER, HE WILL SEEK US OUT.
DO I HEAR HIM AT LAST?
Plap Plap Plap Plap Plap Plap Plap
WELCOME BACK, MY LORD.
TOOTH-GRINDER, YOU KNOW ME?
OF COURSE, LORD THOR.
HOW MAY WE SERVE YOU?
EVEN WITHOUT AN AMERICAN EXPRESS CARD, ONE COULD HARDLY FAIL TO RECOGNIZE THOR, HOWEVER HIS EXTERIOR WAS DISGUISED.
I MUST RETURN AT ONCE TO ASGARD, TOOTHGNASHER. ONLY THERE CAN I OBTAIN A REMEDY FOR THIS CONDITION.
PERHAPS, NOBLE THOR, YOU SHOULD CONSIDER YOUR MYSTIC MALLET, MJOLNIR.
TAP TAP TAP
I CANNOT WIELD MJOLNIR AS I AM NOW!
BUT OF COURSE! I HAD FORGOTTEN ONE OF THE HAMMER'S MOST IMPORTANT GIFTS.
AND IN THE DARKNESS, THE WORDS SEEM TO GLOW.
WHOSOEVER HOLDS THIS HAMMER, IF HE BE WORTHY, SHALL POSSESS THE POWER OF THOR
EVEN NOW, THE MYSTIC LETTERS APPEAR BEFORE ME!
BUT AS THOR READS AGAIN THE INSCRIPTION HE KNOWS SO WELL...
THERE HE IS WITH THOSE GOATS! I TOLD YOU RIZZO SAW HIM LEAVE THE PARK!
IF WE HADN'T BEEN SO FAR AWAY FROM THAT BLASTED PIPER, WE'D HAVE GONE TO BLAZES WITH THE REST OF OUR PALS!
NOW LET'S SEE TO IT THAT THAT FROG DOESN'T LEAVE HERE ALIVE!

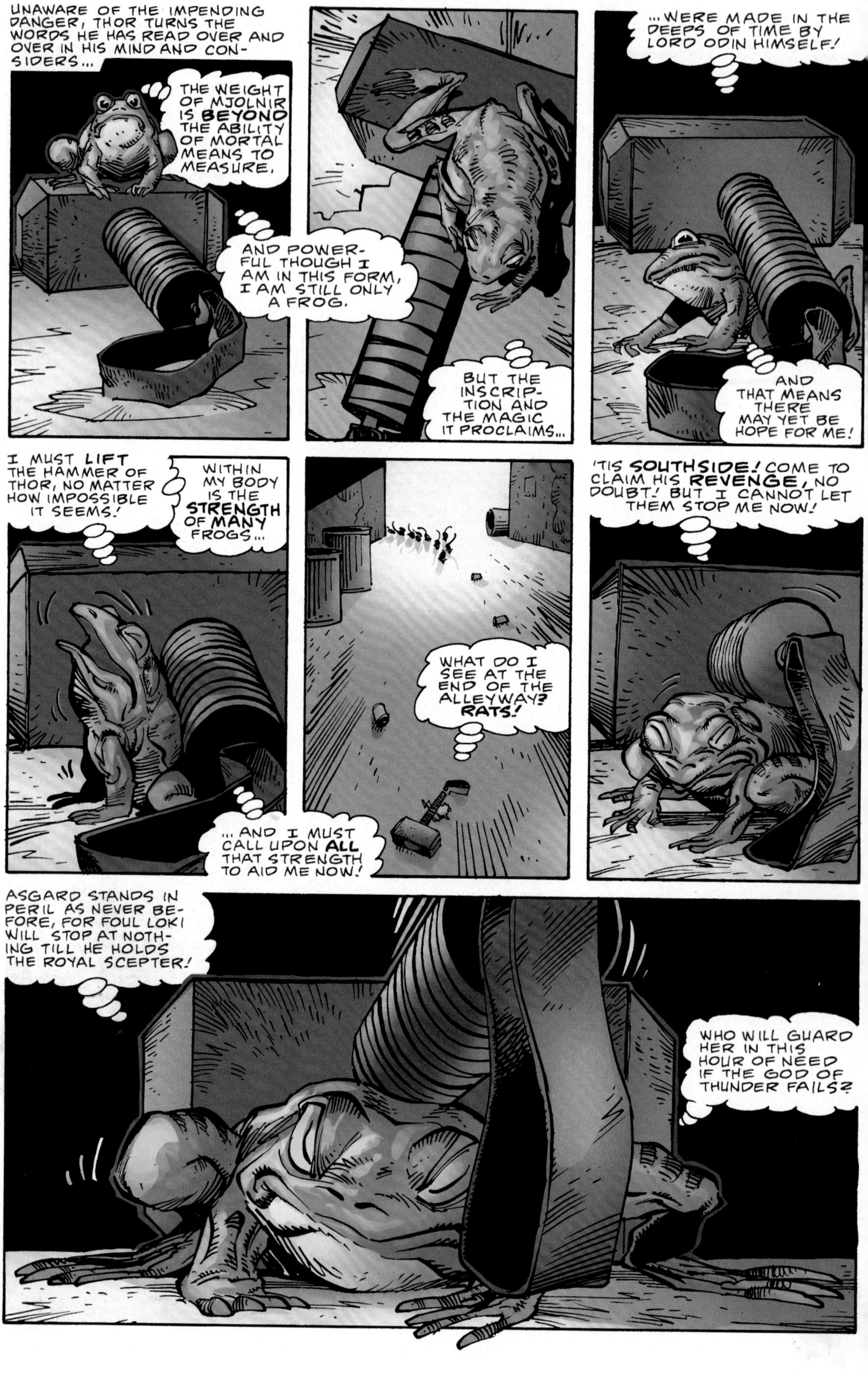
UNAWARE OF THE IMPENDING DANGER, THOR TURNS THE WORDS HE HAS READ OVER AND OVER IN HIS MIND AND CONSIDERS...
THE WEIGHT OF MJOLNIR IS BEYOND THE ABILITY OF MORTAL MEANS TO MEASURE.
AND POWERFUL THOUGH I AM IN THIS FORM, I AM STILL ONLY A FROG.
BUT THE INSCRIPTION AND THE MAGIC IT PROCLAIMS...
...WERE MADE IN THE DEEPS OF TIME BY LORD ODIN HIMSELF!
AND THAT MEANS THERE MAY YET BE HOPE FOR ME!
I MUST LIFT THE HAMMER OF THOR, NO MATTER HOW IMPOSSIBLE IT SEEMS!
WITHIN MY BODY IS THE STRENGTH OF MANY FROGS...
...AND I MUST CALL UPON ALL THAT STRENGTH TO AID ME NOW!
WHAT DO I SEE AT THE END OF THE ALLEYWAY? RATS!
'TIS SOUTHSIDE! COME TO CLAIM HIS REVENGE, NO DOUBT! BUT I CANNOT LET THEM STOP ME NOW!
ASGARD STANDS IN PERIL AS NEVER BEFORE, FOR FOUL LOKI WILL STOP AT NOTHING TILL HE HOLDS THE ROYAL SCEPTER!
WHO WILL GUARD HER IN THIS HOUR OF NEED IF THE GOD OF THUNDER FAILS?

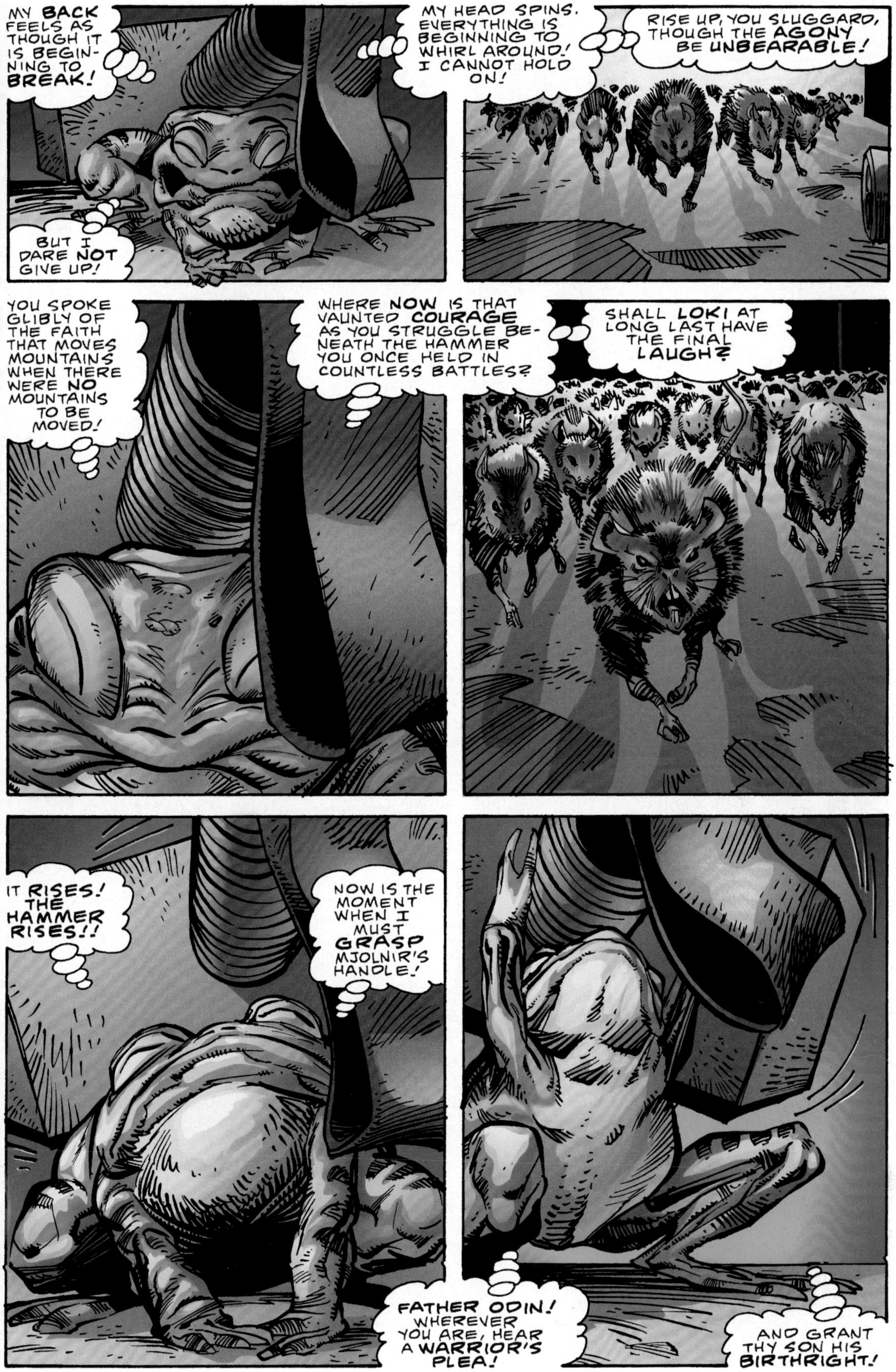
MY BACK FEELS AS THOUGH IT IS BEGINNING TO BREAK!
BUT I DARE NOT GIVE UP!
MY HEAD SPINS. EVERYTHING IS BEGINNING TO WHIRL AROUND! I CANNOT HOLD ON!
RISE UP, YOU SLUGGARD, THOUGH THE AGONY BE UNBEARABLE!
YOU SPOKE GLIBLY OF THE FAITH THAT MOVES MOUNTAINS WHEN THERE WERE NO MOUNTAINS TO BE MOVED!
WHERE NOW IS THAT VAUNTED COURAGE AS YOU STRUGGLE BENEATH THE HAMMER YOU ONCE HELD IN COUNTLESS BATTLES?
SHALL LOKI AT LONG LAST HAVE THE FINAL LAUGH?
IT RISES! THE HAMMER RISES!!
NOW IS THE MOMENT WHEN I MUST GRASP MJOLNIR'S HANDLE!
FATHER ODIN! WHEREVER YOU ARE, HEAR A WARRIOR'S PLEA!
AND GRANT THY SON HIS BIRTHRIGHT!

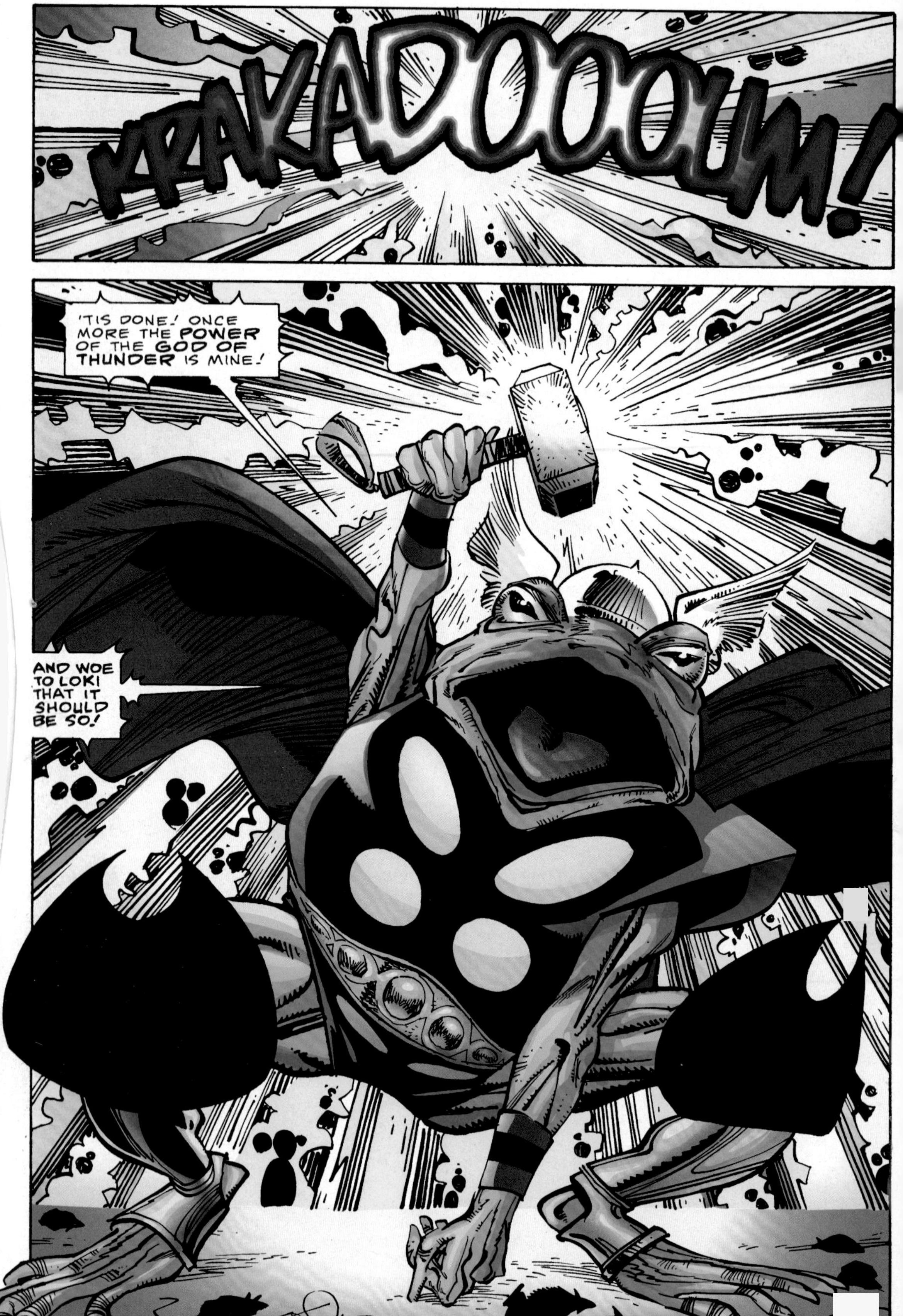
KRAKADOOOOM!
'TIS DONE! ONCE MORE THE POWER OF THE GOD OF THUNDER IS MINE!
AND WOE TO LOKI THAT IT SHOULD BE SO!

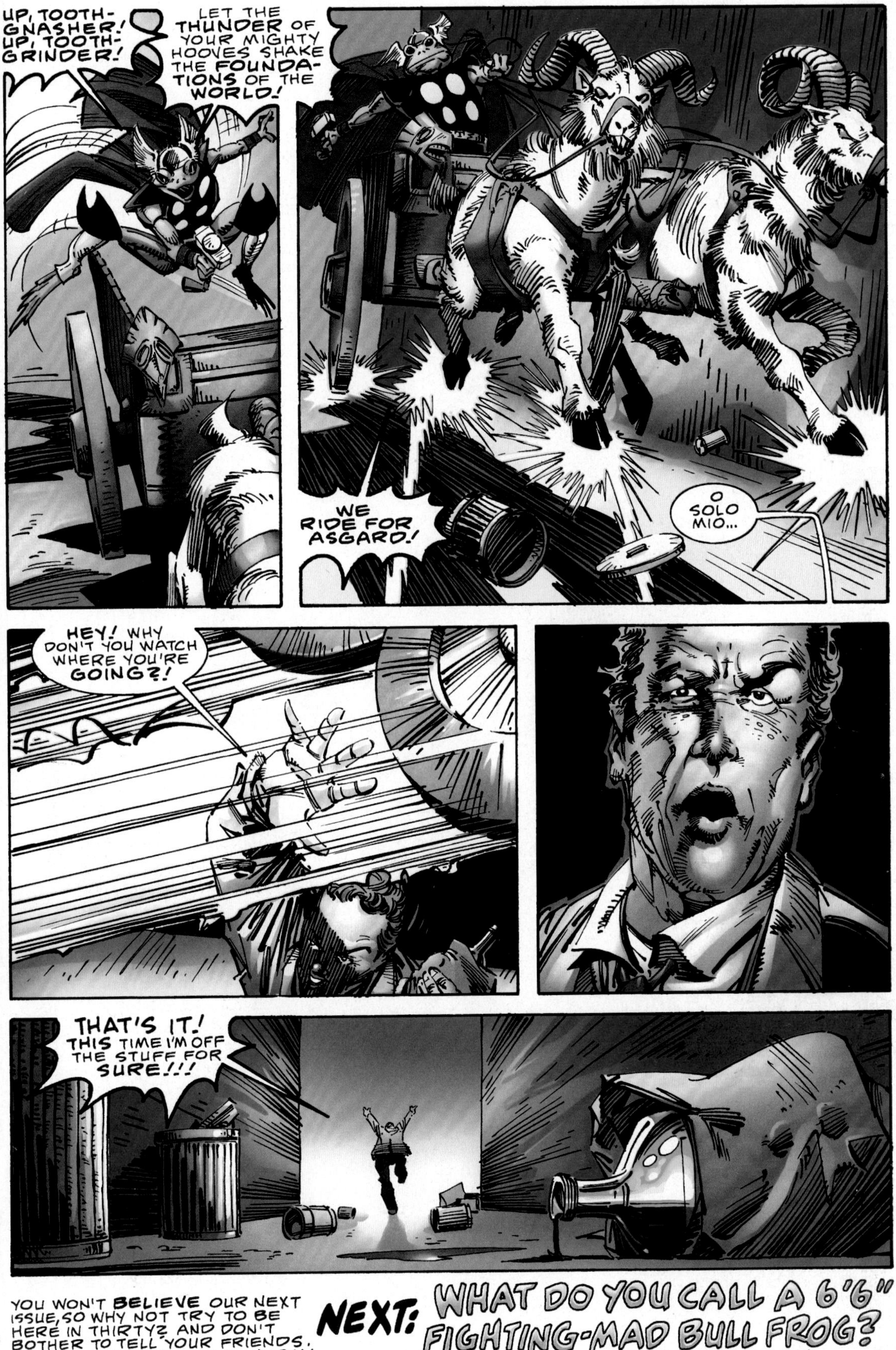
UP, TOOTH-GNASHER! UP, TOOTH-GRINDER!
LET THE THUNDER OF YOUR MIGHTY HOOVES SHAKE THE FOUNDATIONS OF THE WORLD!
WE RIDE FOR ASGARD!
O SOLO MIO...
HEY! WHY DON'T YOU WATCH WHERE YOU'RE GOING?!
THAT'S IT! THIS TIME I'M OFF THE STUFF FOR SURE!!!

YOU WON'T **BELIEVE** OUR NEXT ISSUE, SO WHY NOT TRY TO BE HERE IN THIRTY? AND DON'T BOTHER TO TELL YOUR FRIENDS, THEY WON'T BELIEVE IT, EITHER!!!

NEXT: WHAT DO YOU CALL A 6'6" FIGHTING-MAD BULL FROG?

YOU'RE DARN RIGHT!

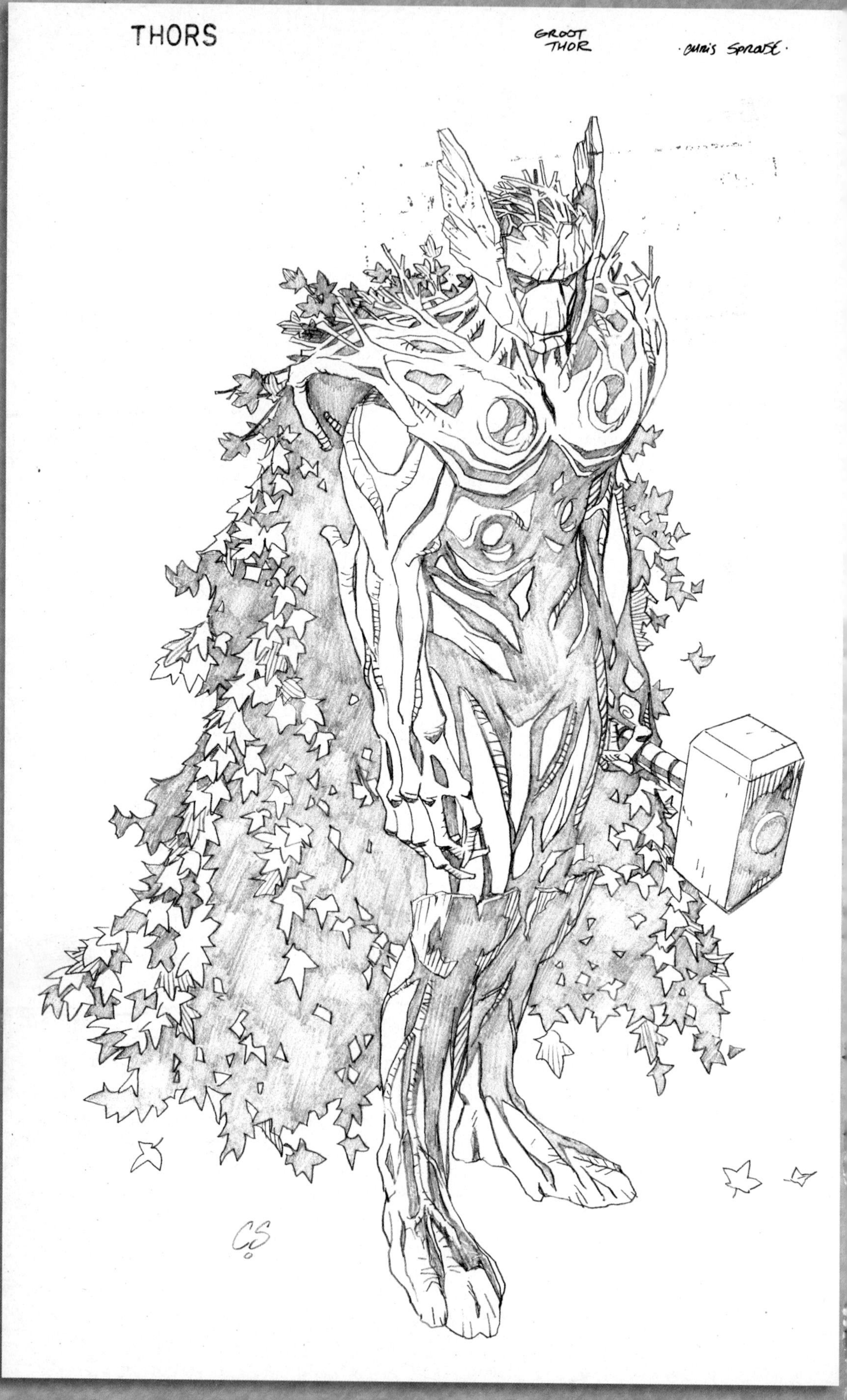
THORS
GROOT
THOR
·CHRIS SPROUSE·
CS

GROOT THOR CHARACTER DESIGN BY CHRIS SPROUSE